2

OPEN
TENNIS
THE FIRST TWENTY YEARS

OPEN TENNIS

THE FIRST TWENTY YEARS

The Players, the Politics,
the Pressures, the Passions,
and *the Great Matches*

Richard Evans

BLOOMSBURY

First published 1988

Copyright © 1988 by Richard Evans

Bloomsbury Publishing Limited, 2 Soho Square, London W1V 5DE

British Library Cataloguing in Publication Data
Evans, Richard, *1939–*
Open tennis: the first twenty years.
1. Tennis — History — 20th century
I. Title
796.342'09'04   GV993

ISBN 0 7475 0175 0

Typeset by Rapid Communications Ltd, London WC1X 9NW
Printed in Great Britain by Butler & Tanner Ltd
Frome, Somerset

CONTENTS

INTRODUCTION

In no sense is this an official history of the first 20 tumultuous years of what we call Open Tennis, and it might not even be an objective one. 'Official', to a journalist, is often just another word for the party line, and, while one struggles for objectivity, it is a far more elusive ideal than many of us like to admit. Writers shed objectivity the moment they start selecting facts which, in itself, is a subjective task.

So, at best, this is a highly personalized account of the game's recent history by someone who, at various times, has worked on both sides of the fence, and if it becomes clear where my sympathies lie, so be it. My loyalties are to the game, not to any political faction, and it never hurts to be reminded that it is the players who make it live. Without their brilliance or merely their honest endeavour, we have nothing. Having trekked after them for so long and worked with them for a while, I appreciate, more than some perhaps, the strength of mind as well as of body that is required to succeed at this most demanding and difficult of sports, and, while in no way excusing the behaviour of a few, I cannot help but admire the talent, dedication and professionalism of the vast majority.

Nevertheless, there is a host of others who toil long hours to make this game work, and it is to officials of every stripe, tournament directors from every continent, agents, referees, umpires and, not least, my companions in the press box and broadcasting booth that I owe a debt of gratitude. Their friendship and co-operation has made this chronicle possible.

Especially, I must thank a few individuals and organizations with whom I work more closely than most — Gene Scott and his *Tennis Week* staff in New York; Tom Clarke, the Sports Editor of *The Times*, as well as the librarians at Wapping who helped me search for some valuable cuttings in the archives; Neil Amdur at *World Tennis*, for providing similar access to back copies; and, as always, my French friends, Jean Courvecelle and his talented reporters and photographers at *Tennis Magazine* in Paris, in particular Serge Philippot and Christophe Guibbaud for their cover photographs.

I have, of course, delved freely into John Barrett's *World of Tennis Annual* and into the *MIPTC Media Guide*, and, of all the books I have consulted none jogged the memory better than Arthur Ashe's superb *Portrait in Motion* — written with Frank Deford — which repays rereading; Jack Kramer's *The Game* and Ted Tinling's *Love & Faults*, a massive volume which Rod Humphries helped to construct.

This, too, is a story of love and faults; of harsh words and of chances missed both on and off the court; of dreams fulfilled and of riches beyond imagining. Most importantly, perhaps, it touches every corner of the globe from the humblest backwaters of the game to the great cathedrals of Wimbledon, Stade Roland Garros and now, in all its modern splendour, Flinder's Park.

We complain of a never-ending season and of too much tennis. There is truth in that but, for me, each year, as each of these 20 past, brings a sense of renewal, beginning with the first warm rays of spring in Monte Carlo and continuing on through the climactic summer. As I wrote somewhere, sometime, life would seem very strange if Paris did not follow Rome with the promise of Wimbledon ahead . . .

R.I.E.
El Castillo de Castellar, Spain.
February 1988

THE BIRTH

His favourite exercise now is to stand on the back porch of his Las Vegas home and drive golf balls out into the Nevada desert. Then he strides out amongst the scrub and cacti and picks them up.

'You get all the exercise a man of my age needs that way,' he says, a twinkle of defiance still gleaming in those dark, beady eyes.

As the long legs carry him out into the pink and purple sunset, it is unlikely that he dwells too much on the circumstances that decreed that the name of Richard 'Pancho' Gonzales would never adorn the honours board that hangs in the hallway of the All England Club all those thousands of miles away. If he did, it would not improve his mood.

Pancho Gonzales never won Wimbledon because, at a meeting of the International Lawn Tennis Federation in Paris in July 1960, three delegates known to be in favour of the motion to introduce the concept of Open Tennis failed to vote. One was in the toilet, one fell asleep and, to complete the farce, a third was absent arranging the evening's dinner entertainment on the *bateaux-mouches*. The required two-thirds majority was missed by the narrowest of margins and while amateur delegates sipped champagne on the Seine that night, the game of tennis found itself anchored to the hypocrisy of amateurism for another eight years.

It was a good thing for the delegates that Gonzales was not present at the meeting. In his heyday he was not a mellow man. Once, at a professional tournament staged by Jack Kramer at the old Madison Square Garden, Gonzales had been infuriated by cameramen's flashbulbs. When he returned to the locker-room, the place shook not merely with the power of Pancho's lungs but with the noise of rackets being hurled against the wall. Like most of the other people present I took cover. Pierre Barthes hid, naked and shivering, behind the shower curtain. Ken Rosewall was under the table. Players were afraid of Gonzales at the best of times. When he was in this mood they had good reason to be. The game might have benefited more had the Gonzales temper been directed against that group of self-serving officials who denied the great Pancho and others of his era their rightful place in the sun.

Until 1968 tennis was a divided game. There were amateurs and there were professionals and heaven forbid that they should ever meet. All those terrific human traits such as snobbism, power complexes and pure selfishness had ensured that any player who signed a professional contract was automatically banned from competing at Wimbledon or any of the other great championships run under the auspices of the International Lawn Tennis Federation (ILTF). It had always been that way. The moment Bill Tilden and Fred Perry turned pro in the 1930s, they were banished to exhibition halls and skating-rinks covered by a wooden court. When Jack Kramer started his professional troupe after the war, the attitude was the same but still Kramer's numbers grew, as one champion after another signed up to secure his future as an honest professional. Those who stayed with the so-called amateur game were forced to put bread on their table by receiving money under it. But that was all right. The establishment figures who still dreamed of a world in which people wrote down 'Gentleman' as a profession in their passports received the 'amateurs' into the citadels of the game and treated them as equals. And the professionals? Well, jolly good chaps and all that but not quite the sort of fellow you'd invite to the club for dinner, what?

We talk blithely of the good old days but although they did indeed have redeeming features that the modern age has lost, they were also great days for racists, snobs and blinkered buffoons. That tennis should have been afflicted by people of that kind three-quarters of the way through what are known as the Swinging Sixties made the sport something of an anachronism, and it was not until a brave man called Herman David, who was Chairman of the All England Club at the time, forced the concept of Open Tennis on to the conservative die-hards of the ILTF that the game was hauled into something resembling the twentieth century.

It should all have happened years before and the fact that the tide of progress was held back for so long had an immeasurably harmful effect on the way the game developed. Had the vast, world-wide family been allowed to evolve naturally, the inevitable squabbles might have been kept under some sort of control and gradual growth could have been achieved with some sort of harmony. After all, in the immediately post-war era when sport was still bigger than the mighty dollar — primarily because television was not there to magnify its importance — professional golf had been able to grow quietly under the widely-accepted auspices of the Professional Golfers' Association (PGA), an organization that was so well established by the time agents and lawyers started waving anti-trust suits at each other that it must have watched the antics being enacted in the name of tennis with bewilderment. Only now is golf, for so long a sport dominated by American ethics and American laws, discovering the legal problems involved when other nations rise to a footing of equal power.

Tennis discovered those problems the instant Herman David, denouncing its ancestry as 'a living lie', kicked Open Tennis out of the womb. The squawling litter's parentage and pedigree were instantly contested by a motley collection of incompetent foster parents — devious and very ambitious godfathers and a whole host of dubious aunts and uncles who, with varying degrees of skill and intuition, spotted gold in the play-pen and made a lunge for it. Several didn't bother to check whether the safety-pins on the babies' nappies were closed and got bloody thumbs as they tried to affix their logos. But a pinprick has never stopped the more ruthless kind in their mindless pursuit of riches, and all but the most feeble were able to line their pockets as the toddlers started to sweat their keep on court.

David had created the opportunity for the biggest sporting gold-rush the world had ever seen by announcing, in 1967, not only that he was going to run a professional tournament for the likes of Rod Laver and Ken Rosewall on the sacred Centre Court at Wimbledon that very summer but that, in 1968, the All England Club Championships would be open to all categories of player and that if the ILTF didn't like it, they could lump it. From that moment on, life in tennis was never quite the same again, but despite the overnight arrival of so many get-rich-quick merchants, those who soldiered on through the early upheavals and lived to tell the tale were almost exclusively people who cared as much for the game itself as for the dollar it was earning them.

For some, money was not even a partial motivation. Derek Hardwick, the last of the old-style amateur presidents of the ILTF before Philippe Chatrier virtually turned it into a full-time, if still unpaid, career, was motivated by many things, including a brilliant mind that was always searching for political power plays. But, by the time he died during the French Open in 1987, Derek had received nothing but expenses for the countless hours he had spent fighting innumerable battles as a member of the Men's International Professional Tennis Council (MIPTC), which had been formed in the mid 1970s in an attempt to give the splintered game some coherent direction.

Hardwick was one of a comparatively small group of people whose long and often heated deliberations in hotel suites all over the world during the past 20 years have been almost entirely responsible for shaping the destiny of the sport. The influences of some is long gone, while that of others is just emerging, but one thing is sure: the great stars of two decades, from Rod Laver and Chris Evert to Boris Becker and Steffi Graf, would not have been presented to their vast world-wide audience in the same manner or in the same places had it not been for the efforts of this opinionated, dedicated and wonderfully diverse group of people.

Despite a strong back-up, particularly from those players who were involved during the formative years of the tour, the independent women's circuit was essentially created by three quite extraordinary personalities — Gladys Heldman, publisher of *World Tennis* magazine and a tireless campaigner for freedom of choice within the game itself; Billie Jean King who, quite apart from being one of the great champions of all time, also became one of the best-known feminists in America, and Joe Cullman, Chairman of the Board of Philip Morris, who answered Mrs Heldman's call for help and married his Virginia Slims brand to a fledgling tour many chauvinists thought would never get off the ground.

All that happened in the early 1970s while the men's game was still struggling to come to terms with the incredible possibilities that Open Tennis in the new televised age had opened up. Mark McCormack, who had eyed the tennis explosion from his near-parallel platform on the 18th tee alongside the two superstars whose careers he helped launch, Arnold Palmer and Jack Nicklaus, was quick to get a foot on the tennis court by signing up Rod Laver, Virginia Wade and others. But McCormack has always tended to stay clear of the game's deeper politics and, before we go any further with this story of power and intrigue, it might be best to introduce four men whose influence, either in tandem or in bitter confrontation, has planted an indelible thumb-print on the destiny of professional tennis.

JACK KRAMER: The 1947 Wimbledon champion, and the man who founded the most famous tour in tennis. Generous, sentimental and as tough as the Las Vegas railroads his father worked on, Kramer was idolized as a player, hated by Gonzales, wooed by the new generation of players who in 1972 made him the first Executive Director of the Association of Tennis Professionals (ATP) and finally vilified by the British press who the following year nominated him scapegoat for the Wimbledon boycott. 'Go Home, Kramer!' screamed the headlines, while the *Evening News* ran an editorial likening him to Hitler. 'Big Jake' may have a big ego — find me a true champion who doesn't — but he was no dictator. A leader and innovator he was, certainly. Having created one tour when he was outlawed from the mainstream of the game, Kramer promptly revealed the traditionalist that lurked beneath the wolf's clothing by devising the format for the circuit that is still in existence today, the Grand Prix. For two years he and I ran the ATP, and had we continued pro tennis would be a different game today.

DONALD DELL: A former Davis Cup player and later a highly successful captain, this Washington lawyer can fling the dirt with the best muck-raking politicians in town. It says a lot about Dell's character that he has a picture of Sir Winston Churchill hanging on his office wall. He understands all about 'in defeat defiance' but it is the bit about magnanimity that he finds hard to grasp. Poor Donald has so many of the right instincts and comes up with so many of the wrong responses. A charmer over dinner and a genuine sentimentalist about his sport, Dell will chew anyone alive over a negotiating table. Business meetings are viewed by Dell as Davis Cup ties in which there has to be a winner. Always late, always on the airport phone two minutes before take-off, Dell is a driven man who eventually drove two long-time friends and partners, Lee Fentress and Frank Graighill, right out of his office. Like many others in the game they could no longer tolerate his ruthless business methods and decided to quit. He lost friends as frequently as he landed huge contracts for his company, Pro Serv, and for his clients, who ranged from his loyal friend Arthur Ashe to Ivan Lendl and, most ironically, Jimmy Connors, who originally, was no sort of friend at all. But to Dell the bottom line would be total control of the game through the ATP. But he trampled on too many people's feelings and never heeded the warning signals. Nevertheless, Dell was a tireless and totally dedicated motivating force in the early days of Open Tennis, and had he married anyone less understanding or loyal than Carole Oscher he would have ended up a very lonely man at the end of his 18-hour days. But the workaholic ethic paid off and Dell was responsible for laying the foundation for the riches that were to flow into the game over the next 20 years.

PHILIPPE CHATRIER: A strange, complex man with the mentality of a dreamer. Unlike most dream merchants, however, Chatrier possessed the drive and the organizational skills to market his vision and make it viable. He saved the old governing body from extinction when he got himself elected President of the International Tennis Federation (ITF) in 1977, and then set all kinds of precedents by remaining in power term after term in the role of an unpaid but very professionally minded ringmaster of the world delegates to whom he likes to refer as his elephants. Thin-skinned, moody and

7

very French despite his fluent English and excellent, broad-minded grasp of the world game, Chatrier is a passionate believer in the ITF's right to preserve the traditional elements of tennis. Biting his lip, he tolerates sponsors and even manages to sound sincere in welcoming their presence in the game. But his real desire is to make tennis independently solvent through gate receipts and television rights. Only the Grand Slam Championships have a real hope of achieving this but Chatrier has come very close in the last few years at Stade Roland Garros, where the French Open, now recognized by many people as the most enjoyable tournament in the world, stands as a monument to his vision and energy. He has found it difficult to win the kind of support he would like from the players — even French stars such as Yannick Noah have fallen out with him — but his friendship with Kramer, whom he idolizes, and formerly with Dell, whom he now barely tolerates, was a pivotal factor in shaping the future of the sport back in the early 1970s.

LAMAR HUNT: The antithesis of the public's image of the Texas oilman, Lamar is not tall, is not ostentatious and does not greet every body with a big 'Howdy!' And even though he owns the Kansas City Chiefs and lives in a Dallas mansion that would make J.R. blink, his instincts are still to fly economy class; to dress like your local bank manager and to grab a bite at the nearest hamburger stall. He was lured into tennis in the mid 1960s by Dave Dixon, a New Orleans promoter who quickly sold out, leaving Hunt with another of those tennis babies. This one was called World Championship Tennis (WCT) and its existence, along with the threat it posed, did as much as anything to precipitate the birth of Open Tennis. During the early years WCT was — as John McEnroe so rightly pointed out last year — the best-run and most respected tour in the game. That, however, did not prevent the Hunt pros from being banned from Wimbledon in 1972, after the All England Club committee had been unpardonably rude to Hunt during his visit to Wimbledon a couple of years earlier. Kramer could never abide Hunt, because this non-athlete had the financial resources to achieve what Kramer had been struggling to achieve through all those desperate years in the 1950s. The bitter relationship between the two men pervaded most of the attempted negotiations that took place between WCT and the Pro Council, which eventually ended in a needless and costly lawsuit, ironically several years after Kramer had retired from the Council. Only now, perhaps, are Hunt's opponents in the game's establishment starting to recognize that he never actually wanted to own the entire game, he never ran out on a commitment and, in those early days of amateurish incompetence, he set standards of professionalism in the running of tournaments that are now considered commonplace. And, even though he could afford it, the whole enterprise cost him a fortune.

On the subject of those Chiefs who are so close to Hunt's heart, it all started in Kansas City, down by the slaughterhouse, where, one chilly February week in 1968, a renegade bunch of young men dubbed 'The Handsome Eight' killed off a sacred cow or two when they played a pristine lily-white game called Lawn Tennis in garishly coloured clothing and encouraged the crowd, such as it was, to shout and scream. David Gray and I, as foreign observers of what looked like a very American spectacle, were witnessing the birth of a lot of things that week. What did Rogers and Hammerstein say? 'Everything's up to date in Kansas City . . . They've gone about as far as they can go . . .'

Well, they hadn't.

KANSAS CITY — AN ICY BEGINNING

Tennis today is very traditional, very conservative. The professional tour is played largely at traditional venues, using traditional scoring — apart from the now totally accepted tie-break — and the players' clothing is, as the Wimbledon rules have always required, 'predominantly white'. This is hardly surprising, because we are living in a conservative age where the young can live out their fantasies through the violent but mostly harmless stars of rock and roll who blare at them through their video machines.

There was less necessity for violence in the 1960s because you could express yourself in so many other ways. In those days, Ray Moore, now all short back and sides and chairman of the Pro Council, ran around the King's Road in Chelsea with his wolfman look and it was quite normal for a guy's hair to be as long as a girl's skirt was short. The world was a trip, man, and nowhere was the psychedelic impact greater than in San Francisco, where the Flower Children in Haight Ashbury were for real and the all-nude strippers in the clubs along North Beach were mostly nice college kids just earning an extra buck.

Given that society was aflame with experimentation, it was inevitable that a sport still run by a breed of men who had never heard of Bob Dylan, let alone LSD, should find itself being jolted out of its moribund state by new promoters with new ideas. Tennis was simply too good a sport, too alluring and too saleable to be left out of the mainstream of exploding innovation.

So it was that we found ourselves down by the stockyards in Kansas City during the cold, snow-flecked, first week of February 1968. Just how a New Orleans promoter called Dave Dixon had got us there is a story all in itself. But got us there he had, and David Gray and I were left to work out how best to explain to our readers back in England why their beautiful game was being played on a synthetic court laid on ice in an arena so near the slaughterhouses that the smell of cattle troubled the nostrils.

And that was only the where of it. The manner in which the game was being played was even more troubling for the purists.

An abomination of a scoring system, devised by that restless New England aristocrat Jimmy Van Alen, had the players fighting over two sets of ping-pong scoring (the first to 31 points) and, if the sets were split, deciding the match with a nine-point tie-break. The coloured clothing worn by Dixon's troupe provided a culture shock all of its own. Roger Taylor wore fire-engine red, Pierre Barthes wore blue and John Newcombe's shirt and shorts could best be described as the colour of rust. Oh, and the crowd. Such as it was, it was encouraged to make a noise. Not just between points but any time. As an incentive, an idea was imported from the preliminary event the troupe had held in Australia the week before. In brief, it entailed giving away a bottle of perfume to all the women if their nominated player won and a bottle of cologne to all the men if he didn't. In Sydney it had been used when Taylor, the women's choice, was playing Barthes. Roger knew the idea was working when a little man jumped up as soon he broke Pierre's serve and yelled, 'Drop dead, Pommie!'

On hearing about it in Kansas, the local Revlon representative got so excited that he had 3000 bottles of lotion and cologne sent in. Considering the whiff from the stockyards it was something of an inspired move, but it led David Gray to wonder, in his *Guardian* report, if all this was merely giving us a fascinating glimpse of what Wimbledon would be like in 1984. We all used Orwell's chosen year as a sort of yardstick in those days but by the time it arrived David was no longer with us. He had done his bit in the meantime, however, to ensure that Wimbledon remained recognizable.

Considering what David and I witnessed in Kansas City, followed as it was by the introduction of the equally revolutionary concept of World Team Tennis, the miracle is that the game has changed so little. But I think we both realized at the time that this was a necessary adventure that had to be taken to the very boundaries of possibility before a less extreme form of modernization would become acceptable. So although his presence in the game was fleeting, Dixon's promotional daring should not be brushed aside as some irrelevant aberration. He may have started life as a plywood manufacturer but many of his ideas were more solid than his former product, and when he finally tracked a phantom group of ailing pros to the unlikely venue of a virtually deserted hall in Rochester, New York, he was shrewd enough to understand what he was witnessing. 'Everything was wrong except the tennis, which was wonderful,' Dixon told us. That would have been right. The tennis was being played by Rod Laver and Ken Rosewall.

As it happened Dixon did not get Laver and Rosewall, who were in the act of joining a new group, organized by former US Davis Cup captain George MacCall, that would consist largely of the remnants of the old Kramer tour plus some new additions such as Roy Emerson and Fred Stolle. That didn't bother Dixon because he felt that younger players would be more open to new ideas. But to make it work he needed two men — the previous year's No. 1 player in the United States, Dennis Ralston, and the reigning Wimbledon champion, John Newcombe. MacCall hadn't made a move for Ralston and, as an American, Dennis was quick to understand Dixon's overtures. Newcombe and his great doubles partner Tony Roche, however, were still a little green about the big, brash world of sports promotion in the States, and they needed a little inducement. Twenty years later, revisiting Dallas for the WCT Finals in his role as television commentator for CBS, Newcombe recalled the way he and Roche were conscripted:

'I was staying at the Roosevelt in New York just prior to playing Forest Hills,' Newk told me. 'It was 1967 and I had just won Wimbledon. One morning Rochey calls me up from his room and says, "How'd you like to make a million dollars?"'

'Well, I was clearing about $15,000 a year as the No. 1 amateur in the world at the time so it sounded pretty good. I was getting $500 to play Forest Hills and that was supposed to cover two weeks of expenses in New York for my wife and myself. I used to have brown toast and beans for breakfast and at night Angie and I would often eat at the Horn & Hardardt cafeteria. So when Rochey said two guys called Dave Dixon and Bob Briner wanted to meet us, I said "When?"'

Dixon's softening-up procedure on the two wide-eyed young Aussies began immediately. Within minutes of their first meeting him, Newcombe and Roche were told to walk across Madison Avenue to Brooks Brothers and order themselves a suit. Dixon, with the massive figure of his Texan henchman Briner lurking in the background, seemed to be flush with cash — although he hinted that it wasn't all his own. There was a wealthy partner involved, he said, whose name could not be revealed just then. 'Go and get your suits, guys,' said Dixon. 'Then we'll talk.'

It did not take Dixon long to come up with the name of his partner. It was Lamar Hunt — although the name meant nothing to Newcombe and Roche. 'But when he told us Lamar had a cousin called Al Hill, that rang a bell because Al had been playing on the Trinity College team and some of us had practised with him,' Newk explained. 'So we called Al to get a bit of background on these guys and eventually ended up signing for $1,000 down with a $55,000 a year guarantee. It seemed huge to us but my lawyer pal Parker went nuts when I told him. "How could you do that? You've left yourself no room to negotiate!" We were so naïve.'

Naïve or not, Newk and Tony had taken a calculated gamble with their careers. This was September 1967, and although the rumblings of discontent were growing, there was still no guarantee that Open Tennis would arrive in the immediate future. Newcombe had effectively signed away his Wimbledon title just as his great line of Australian predecessors had been forced to do for the previous 15 years.

Dixon, however, was inadvertently making sure that Newk would not have to miss a beat as far as the defence of his Wimbledon crown was concerned. By going after Cliff Drysdale and the two beaten semifinalists of that year — Taylor and the tall, sardonic Yugoslav Nikki Pilic — Dixon merely helped to make up the mind of a man whom he did not know and whom, to my knowledge, he never even met. That man was Herman David, who had already broken with tradition by staging a professional championship on the Centre Court at Wimbledon in August of that year — a well-attended experiment, which had been won by Laver — and was now watching not merely the reigning Wimbledon champion but an entire supporting cast disappearing into the professional ranks.

Within a matter of weeks David would publicly denounce the amateur game as 'a living lie' and, with the full backing of the All England Club committee, throw down the gauntlet by stating flatly that Wimbledon in 1968 would be open to all categories of player, amateur and professional alike. The collective gasp of amazement and, in many cases, horror was heard from Rome to Rangoon, but one would have needed to belong to an extremely intransigent species of ostrich not to recognize the accuracy of David's assessment of the state into which tennis had got itself.

Within a week of the All England Club Chairman's declaration, the *Sunday Times* Insight Team produced a two-page spread that offered more proof than was needed of the truth of David's 'living lie' statement. Accurately depicting the players' tea-room at Wimbledon during the Championship as an open market with tournament directors from around the world bartering for the services of 'amateur' players, the article offered up the next best thing to a ranking list of the day.

From the bottom up, it listed such players as Britain's Mike Sangster, the great bearded Dane Torben Ulrich and Australia's

Owen Davidson as being in the $300-400-a-week class for under-the-counter payments. Pilic, Wilhelm Bungert of West Germany, Thomas Koch of Brazil and Marty Mulligan, the Italian-based Australian, were said to be worth up to $500 a week. A select quartet comprising Newcombe, Roche, Sweden's lanky Jan-Erik Lundquist and Rafe Osuna, the delightful Mexican who was later killed in an air crash, were named as $700-a-week players. Roy Emerson and Cliff Drysdale were listed at $900, with Manolo Santana, the Wimbledon champion of 1966 and winner of both the French and the Forest Hills titles, top of the heap at $1,000. That was the shady world of tennis 'shamateurism' as laid out for all to see in *The Sunday Times*.

Actually the figures were a little conservative. 'Emmo and I were getting 15 hundred a week,' Santana told me recently at his sumptuous club next to the Hotel Puente Romano in Marbella. 'We had come to an agreement between ourselves to ask for that and most of the tournaments could easily afford it. Some just wouldn't pay, of course. When I went to Australia in '65 to play the Davis Cup final, the Australian LTA wanted me to play in their Championships. But when I told them the price, they refused. So I didn't play. When Emmo played in Spain he got paid. For a couple of years it was simply better for us to remain amateur because all the other top players had turned pro. If I had turned I would have gone to MacCall, but in the end I stayed with the 'shamateur' system, embarrassing as it was. I was relieved when Open Tennis came in. It ended all that hypocrisy for everyone.'

It also ended the need for players to run around the world practising their letter-writing skills as well as their backhands. It would seem inconceivable for a modern day pro to have to carry a briefcase full of correspondence with him on tour, just to ensure that he had somewhere to play in a couple of months' time. 'But that's what I had to do for years,' recalled Boro Jovanovic, one of the great clay-court experts of the day, who now runs a restaurant in Zagreb. 'I had to remember all the names of all the tournament directors' wives and write to thank them for everything they had done for me last year and please could I play again next year. Only then did you start negotiating for expenses and maybe air tickets. Agents? Hah, what were agents? We did everything ourselves.'

With his dark good looks and five languages, all spoken in a deep, cultured voice, Jovanovic found all this a great deal easier than a lot of players, but most of them, out of necessity, got by. (Heaven knows how some of today's pros would manage if they suddenly had to write a letter! It might be fun if the ATP road managers and the management companies went on strike for a while so we could find out . . .)

But the days of letter-writing were over for Dixon's group which, in another inspired promotional move, had been dubbed 'The Handsome Eight'.★ They were now under contract to an organization with secretaries and telephones and a mapped-out itinerary of where they were supposed to play on any given day. Their main task in Kansas seemed to revolve around kitting themselves out in their weird new gear and then wearing enough of it to avoid catching pneumonia on court. The temperature was two degrees below zero outside and colder, if anything, inside the arena, where the fast astroturf carpet did not entirely cover the ice-rink. Apart from keeping pneumonia at bay, it was a miracle no one broke a leg. Ralston, chasing a lob, found nothing but ice beneath his feet and eventually ended up skidding the last 10 yards of his fruitless journey.

But the crowd, filling about one-sixth of the 6000-seat hall, loved it and did their best to create the kind of atmosphere the promoters were hoping for.

The players had been grouped according to continent, to create a team format that probably confused the middle-American patrons even more, considering their hazy understanding of geography. Nevertheless Ralston, remaining upright, gave America a 1–0 lead over Europe by beating Barthes 31–27, 31–29. For this Dennis received $620 and Pierre $380. Declaring himself desolated at having lost for Europe and not bothered about the money, Barthes proved it by blowing his entire bonus cheque on a series of midnight phone calls to a girl he had just met in Paris. Now, with three children and after 20 years of marriage to Carolyn, Pierre looks back on it as his best investment.

But, with the benefit of hindsight, one can see that it was not the ice or the coloured clothing or the rock-and-roll dancers produced to entertain the customers in between matches that proved to be the most remarkable aspect of this strange adventure in Kansas City. It was the future that was remarkable. These eight young men were not merely handsome but soon to be blessed with the future that virtually any professional athlete of that era would have settled for. Even today, stardom at 22 does not ensure security at 42 for a pro athlete, but, although they did not know it, The Handsome Eight were boarding the gravy train in Kansas and it would carry each one

---

★Nicknames for tennis players were hardly an innovation, however. Maurice McLoughlin, US champion in 1912, was popularly known as 'The California Comet' and Norman Brookes, Wimbledon winner in 1914, was referred to as 'The Wizard'.

of them, through innumerable stops and many a jolt in the night, to positions today that typify the success of the game as a whole.

John Newcombe, who went on to win two more Wimbledons, marketed his moustache to such good effect that he is now a Sydney-based millionaire, free to pick and choose his assignments. Tony Roche has, in the last few years, become recognized as one of the world's premier coaches, by helping Ivan Lendl to consolidate his position as the World No. 1. Equally successful as a coach, Dennis Ralston went on to captain the US Davis Cup team, to coach Chris Evert and to enjoy his current position as Director of Tennis at the Southern Methodist University in Dallas. Butch Buchholz, previously one of the Kramer pros, had a spell as Executive Director of the ATP and then fulfilled a long-held ambition to establish another two-week championship for men and women, which he eventually settled on Key Biscayne.

Cliff Drysdale, like Newcombe, invested well and, apart from managing numerous business interests, has made a name for himself as one of the best television commentators on the game, working mainly for the ESPN sports network. Pierre Barthes, Tennis Director at the plush Paris Country Club, is also part-owner of Europe's largest tennis camp at Cap d'Agde. Roger Taylor also has financial interests in his Portuguese tennis club and has built up his own holiday travel business in Wimbledon. Nikki Pilic, fated to become the *cause célèbre* of the 1973 Wimbledon boycott, recently took up West German nationality so that he could accept the post of the German Davis Cup team captain. Nikki used to boast that he and President Tito owned the only two Mercedes in Yugoslavia. Now, having joined the nation of the land of the Mercedes, Pilic is still viewing the world from a very comfortable seat.

In due course much of the upholstery would be provided not by Dixon, who faded from the tennis scene, but by his Texan partner. I think it was in a suite of that Kansas City hotel, amidst all the paraphernalia of a tennis player's wardrobe, that I first met Lamar Hunt. At first glance he was indistinguishable from some of his young aides — such as Ron Bookman who had been hired as the tour's first PR man. Of medium height, with glasses and a conventional haircut, Lamar was one multimillionaire who had no trouble losing himself in the crowd. If Hollywood had come up with this understated son of the notorious H.L. Hunt as a prototype for an oil tycoon, J.R. and *Dallas* might never have been born.

As he handed out the coloured shirts like some clothes company rep, only the winning smile and the glint in the eye hinted that this was the man who had taken on the entire American Football establishment and, in defiance of the National Football League, had created his own league. There was nothing understated about that, but, as the tennis establishment was about to discover, Lamar's bite was always worse than his bark.

Years later, gazing out over the Dallas skyline from his favourite table at the Tower Club — those without an oil well need not apply — Lamar was still smiling, even if a certain wistfulness had set into the largely unchanged features.

'Obviously with hindsight, there are things we would have done differently,' he said. 'For a start we would not have got into it at all if we had foreseen the size of the financial burden.'

Passionately well-versed in the grid-iron game, Hunt was an innocent as far as tennis was concerned when Dixon first approached him. 'I only knew the names Gonzales, Laver, Rosewall because I read the sports pages. When Dave told me none of them was allowed to play Wimbledon I was shocked. I had no idea.'

Initially Hunt's interest in The Handsome Eight was 25%, with his relations, the Hill family, owning another 25% and Dixon the rest. Then, after the Kansas episode had been followed by a few empty stadiums in Florida, Dixon phoned Hunt to say he was financially over his head.

'So we took it over,' Lamar said — with remarkable nonchalance, considering the fortune that had disappeared into the coffers of World Championship Tennis in the intervening years. 'And I found myself taking a crash course in tennis politics. I must admit much of it shocked me.'

Tennis politics at the time was shocking in every sense — shocking certainly for the convoluted contortions its leading figures put themselves through in a belated effort to face up to some very basic facts of life, but shocking mainly for the sheer hypocrisy that lingered behind so many decisions. But with George MacCall, with his furrowed brow and lop-sided grin, running the rival pro tour with names such as Rod Laver, Fred Stolle, Ken Rosewall, Pancho Gonzales, Andres Gimeno and the new recruit Roy Emerson under his wing, amateur tennis could no longer live the life that Herman David had so rightly accused it of living. The game was up. But there were still some cards to play.

3

CORONADO AND CONFUSION

From the eye-popping experiments of Kansas City, David Gray and I moved back into the old familiar world at an annual meeting of the United States Lawn Tennis Association (USLTA), which that year was being held at one of America's landmark hotels, the Del Coronado, which sits in timeless splendour on the edge of the Pacific, close to San Diego. Ever since the British LTA had elected to turn Herman David's threats into official policy, the amateur game had been turned on its head, and here in Coronado confusion reigned.

The October Revolution that had taken place inside the British game the year before had virtually ensured that the structure of the world-wide game would never be the same again. The British call for an end to the distinction between amateurs and professionals, coupled with Herman David's vow to allow anyone and everyone to play at Wimbledon, was as radical a piece of legislation as could have been imagined. With LTA officials Eaton Griffiths, Derek Hardwick and Derek Penman in the van of the movement, the Association acted with a courage and a vision that were quite out of keeping with its performances, either before or since. How an organization that had taken such a dynamic stand in 1967 should fall back into a state of apathy in the 1970s as far as the development of British Tennis is concerned remains one of the game's saddest mysteries.

Nevertheless, the turmoil that existed in world tennis throughout the winter of 1967-68 was almost entirely the LTA's doing. The reaction amongst the various national federations was mixed but, initially at least, there was a heavy bias in favour of those who were in love with the word 'amateur', afraid of the word 'professional' and desperately anxious about what Open Tennis would do to the perks and the stature that came with their honorary jobs. Some, in the smaller nations, who had been fed the party line by the autocratic ILTF Secretary, Basil Reay — who was not beyond telling some African or Asian delegate to shut up and listen — simply didn't understand what was going on.

That was hardly the case in Coronado. Admittedly there were a few delegates who might have had difficulty spelling 'Wimbledon', but the leaders of the USLTA were politically savvy, even if many instinctively shied away from the brave new-world that was rushing towards them. Happily for the future prosperity of the game, the President that year was one of the few men of real stature to have emerged from the general level of genial mediocrity that exists in so many amateur sporting bodies. Tall, distinguished and as articulate as his legal training at Harvard would suggest, Robert J. Kelleher was firmly of the opinion that the time for pussyfooting around the subject of Open Tennis was long gone. While recognizing that he could not lead his vast, diverse body of delegates quite as far down the revolutionary trail as Britain would have liked, he was determined to gain a majority support for the principle of self-determination for those nations who wanted to test the Open Tennis waters.

During five long days of committee meetings and huddled confabs in the endless corridors of the old hotel, Bob Kelleher was made painfully aware of just how much resistance there was to the progressive attitude he and his supporters were promoting. 'Lawrence Baker, one of the stalwarts of the USLTA, was adamant in his anti-Open Tennis stance,' Kelleher recalled when he looked back recently. 'Baker said it would be like opening the temple to the money-changers, and when I pointed out that the money-changers were already there but simply under cover, he just shrugged and said, "Oh, it isn't a perfect world." '

This kind of attitude merely exasperated Kelleher, who was determined that the meeting send out a clear signal to the ILTF to the effect that the USTLA would cut its ties with the world body unless, as Bud Collins of the *Boston Globe* so accurately put it, 'that stodgy, antiquated body reforms and permits self-determination by all nations on the matter of open events . . .'

But the fears of the old guard had to be heard, and some of them were moving in their sincerity. One of Kelleher's predecessors, Martin Tressel, from Pittsburgh, had gone blind since completing his presidential term twelve months before, and his remarks carried a particular poignancy when he rose to speak to the huge gathering of delegates from 17 sections across the country.

'You make a mistake in pointing a shot-gun at the ILTF with this resolution,' said the 68-year-old speaker. 'They've been shot at before. You shouldn't raise false hopes that the ILTF will change. If we go ahead with this they may throw us out and then we'll be out of the Davis Cup, too.'

Kelleher knew that Tressel was voicing the fears of some of the more timid traditionalists as well as of those who frankly hated everything to do with the professional game. His supporters had also been accused of acting like 'pawns of the British' by Baker and others. So it was with a certain alarm that he greeted the sudden appearance of Britain's 'two Dereks', as they became known. Derek Hardwick, a feisty, bow-legged farmer with a political mind that worked like a scythe, and Derek Penman, an upright, patrician figure whose bearing belied his revolutionary ideals, had arrived in San Diego at the end of a round-the-world tour aimed at drumming up support for Britain's position.

The two Dereks had spoken at the AGM of the Australian LTA in Melbourne — where, interestingly, Harry Hopman, whose talents as a coach had produced so many champions for the professional ranks, had voiced the strongest objections to their plea for progress — and had met, briefly, with New Zealand officials during a stop-over at Auckland Airport. Now they were hoping to give a boost to the progressive forces in America but Kelleher was afraid their presence might antagonize people rather than activate the kind of support he was seeking.

'Frankly I wasn't expecting the two Dereks to just show up like that and my first reaction was to get them the hell out of there,' said Kelleher. 'So I hid them in a hotel downtown until I felt the mood was right for them to make an appearance.'

Kelleher's instincts were right. Neither of the two Dereks was interested in putting across their point of view in guarded, diplomatic terms. They had laid it on thick with their own councillors back home and were determined to do the same abroad. Both felt they were leading a moral crusade, and Penman's speeches to the LTA Council on 5 October and 14 December 1967 reflected that feeling. Given that his words helped set in motion the most dramatic change that has been effected in any major sport this century, it is worth quoting extracts from one of his speeches.

'The first point I would like to make clear,' Penman began while addressing the December meeting in London, 'is that, despite the impression that some people may have, the main object of this resolution is not that we should have an Open Wimbledon but that we should remove sham and hypocrisy from the game . . . For too long now we have been governed by a set of amateur rules that are quite unenforceable. We know the so-called amateur players bargain for payments grossly in excess of what they are entitled to but without which they cannot live. We know that tournament committees connive at this, else there would be no players at their tournaments. We feel we owe it not only to ourselves but to our players to release them from this humiliating and hypocritical situation and that the players should be able to earn openly and honestly the rewards to which their skill entitles them.'

Even in Britain this had caused a bit of puce-faced spluttering from the old guard but in America, where certain traditions can be just as jealously defended, it was too big a pill to swallow whole. Nevertheless, Kelleher kept hammering away, even though he was disappointed by the word that arrived from Australia, in the middle of the most intense lobbying, to the effect that the Australian LTA would favour reform but only with the consent of the ILTF. However, on closer inspection it appeared that the Australians were giving themselves greater flexibility than their official statement suggested, and Penman, stoking the fires of encouragement, announced that he and Hardwick were delighted. 'It was more than we expected,' Penman said.

Heartened by this, Kelleher launched his final attack. Pounding at the core of the resolution that empowered him to break with the ILTF if necessary, Kelleher told the delegates, 'This isn't an empty threat, nor is it merely a vote saying we favour open tournaments, such as we took prior to the 1967 ILTF meeting when Open Tennis was once again disapproved. Our resolution directs me to say to the ILTF, "You have failed to promulgate and enforce realistic and practical amateur rules. Therefore the time has come to take away from the ILTF all but small responsibilities. . . ." '

This was strong stuff, but once another resolution calling for the British solution — a complete abolition of the distinction between amateurs and professionals — had been unanimously voted down, Kelleher won a historic victory by getting the main resolution passed by 16 sections to one, a total of 102,064 votes to 9,978. The dissenting voice came from the middle States (Pennsylvania and Delaware) — an irony, as it turned out, because it was here, in Philadelphia, that the Fernbergers, within a few short years, were to build the most progressive indoor event of the new Open era.

As David Gray, Bud Collins and most other observers agreed, it had been a triumph for Kelleher's far-sighted determination to take the game in America into the modern age, and he had managed it despite one tactical slip that rapid staff-work covered up just in time. Several months before, Kelleher had given Bud Collins an interview for use in *Sports Illustrated*, in which he had referred to Baker as a 'stuffed shirt' and said that he was taking on the presidency only to stop it going to 'one of those backward old goats'. Not surprisingly the *Sports Illustrated* sub-editors seized on this, to come up with a headline that read, 'Open-minded boss for a bunch of old goats'.

With classic timing, this issue was due to go on sale on the

Wednesday morning of the Coronado meeting, just a couple of hours before Kelleher would be asking for the old goats' vote. Plunging into the petty cash, Bob Malaga, Kelleher's executive secretary, immediately sent out teams of helpers to buy up every copy of *Sports Illustrated* that was on sale in the vicinity of the hotel. By the time any of them had a chance to discover that they were a stuffed shirt or an old goat, most were already wearing Kelleher's colours.

Victory for the progressives at Coronado made it virtually certain that Britain would not be isolated and that some form of Open Tennis would emerge from the battlefield before the year was out. But the shooting had not stopped. The game was being splintered in unimaginable ways. The Australians were in the hopeless position of being led by a man who was quite openly in conflict with the view of the vast majority of his delegates. 'Big Bill' Edwards told my *Evening News* colleague John Oakley, 'I am still firmly convinced that a switch to Open Tennis would be suicidal, but this is only my personal view. It is certainly not the view of the Australian LTA. Five of the six states have voted for Open Tennis, so if America goes ahead with its threat and pulls out of the ILTF, it looks as if Australia will have to do the same.'

I never met Edwards, but from everything he said at the time, 'Big Bill' appears to have been a big bureaucrat — one of those people who hide behind the world 'official' and refuse to recognize reality unless it carries a stamp of approval. Writing in the *Melbourne Herald* at the height of the crisis, Edwards said that red-herring words like 'hypocrisy' and 'shamateurism' only tended to confuse the real issue. The real issue, according to Edwards, was that at the ILTF meeting in Luxembourg the previous July, the proposal for Open Tennis had been rejected by 33 nations, with only 10 in favour. No matter that half the small nations had no clue what they were voting for; no matter that vested interest was rife and his little red herring called hypocrisy rampant. None of that concerned Edwards. His main concern, as stated in his own words, was to ensure that no decision be taken as a result of 'British brinkmanship stemming from petulance because it cannot get its own way'.

In the early months of 1968 there was no doubt that Britain was out on a very long limb and was, in fact, faced with expulsion from the ILTF and therefore from the Davis Cup as well. And no one was more determined to see Britain kicked out than the man who just happened, at the time, to be President of the ILTF. Giorgio de Stefani had been a pre-war star of the Italian Davis Cup team. I thought I detected a certain malicious satisfaction in his announcing in January that, 'because of its anti-democratic and illegal' unilateral decision to admit professionals, Britain would be excluded from all international events. Well, I thought, wasn't that rich. 'Illegal' did he say? How illegal was it under the ILTF's own sweet rules, or anybody else's for that matter, for an amateur body to pay amateur players simply to remain amateur? If that ludicrous process did not define the meaning of the word 'shamateur' then I didn't know what did.

In the late 1960s I was a foreign correspondent for the London *Evening News* and was based in New York, but I had still managed to stay close to the tennis scene by taking time off to cover Wimbledon and the Forest Hills every year and it had been only a few months prior to de Stefani's pronouncement that Nikki Pietrangeli, the classic clay-court stroke-maker of his day and a hero in Italy after twice winning the French Championships, had been telling me a few home truths about life on the Italian Davis Cup squad. Our conversation had been off the record. Now I felt it was time to put the public record straight.

So I phoned Nikki at his flat in Rome from my office in Rockefeller Plaza, and I like to think that the result of what Pietrangeli openly admitted to me that day helped to drive another long nail into the coffin that would soon contain a terminally ill 'living lie'.

Pietrangeli said that he had been on the point of signing professional forms with Jack Kramer a couple of times in the early 1960s, but that on each occasion he had been dissuaded by the Italian Federation, of which de Stefani was President. 'I'm not prepared to say how much, but they paid me money,' said Nikki.

That was all I needed. The story was prominently displayed on the front page of the *Evening News* on 11 January 1968 and de Stefani, as well as, I am afraid, poor Pietrangeli, spent the next 24 hours being hounded by reporters. It was, after all, only three days after the ILTF President had handed out his imperious ruling on Britain's status in the game.

In *The Times* Rex Bellamy picked up the story and quoted de Stefani as saying that 'someone' in the Italian Federation had 'arranged' for Pietrangeli to withdraw from his professional commitments (Nikki, at one stage, had actually signed a preliminary agreement). De Stefani went on to admit, 'We certainly helped him but he did not get money from the Federation for this purpose. Any such idea is absolutely untrue.'

Bellamy added, 'This confused double-talk presumably means something to Dr de Stefani though it may not mean much to anyone else . . . But Pietrangeli's admission has done Britain some good and the ILTF some harm. The "floating voters" of the world may now be thinking that Dr de Stefani should put his own house in order before making holier-than-thou statements to other people.'

The ILTF's defences had already started to look flimsy and this revelation merely blew a few more holes in them, while, on a personal level, they made de Stefani simply look silly. But the battle continued, moving within the space of a few days from Coronado to Paris, where Kelleher rejoined Hardwick and Penman at a special meeting of the ILTF. No matter what kind of brave statements de Stefani and others were making in public, the ILTF realized their position was crumbling, and frantic efforts were being made by some of its more imaginative leaders to come up with compromise solutions. One such leader was Jean Borotra. 'The Bounding Basque' had enchanted crowds and enraged opponents during his extravagant years as one of France's 'Four Musketeers'. Now President of the French Federation, Borotra had been a driving force on what the ILTF liked to call its 'committee on amateurism', and as soon as Kelleher, accompanied by his vice-president, Alastair Martin, arrived in Paris, Jean bounded into the Hilton for a breakfast meeting.

Talking in his voluble, machine-gun English, heavily accented but very precise, Borotra spelled out his ideas for a compromise. They were geared, quite genuinely, to finding a solution that would satisfy the British, but stopped short of the desperate idea of abolishing all distinctions between amateurs and professionals. It was here that the idea of the dreaded authorized player was born.

To his surprise Kelleher found himself invited to a meeting of European nations at the Hotel Scribe, which sits in the shadow of the Opera House. 'I was even more surprised when they asked me to preside,' Kelleher recalled. 'I didn't even know what I was doing there at first, but I sat down at this long, green-baize table and tried to explain the resolution we had passed in Coronado — a position from which we would not budge.'

Unlike some of his brash, stetson-hatted, cigar-chomping successors, Kelleher was just the kind of civilized American to whom a roomful of Europeans were prepared to listen, and although the USLTA President could not kill off the authorized-player idea, a motion along the lines of the American resolution was passed at the general meeting the following day.

The weeks between that Paris meeting and the emergency general meeting of all ILTF delegates to be held on 30 March, also in Paris, were crucial to the future structure of the game. The danger of a breakaway by Britain, the United States, Sweden and other like-minded nations was still very real, and when the ILTF came up with the authorized-player concept as a solution, it was met with scorn by Penman, Hardwick and their colleagues.

In simple terms, authorized players were to be a species who would be allowed to accept prize money at certain designated tournaments but who would still remain under the jurisdiction of their national association. Other players would then fall into one of two categories, either that of amateurs or that of those professionals under contract to pro promoters. It was a desperate attempt by amateur officials to cling on to a game that was slipping away from them and the LTA, still fired with revolutionary zeal, were quick to spot it. 'What we want is honesty in the game and what they are suggesting is not honest,' Hardwick said flatly. The official LTA statement was no gentler.

'The authorized player is the quintessence of hypocrisy. It is no cure for shamateurism as we shall still get players who are not authorized but are still receiving money under the table.' The LTA also believed that it was 'unworthy and illogical' for the ILTF to propose that authorized players be allowed to compete in the Davis Cup while genuine professionals were barred. They were right. The idea of the authorized player was an anachronism at birth and died after a short and useless life a couple of years later.

Under the circumstances it was surprising that it was given life at all but, in fact, Britain backed down a bit in the weeks leading up to the 30 March meeting, which was held at the Automobile Club on the Place de la Concorde, a suitably revolutionary site. Yet the result was not as bloody as many had feared. In return for getting everyone to recognize the reality of Open Tennis and also for being allowed to call their own players what they wished, Britain conceded to the ILTF the idea of the authorized player for those nations that insisted on nurturing the little devil as well as the proposal that nations limit the number of Open tournaments they staged.

No one was defeated. Honour was satisfied — but only fools failed to realize that the game had been irrevocably changed.

4

GONZALES–PASARELL

Charlie Pasarell, the Puerto Rican who was on the same college team as Arthur Ashe at UCLA and went on to be ranked No. 1 in the United States in 1967, will never be remembered as one of the great players of his era. He never reached even the semifinal of a Grand Slam event and his Davis Cup career was brief. Yet the name of Pasarell is inextricably linked with the history of Wimbledon and with some of the greatest matches ever played there.

In fact for three years, from 1967 to 1969, Pasarell very nearly took over the Centre Court during the opening days of the Championship and made it a showcase for his own muscular gifts. The fact that he was victorious in only one of the three epic battles he fought may have been very painful at the time, but, in retrospect, the result was less important than the matches themselves and the manner in which the protagonists fought the good fight.

Lack of speed and a less than energetic attitude towards training probably prevented Pasarell from doing full justice to his ability. When we were on tour together in Africa in 1971, Ashe would tell the kids, 'Watch Charlie play and copy his strokes. He's got the best strokes in the world.'

'The Pasarell Years' began with a bang in 1967 when he shocked Wimbledon on the opening day by defeating the reigning champion, Manolo Santana. Charlie wrote himself into the history books that day because never before, nor since, has the defending men's singles champion lost in the first round. Santana, such a favourite with the crowds when he had beaten Dennis Ralston in the final the previous year, was never really in the match against Pasarell, who bombarded him with his heavy serve delivered off a powerful, cork-screw action.

The next year, when Open Tennis arrived, Ken Rosewall marked his return to Wimbledon after a 12-year absence with a match against Pasarell that few in the audience will ever forget. Frequently interrupted by rain, it occupied the whole of the first Friday's playing time and eventually went to Rosewall 7–9, 6–1, 6–8, 6–2, 6–3. Often interrupted matches lose their rhythm and the standard of tennis declines. Not so on this memorable occasion. Each time the players returned, battle was immediately enjoined with even greater intensity and skill. Perhaps the rest periods helped Pasarell maintain the ferocious velocity of that serve, and maybe Rosewall's little legs — not young even back in 1968 — benefited from occasional respite, for they were having to carry him over the grass at incredible speeds to meet the Puerto Rican's powerfully angled volleys.

What a contrast they made! Rosewall, small and neat, not a hair out of place — a deliberate man who calculates every shot to the inch and matches a computer-like brain with strokes of precision and beauty. In contrast Pasarell looked like some half-tamed warrior, hitching up his pants as he swaggered, splay-footed, across the base-line, gripping his racket like a tomahawk. Power and blood and guts were his stock-in-trade and when he led 4–0 in the third set and then, despite an Australian recovery, still reached set point at 5–4, it seemed that power might win the day.

But Rosewall met that crisis with an angled forehand so surprising in its design and so lovely in its execution that a collective gasp was heard around the Centre Court. Even though Pasarell eventually snatched the set 8–6 (no tie-breakers in those days, remember), the memory of that incisive forehand lingered on and soon the Australian's accuracy began to overcome the American's power. So Pasarell lost in the end, but not before he had roused the crowd with a few more defiantly explosive blows, and when it was finally over, dusk was settling over the Centre Court and people were loath to go home. It had been one of those matches one never wanted to end. 'But in some ways it never will,' wrote Rex Bellamy in *The Times* the following day, 'because it was a match we shall tell our grandchildren about.'

So Charlie Pasarell, who was a mere private in the United States Army at the time, had established himself as a fighter of much higher rank as far as the Centre Court was concerned, after two consecutive performances of such power and purpose. But amazingly the best was still to come. For sheer drama, emotion and excitement the third year outstripped everything that had gone before, because in 1969 Pasarell found himself facing one of the legends of the game in a match that was to break records for longevity and go down as one of the most incredible battles ever witnessed at Wimbledon.

That year Pancho Gonzales, twice United States champion at Forest Hills in the late forties and a giant presence on the Jack Kramer pro tour all through the fifties and early sixties, was 41 years old. At such an age most professional athletes have long since retired from the top flight of competitive play but Gonzales, despite flecks

27

of grey in his black mane of hair, was still a ruggedly fit and durable athlete.

But against a man 16 years his junior, he was obviously going to face a formidable task on the fast grass court that gave so much assistance to Pasarell's powerful serve. Gonzales, however, was determined to prove that when it came to serving, no one in the history of the game had possessed a more fluent, majestic or accurate delivery than the great Pancho himself. If proof was needed of this, Gonzales provided it with the most amazing feat in a seemingly interminable first set, when from the time the score reached 4–5, he served to save that set no less than *eighteen* times. Even then Pasarell needed a lob that landed somewhat luckily on the back edge of the base-line finally to break the Gonzales serve and so win the opening set 24–22. The 46 games played in that set equalled the record set at Wimbledon in 1962 by Nikki Pietrangeli and Nikki Pilic. But on this occasion there was much, much more to come.

Aggravated at losing a set after saving 11 set points, Gonzales soon found other things to anger him apart from the increasingly confident nature of Pasarell's game. The light was fading. At Wimbledon in the high-summer months, it is possible to play tennis until 9.30 pm or even later if the sky is clear. But an overcast evenings the lights fades much more quickly from the Centre Court, where the covered stands cast their own shadows even on the brightest days. .And so as the second set began, long past seven o'clock, the light was worsening and Gonzales' eyes started straining to pick up the ball in the gathering gloom.

It was then that the immensity of the drama started to unfold. The Centre Court at Wimbledon is an intimidating arena; it is, in a sense, a cathedral of the game and even the noisiest and most extrovert personalities tend to be dwarfed by its all-embracing atmosphere. Prior to the McEnroe era very few players misbehaved on the Centre Court. Like a temple, it is not a place where one easily raises ones voice. It takes a very big personality, a giant in every sense to do that — but of course Pancho Gonzales is and always was just such a man. Of all the potentially explosive personalities I had seen play, only Gonzales, up to that time, had the grandeur and the arrogance to dominate the Centre Court through the sheer power of his personality.

As the light continued to fade and Pasarell's serves continued to blaze down at him, Pancho prowled the base-line like some caged and tormented lion. Finally he could take it no more. 'Get the referee!' he roared. 'How the hell can I play when I can't see?'

To hell with history and tradition and the way things were supposed to be done. No matter that this was Wimbledon, Pancho Gonzales was just trying to win a tennis match and he knew that if he was forced to play much longer in that kind of light, his 41-year-old eyes would lead him to defeat.

But the response from the Wimbledon hierarchy was typically aloof. Even when light rain began to fall from leaden skies, the referee, Captain Mike Gibson, stood stony-faced at the end of the court, his military moustache twitching from time to time as if the conditions were to be gauged by the occasional sniff and, for what seemed like an eternity, did nothing.

Gonzales continued to rant and rave, trying vainly to hold the rampant Pasarell at bay in between ever more ferocious demands that play be halted for the night. Once he threw his racket down by the umpire's chair and it hit the BBC courtside microphone. To people watching on television, the explosion sounded like the end of the world. Their screens were filled with a close-up of the Gonzales scowl, and, with the light so bad, the whole face was tinted green, making him look like some great Aztec god — an awesome, fearsome sight.

Captain Gibson was either frozen with fear or completely unmoved — I suspect the latter — because, despite the rain and the dying light, he did nothing until Pasarell had wrapped up the second set 6–1, leaving Gonzales to storm off court with boos and whistles ringing in his ears. In those pre-McEnroe days, the Centre Court crowds were not accustomed to people who challenged the very fabric of etiquette and traditional behaviour.

The arguments were still raging when the two men returned to resume the battle the following day. Few doubted that Gonzales' hopes of victory were virtually beyond the realms of possibility.

There was nothing about the opening games of the third set to suggest otherwise. Gonzales' serve was getting shorter, Pasarell was piling on the pressure and, occasionally, Pancho started to look as old as he was. Once the Puerto Rican unleashed a serve straight at Pancho's stomach and the 41-year-old reflexes were tested to their utmost as he doubled up defensively, protecting himself with his racket.

But the set wore on and the expected collapse never happened. Strangely, Pasarell was using fewer of the lobs that had served him so well the previous day and his forehand started to jerk nervously whenever he manoeuvred Gonzales into a vulnerable position.

Charlie's serve was also becoming erratic. With the score at 13–14, he served three aces, but at 14–15 he produced two double faults, which cost him the set and, psychologically, cost him a great deal more in confidence. Gonzales smelt blood. He knew where to look for it, too, because he had coached the young Pasarell often enough in the past when Charlie had visited him in Las Vegas, and there was nothing about the technical aspects of his opponent's game that he could not analyse.

However, there was not much analysis needed as the fourth set came to a comparatively speedy end with Pasarell delivering another double fault to lose 3–6. Now, more than ever, it was an endurance test and, again, it seemed impossible that Gonzales would survive. He was looking more exhausted by the minute, hanging his head to let the sweat drip off him and leaning on his racket for support between points.

But if the body was wilting, the mind was still sharp. In fact that was true of both men, for every possible variety of serve was coming off their rackets — spinning, cut, angled, short, deep or just plain fast — and the base-line rallies, whenever they were allowed to develop, were probing affairs, full of carefully stroked shots.

Suddenly Pasarell arrived on the brink, forcing Gonzales' back to the wall at 0–40, 4–5 in the final set. The lob reappeared in Pasarell's repertoire but two of them now landed inches out and Pancho saved the third match point with a centre-line service winner. Seven deuces were needed before Gonzales clawed his way back to safety at 5–5. The tension was becoming unbearable.

By the time Gonzales had pulled himself out of yet another 0–40 situation at 5–6, spectators were on the point of hysteria. A smash, a sweetly angled volley and another fine service had enabled Gonzales to escape a second time, but could he last much longer? Surely the younger man's stamina would tell in the end. Indeed, at this stage, Pasarell seemed to be getting stronger and, at 8–7, he reached match point on the Gonzales serve for the seventh time. A hush fell over the Centre Court. Could this be it? Up went another Pasarell lob as Gonzales' tired old legs carried him to the net but, as gasps were emitted all around the arena, the ball again landed inches long.

Impossible as it seemed at the time, it proved to be Pasarell's last gasp, for suddenly the Puerto Rican cracked. Inexplicably for a man who seemed to have had his ageing opponent on the rack, Charlie lost 11 consecutive points and suddenly, out of nowhere, the incredible Pancho Gonzales had survived long enough to claim a famous victory. The score was 22–24, 1–6, 16–14, 6–3, 11–9. Over the two days they had played for five hours and 20 minutes — and this in an era when players did not sit down during the change-over and generally played their matches at a faster pace than the stars of today. The total of 112 games exceeded by 19 the previous record for the longest match ever played at Wimbledon, staged 16 years before by those two long-time rivals who knew each other's play so well, Jaroslav Drobny and Budge Patty.

But Gonzales' triumph over Pasarell was something else altogether. It transcended the ordinary tennis match by virtue of its drama, emotional impact and hair-raising excitement, as well as its length. Inevitably one felt sad for Pasarell, but it was fitting that Pancho Gonzales, who had been denied the right to parade his greatness on the world's greatest tennis stage for so many years because of his professional status, should have managed, in the dimming twilight of his career, to show the Wimbledon crowd just what he was capable of. And what might have been.

5

A NEW ERA

No one needed to explain to Donald Dell about change or the dawn of a new era. Like a bloodhound on the scent, ears pricked and teeth bared. Dell had been sniffing the winds of change for months, and when Open Tennis finally arrived he was already into his stride. Grasping the vast possibilities that awaited anyone with sufficient drive, imagination and organizational skill, Dell was planning a complete restructuring of the old amateur game before most people understood what he was talking about.

Having terminated his own Davis Cup career in the mid 1960s to take over as captain of a powerful United States team, this Yale law graduate was already making a name for himself as a demanding, inspirational leader. On graduation he had left home in nearby Bethesda, Maryland to rent a Georgetown house in the nation's capital with two college chums who would soon become his partners, Lee Fentress and Frank Craighill. He took a job as top aide to Sargent Shriver at the Office of Economic Opportunity, a government department that had sprung from Shriver's time as head of the Peace Corps. The Kennedys were still a powerful force in Washington and not only was Shriver the dead President's brother-in-law, but also Dell, by instinct and conviction, was a Kennedy man.

All that winter of 1967–68 Robert Kennedy agonized over whether he should run for the presidency. When the Vietnam War became too big an issue for him to ignore any longer. Kennedy threw his hat into the ring, gathered about him many of his brother's former aides and then asked America's young Davis Cup captain to play a key role in his campaign.

'Bobby wants me to be his advance man,' Donald told me on one of my frequent visits to Washington. 'Obviously it's an unbelievable challenge, but I don't know whether I can throw everything I am building here to one side and take the time.'

What Dell was building was a managerial organization that would have a lasting effect on the way professional tennis was reared and moulded over the next decade. He had left Shriver by this time and with Fentress and Craighill at his side, had already apprised his Davis Cup squad of his dream. 'Stick with me and I'll make you millionaires,' Dell told Arthur Ashe, Stan Smith, Bob Lutz, Dennis Ralston, Charlie Pasarell and Marty Riessen. Give or take a few cents, not to mention a few investments that ended in disaster, Dell was as good as his word.

You could never accuse Donald of not knowing where he was going. The Kennedy offer was professionally and emotionally tempting. Although Fentress, who took leave of the new firm of Dell, Fentress & Craighill to run the RFK campaign headquarters in Indianapolis, was a closer family friend of the Kennedy clan, Dell was also deeply committed to the cause and, apart from anything else, he knew that if he turned the offer down he would be jeopardizing his chance of getting a White House staff job should Kennedy win.

But in one of those decisions that might just conceivably have changed the history of the world, Dell said no. As the candidate's advance man, Dell would have had a major say in where Kennedy spoke, which routes he travelled, which hotels were used in cities across the nation. It is quite possible, of course, that Dell, too, would have chosen the Ambassador Hotel as the location for Bobby's victory party on the night he won the California primary and that he, too, would have had the candidate take a short cut through the kitchen pantry. It is highly probable that nothing he might or might not have done would have prevented a lone assassin from shooting a man who was primed and ready to become one of the great presidents in the history of the United States. We shall never know.

It would be unfair to suggest that Dell made the wrong decision either personally or professionally. It was a tough choice and it took courage to resist the magnetism of the Kennedys. Yet a few precious months in the close company of such an extraordinary man might have taught Dell many things he needed to learn. In the years that followed, Dell built his career by behaving in much the same manner as the tough, ruthless baby brother who had become President Kennedy's Attorney General. But Jack Kennedy's death had turned Bobby into a far more introspective, caring human being. All through the final months of his life, Bobby was growing in stature, in compassion and in his awareness of the hopes and aspirations of people poorly placed to realize the American dream.

Uninterested in adulation, Bobby sought out opposing views and listened. He received an earful at an airport in Indiana one night from a group of young supporters of Eugene McCarthy, his rival for the Democratic nomination who seized the youth vote by announcing his anti-war candidacy before Bobby. Later, back on the campaign plane, he stopped in the seat next to mine for a moment as he moved around the cabin, and said, 'I understand completely why those kids are for McCarthy. But it's so frustrating because, in the long run, I know I will be able to do so much more for them.'

Kennedy may or may not have had a premonition about his own death but he knew that no matter what happened, McCarthy would never make it to the White House.

Dell was devastated when Bobby was killed, but he found no reason to search his soul as Kennedy had done when the President died. Obviously the strong family ties were missing, but Donald might have avoided much of the hostility he has engendered had he listened more closely to what his friend was saying in the last months of his life. Instead, Dell ploughed on with even greater energy and ambition, cutting swathes through meetings with people who opposed him, his natural charm and *bonhomie* always threatened by a sudden outburst of temper. He built a power base and became a bully. Friends recoiled and partners deserted him — Fentress and Craighill both leaving to form their own management company. One-time allies such as Philippe Chatrier would no longer speak to him. The ATP, which Dell had been instrumental in forming, drove him out of the organization when the Board of Directors voted to replace him as their legal counsel. So was Donald Dell destroyed? Far from it. Holding his head high, no matter what kind of bruising his pride had suffered, Dell continued — and continues — to master-mind the activities of Pro Serv and its television affiliates, drawing Ivan Lendl and Jimmy Connors — once a bitter foe — into the company as big-time clients and retaining the loyalty of Arthur Ashe and the man Arthur discovered on a Dell-inspired tour of Africa, Yannick Noah.

So, from all this, it can be seen that Dell is remarkable. Had he not been, professional tennis would be a different sort of game today — quite possibly not as popular, quite certainly not as rich. Because back in 1968, Mark McCormack, who began his career in Cleveland managing Arnold Palmer, might have been casting a first wary eye at tennis and Chatrier might have been plotting how best to storm the French game's Bastille at Stade Roland Garros, but it would all have taken a far, far longer time to blossom into the multimillion-dollar business it became had not Dell and one other man brainstormed and barnstormed their way through the decaying fortress of amateur tennis. The other man was the old pro himself, Jack Kramer.

Like any budding politician in Washington, Dell needed an old pro to hold his hand and help him plot a path through the minefield that lies in wait for any young upstart seeking to overthrow the established order. No one could have been better suited to the task than Kramer, a former outlaw who was now prepared to ride with the sheriff's posse — provided that the trail was of his own choosing.

Kramer had his trail all mapped out. It was to be called the Grand Prix and would wend its way around the world, linked by a points system that would bring cohesion and understanding to the disjointed tournament circuit. If the ILTF were interested in this kind of idea, then Kramer was ready to come in from the cold and help them. Like Charles de Gaulle waiting in his little village of Colombey-les-Deux-Eglises for the call to become President of France, so Kramer had retired to the family home in Bel Air since giving up an active role in the pro tour he had founded. And there he waited. Various attempts had been made to lure him back into the mainstream of the game but, like *Le Grand Charles*, Big Jake had a political nose and he was waiting until the time was right.

Obviously the time had not been right back in 1960, when a very young Chatrier had organized a dinner for Kramer and Jean Borotra, then the leader of French tennis. 'I wanted to persuade Jean to have Jack come back into the official game and organize a professional department of the ILTF,' Chatrier explained. 'I tried to make Jack see that his tour was not going anywhere; that the Kramer Cup Tony Trabert and the boys had started in Jack's name would never capture the imagination of the public like the Davis Cup; that the future lay with the traditional tournaments. But we missed voting in Open Tennis that year, and anyway I realized during the dinner that there was still too much suspicion and pride dividing these two great Wimbledon champions.'

To an even greater extent than Dell, Chatrier had vision. He foresaw what was coming, even though his patience was sorely tested by his having to wait for it, and by 1968, when he became Dell's counterpart as captain of the French Davis Cup team, he was busy organizing an in-house revolution that would set him off on a road to a position of more permanent power than anyone else in the game has ever enjoyed. It began with the installation of the amiable 1946 French champion, Marcel Bernard, as President in place of Borotra. Having got himself elected as Vice-President of the French Federation, Chatrier then bided his time until 1972 to take over in name. In reality Chatrier had been the driving force behind the restructuring of French tennis and, indeed, together with Kramer and Dell, of the world game, for the previous four years.

Just as Chatrier had been great friends with Tony Trabert when Tony was running the new-style Kramer tour from Paris in the early 1960s, so Philippe now grew closer and closer to Jack himself. And when Jack made one of his frequent visits to Paris, Donald was almost invariably with him.

It was in 1969 in Chatrier's old apartment just off the Avenue des Ternes in the 17th *arrondissement* that the first of what was to be a whole series of meetings between this formidable trio took place. Unlike the meetings that became the focal point of Dell's whole career — he was always having 'meetings' — there was no structure to these talks; just three increasingly close friends arguing passionately and endlessly about how the game of tennis should proceed. I joined them one evening in early 1969 and as Madame Chatrier — the former British player Susan Partridge — appeared occasionally to refill the men's glasses, Kramer produced the blue-print for his Grand Prix concept out of his bulging briefcase.

On arrival I had timidly mentioned some thoughts I had been having about a points table for the top players (neither the ATP nor the computer was in existence then, of course), but Kramer cut me short. 'Been reading my mind, kid,' he laughed. 'Here, take a look at this.'

It was all there, the basic structure for a world-wide system that would get off the ground within a year, originally under the Pepsi-Cola banner, and finish its first year of activity with a Masters tournament played in Tokyo, in the dankest, coldest stadium I have ever seen. Stan Smith just had time to win the first prize of $15,000 before flying off to army boot camp in California, and although the amount of money was miniscule compared with the gold-rush that Kramer had unleashed, it still made Stan one of the richest recruits in the US Army.

The system, not so different from that of the motor-racing Grand Prix, was basically simple. Points would be awarded round by round in numbers linked to the overall prize-money level of the tournament and, at the end of the year, the top eight points finishers would qualify for the Masters and the top 30 would claim graduated levels of bonus money. In 1970 the top prize was $25,000. Six years later, when Raul Ramirez finished top, it had risen to $150,000. In 1987 Ivan Lendl received $800,000 for finishing in first place. One could say that Jack's little idea was quite a success.

But it wasn't, of course, that simple. The game in the late 1960s was in an inevitable state of upheaval and, aided by Chatrier from his power base in Paris, Kramer and Dell worked harder, longer and in more places than it would be possible to document or remember. They were to be found in hotel lobbies and hotel bedrooms, in airports and clubhouse lounges. They met with tournament directors and sponsors and television agents. They'd argue over soused herring at the Grand Hotel in Stockholm and over a *filet mignon* at the Westbury in London. If it was Philadelphia one night, it could be Rome the next. With increasing frequency, Dell would suddenly announce, 'God, I'm exhausted,' and lurch off in search of the only place where he could really relax — a hotel sauna. Occasionally Kramer, stubbing out his cigar, would join him in the steam and the friendly arguments would continue. They made an amazing pair.

Ironically, of the three women in their lives it was Susan Chatrier who decided she could no longer handle an introspective workaholic. Since their divorce Philippe has never remarried. Somehow Carol Dell, a beautiful Pan Am stewardess, and Gloria Kramer, who gave Jack five sons, have stayed the course. Heaven knows how. Carol could have put up with the impossibility of trying to build a life around a man who was always late, never stopped working and was rarely off the phone only through a strong streak of self-sufficiency and a steel-willed determination to make the marriage succeed. Because she is a very rare and intelligent woman, it has.

Gloria Kramer shares Carol's will of steel, although the size of her personality would brook no rival. Basically, 'Fou-fou', as Jack calls her, is a riot. If anyone ever made a film about the Kramers, it would take Angela Lansbury to portray Gloria properly — and even she would have to stretch herself. Whenever Jack's obsession with the game that ruled their lives became too great, Gloria would tend to take it out on his American Express card. The British photographer Arthur Cole and I went shopping with the Kramers in Hong Kong one year. You have never seen so many happy shopkeepers. 'Darling, you look a vision,' Gloria would cry as she swept another shirt off the counter and held it up against Arthur or myself. In those Kowloon shopping arcades that go on for ever, Jack was always three boutiques to the rear, signing the bills.

But if Kramer had been given a new lease of life by the advent of Open Tennis, so, too, had many of his former players. Frank Sedgman, revered by his peers and by the generations that followed as the perfect role model for an Australian sportsman, was one of the first to seize the opportunity of returning to the Wimbledon stage he had left 16 years before. Sedgman was 40 in 1968 but, as his exploits on the Grand Masters tour proved many years later, fitness had always been a Sedgman hallmark. Unfortunately Lew Hoad, next up amongst Hopman's Aussies to win Wimbledon, could never make the same claim. Hoad was as strong as an ox and as talented a player as has ever set foot on a court. There are those who insist that, on his day, Hoad was the greatest player of all time. But his days were numbered by a chronic back injury and an insistence that life was for living. None the less Lew still had plenty of tennis in him and he, too, was anxious to return to what was going to be a historic Wimbledon — the first Wimbledon since Bill Tilden had turned pro in 1930 to include every player of sufficiently high standard who wanted to play.

Like the two Panchos, Gonzales and Segura, like Ken Rosewall, Barry MacKay, Andres Gimeno and all the other pros who had been banned from the cathedrals of the game for so long, Hoad wanted to be part of the new era, but would his back stand up to it? What kind of pain barrier would he have to pass through to make himself truly competitive again?

One night in early 1968 we were talking about this over a dinner organized in New York by Gene Barakat, a former New Zealand rugby league player who later became Eileen Ford's right hand man at the Ford model agency. The chance of being introduced to some stunning woman was only part of the attraction of dining with Gene. As an athlete he spoke the Aussies' language and, in the absence of anything more alluring that particular night, four of us — Barakat, Hoad, Roy Emerson and myself — retired to my apartment on East 57th Street for a night-cap. I remember the evening particularly because it brought home more forcibly than ever before the esteem in which Hopman's generation of Australians held one another. All young athletes tend to idolize their immediate predecessors — witness Bjorn Borg and the Swedes — but the Australians of that golden era had something very special going between them. Somehow they managed to be the fiercest competitors on court and yet best mates off it, even to the point of self-sacrifice.

'You should give it a real go, Hoady,' Barakat was saying as I searched my fridge for another beer. 'As long as your back stands up to it, you can still beat the shit out of most guys on the tour.'

Hoad was standing by the window, staring out over the Manhattan skyline, his blond hair illuminated at two-second intervals by a flashing neon sign across the street. Suddenly Emerson interjected.

'Look, mate, I'll tell you what,' said Emmo. 'I'll take six weeks off and I'll train you. I'll work you to the bloody bone so that you can get in shape to play your best tennis. Then Gene will be right. You will beat the lot of us.'

It was an extraordinary offer. This was not some middle-ranked pro speaking but Roy Emerson, one Wimbledon champion talking to another. Here was a man who still had aspirations of winning another title himself, yet was offering to help decrease his chances of doing so by sharpening up one of the greatest talents in the game. What was the motivation? Certainly not money. That simply didn't come into it. No, like many great performers, Emerson was in awe of genius and was a big enough man himself not to feel threatened by it. He loved the game of tennis and he loved Lew. He simply would have considered it a privilege to help elevate both to the highest possible level of which man and his sport are capable. As it turned out Hoad never took up Emmo's offer, and although he did reappear at Wimbledon, momentarily rekindling memories of his greatness on the Centre Court, his back imposed hopeless restrictions. For Hoad, Open Tennis had taken too long in coming, just as it had for Gonzales, and if one could point out, equally, that the delay had had the opposite effect on Emerson's career, allowing him to win titles when Laver, Rosewall and other rivals were banned, the sheer weight of Emmo's achievements during those years in the 1960s mark him down as a very special competitor. He finished with more Grand Slam titles in singles and doubles (28) than any other player in history, and that included winning all four Grand Slam singles titles *at least* twice. When one considers that Borg, McEnroe, Connors and Lendl have not, as yet, been able to win all four titles even once, Emerson's achievement overrides the obvious fact that the competition was marginally easier. But, as that evening proved, no one needed to tell Emmo about levels of excellence. 'I'm not in your class, mate,' he said, clutching my last can of beer and looking Lew straight in the eye. From one champion to another I thought that was a pretty classy sort of thing to say.

Several years later there was another lovely example of how the likes of Hoad, Laver and, in this instance, Rosewall were revered by their peers. Sherwood Stewart, a great doubles player who has since challenged Kenny himself for longevity on the pro tour, was playing his boyhood idol for the first time in the Australian Indoors in Sydney. Bud Collins described what happened. 'One point will stay with the witnesses for a long time, a furious duel of cross-court backhands, each hit faster and lower than the one before. These skimmers continued for a while until Rosewall got bored. Whack — with that undetectable change of direction at the last instance of his swing, Kenny drove down the line, tangle-footing Stewart who collapsed on the court in a wild giggle. "I don't believe it, but I've seen it now!" Sherwood shrieked as he rolled on the asphalt. "Isn't he something? How much," he yelled at Rosewall, "do you charge for a lesson?" '

The respect, even the awe, was genuine not just on Stewart's part but on the part of most of the journeymen pros who travelled with the greatest practitioners of their craft. It is true that the tour was a more carefree and friendly set-up in those early days, but I don't think professional respect between players has diminished. A locker-room will still empty when a player of Miloslav Mecir's special skills is playing particularly well, and even a lower-ranked player like Ramesh Krishnan will be admired purely for his simplicity of style. Once, when the little Indian was engaged in a superb match against Mats Wilander in the Seiko Classic in Tokyo, a whole group of players stood around at the courtside shaking their heads in wonderment and admiration at the standard of stroke-play they were watching.

But back in 1968 it was the pros who were feeling the pressure to perform, no matter how much they were idolized by the younger generation who were waiting for them in the newly designated Open tournaments. When the first such tournament was played, in the damp little English seaside resort of Bournemouth in April of 1968, the results, quite apart from the historic nature of the event itself, made headlines around the world. Mark Cox, the Cambridge Blue with the thatch of blond curls, could not have looked more like a pink-faced English amateur but, as he was to prove often enough on the WCT tour in later years, his game was a lot rougher than his retiring personality would have you believe.

Cox's left-handed game packed what the pros like to call a 'heavy' ball and it proved too heavy not only for Pancho Gonzales in the second round but also for Roy Emerson in the third. Rex Bellamy, who watched it all in amazement, commented in *The Times*, 'To beat Gonzales over five sets in 2¼ hours was astonishing. To beat Emerson 6–0, 6–1, 7–5 in an hour less was ridiculous. To pack both performances into 26 hours was to play tennis that dreams are made of — and Cox did exactly that. The mind boggles at the audacious enormity of his achievement.'

Revealing the cool analyst that would later become such a valuable asset to the BBC Television commentary team, Cox refused to get quite as carried away. 'These fellows are under a lot of pressure this week,' he said, 'It's as if they've got weights round their legs. They are frightened to lose and are therefore not doing themselves justice.'

Rod Laver restored professional pride by beating Cox in the next round but it was Rosewall who went on to win the first ever

Open tournament at that little West Hants Club which, regrettably, no longer offers the good citizens of Bournemouth a chance to watch springtime tennis in a nice English drizzle. A combination of finance and the weather killed it off. But the British Hardcourt Championships' place in history is assured.

That first Open event offered a total prize-money purse of £5,490 — Cox, with his customary caution, had elected to play for expenses only — and when the long-awaited Open Wimbledon arrived, everyone marvelled at the total pot of £26,150. Today, that amounts to slightly less than the winner would expect to receive at an average Super Series Grand Prix tournament.

But money was not the motivation in 1968. As it had been in Paris two weeks before, when huge crowds made the most of the chaos on the Left Bank to welcome great names back to the old concrete fortress of Stade Roland Garros, the atmosphere was one of celebration. It was as if a huge family quarrel had ended and we were all brothers and sisters again. Players wandered around the grounds of Roland Garros and the All England Club bumping into old foes and old friends who were usually one and the same and kept on exclaiming, 'Great to see you! I don't believe this, do you?'

No one really believed it because a year before, even a few months before, the whole idea had seemed an impossible dream. But now, at Wimbledon there were no fewer than 13 former champions in the field (nine men, four women) and the entry was so strong that the reigning champion, John Newcombe, was relegated to No. 4 seed. But it was a reunion for all ages. In the veterans' draw, two of the real pioneers of the professional game, Don Budge and Bobby Riggs, both pre-war champions, had returned to drink from the well that had been off-limits for so long.

Rosewall, winner at Bournemouth, winner in Paris, quickly held centre stage at Wimbledon, too, with a match of sublime contrasts against the muscular Charlie Pasarell — the foil and the sabre — the new generation of budding stars from the amateur game pitting their talents against the old generation of pros. This was what Wimbledon 1968 was all about, but although Rosewall survived Pasarell's onslaught, winning on grass — as opposed to the clay of Roland Garros, — proved to be beyond him. Instead it was his red-headed rival with the mighty left arm, Rod Laver, who returned to Wimbledon after a six-year absence and never broke stride. 'As I was saying before I was so rudely interrupted,' the great *Daily Mirror* columnist Cassandra had written on resuming his column after the Second World War. Laver was just as imperious, just as disdainful of the passing years. Champion in 1961 and in 1962, he swept through the new Open field like a king sweeping squatters out of his castle. Tony Roche was the last to go but in the end it did not take long. Precisely 60 minutes, in fact, for a final that was a mere exhibition of Laver's extravagant skills.

The first Open Wimbledon wrought no particular changes in the women's game because all the top players of that era had remained amateur, as much by force of circumstance as for any other reason. They were not, as yet, a big enough draw card to attract a pro promoter, although there was at least one player on the tour who had no intention of allowing that situation to continue for much longer. Happily for the women's game, the player concerned was the reigning Wimbledon champion as Open Tennis hove into view, and Billie Jean King showed just how wonderful she thought it was by defeating the ebullient Australian Judy Tegart, 9–7, 7–5 to win the title for the third consecutive year.

For Billie Jean, the acceptance of professionalism in tennis was a cause for celebration. In this and in many other respects this frumpy little Californian with the big spectacles and even bigger personality was the antithesis of the typical English schoolgirl brought up on a diet of tennis and jolly hockey sticks. Although an outside portion of talent and determination set her apart, Christine Truman, as she was before marrying a Wasps second-row forward called Jerry Janes, typified the British attitude and I can just imagine her saying — at the time if not now — 'Turn professional? Oh, dear. No, I don't think so, do you?'

That kind of attitude — and I am putting words into Christine's mouth only to make a point — left Billie Jean speechless, which was unusual, to say the least. To her, professionalism seemed a natural part of growing up. Her brother, Randy Moffitt, was a professional baseball player and, as soon as she was old enough to realize that her chances of playing pro ball, as they would call it in America, were considerably less than zero, she turned to tennis and dreamed of Wimbledon. Now, at least, Wimbledon and professionalism were not mutually exclusive and, as we shall see, Billie Jean's dreams did not take long to encompass the new possibilities.

Ironically it was one of those terribly British schoolgirls who deprived Billie Jean of her US title when the first Open championship was held at Forest Hills two months later. Virginia Wade who, like Miss Truman, was hardly a typical product of her genteel background, used the only top-quality serve ever produced by a British woman player, to beat Mrs King in straight sets, thus becoming the first English woman to win at Forest Hills since Betty Nuthall in 1930.

But, as at Wimbledon, it was the men who demanded most of the attention as the contract pros tried to come to terms with a whole generation they had never seen before. This was unsettling for a group of players who had become used to knowing every quirk and weakness of the man on the other side of the net in the tightly-knit little world of the old pro tour. Some found it more unsettling than others and none more so than Andres Gimeno, the delightful Catalan whose factured grammar never put more than a punctuation mark in his stream of funny stories. At Wimbledon Gimeno had suffered the unfunny experience of losing to an amateur, Ray Moore, whose appearance was to go through many guises before, some 18 years later, he would end up as Chairman of the Men's International Professional Tennis Council. In 1968 Moore was just another young South African with a not-so-good serve, who had bamboozled an old pro with a mixture of deft volleying and surprising tactics. Or at least surprising to Gimeno, who had never heard of Moore before.

The experience had made Andres even more nervous of what lay in store for him at Forest Hills, and his Aussie mates did nothing to alleviate his fears. John Newcombe and Tony Roche were quite merciless when I joined the three of them for a pizza dinner in the Pan Am Building on Park Avenue one night before the first US Open began.

'Moore's not the only good youngster out there, you know,' said Newk helpfully.

'Too true, blue,' added Rochey, 'We've got a couple of Australian kids coming along nicely. John Alexander and Phil Dent. J.A.'s got a big first serve, ideal for grass, and Philby's just an all-round talent.'

'Really?' said Gimeno, trying hard not to look concerned.

'Yeah, and then there's Izzy El Shafei,' Newk went on. 'Heavy leftie serve. You know how dangerous that can be on grass.'

'Not really,' replied the Spaniard morosely. 'You see I haven't played on grass very much. Anyway, this Izzy, he's Moroccan, no?'

'No mate, Egyptian actually,' said Newk, trying to hide a smile behind the beginnings of what would become a famous moustache. 'Straight out of the Cairo bazaar. He'll beat you at backgammon before he does you at tennis.'

'And you want to try and avoid Dick Crealy,' added Rochey. 'He's another Aussie with a huge first serve.'

'And his second serve?' asked Gimeno apprehensively.

'No, you can forget about Creals' second serve, mate,' said Newk, offering Andres the first lifeline of the evening. 'His second serve wouldn't hurt a fly.'

'Phew, that's good to know,' replied Gimeno with a twinkle in his large brown eyes. He knew he was having his leg pulled but, equally, he was afraid there was more than a grain of truth in what they were saying. 'I'm not sure Open Tennis was such a good thing. Half these guys I never heard of and the other half, they all play like crazy. I think maybe I prefer to play Gonzales or Laver in the first round. At least I know what to expect!'

Poor Andres. Against all the odds known to man, he drew Ray Moore for the second time and lost again, with the score an embarrassing 4–6, 6–1, 6–2, 6–1. It took Gimeno a while to sort out the brave new world of Open Tennis but, happily, he managed it in time to win the French Open title in 1972 at the ripe old age of 34.

But there was a bigger upset than Moore's defeat of Gimeno at this historic Forest Hills. Rod Laver, who was expected to produce a repeat of his Wimbledon triumph, went down in the fourth round to Cliff Drysdale, another South African who used his stinging double-handed backhand to demolish Laver's game, winning 6–1, 6–1 in the fourth and fifth sets. That opened up the field considerably and Arthur Ashe grabbed the opportunity to become the first black man ever to win the United States title. Against Tom Okker, whose mercurial speed quickly had him dubbed 'The Flying Dutchman', Ashe won a thrilling final (played on the Monday because of rain), 14–12, 5–7, 6–3, 3–6, 6–3.

That an American amateur had come through to win the first US Open made the outcome all the sweeter for Bob Kelleher who had fought so hard to bring the professionals back into the fold. The fact that Ashe had had to get past Roy Emerson and Drysdale before overcoming his great amateur rival Clark Graebner in a classic semifinal duel, and that Okker's victims included legendary names such as Gonzales and Rosewall, only made their achievements more rewarding. Kelleher, sensing what it would mean to him, insisted that Ashe's father join him on court for the presentation ceremony, but it took a bit of encouragement to get Mr Ashe out there because the public-parks policeman from Richmond, Virginia was overcome with a mixture of emotion and stage fright. Eventually father and son embraced and no one was applauding harder than Althea Gibson, who remains the only black American woman to have won her national title. Althea knew better than anyone just what it had taken for Arthur to get his hands on that Cup.

However, it was Okker who got his hands on the money. All $14,000 of it because, under the timid compromise that had been worked out in Paris, Tom, having chosen to become an authorized player under the Dutch LTA, was eligible to accept prize money, while Ashe had remained an amateur, because he wanted to continue playing in the Davis Cup. So, while the sporting world acclaimed a new hero, it also laughed at the absurdity of a sport that gave the loser the prize money and the winner nothing.

But Ashe was not particularly concerned and neither was his close friend Donald Dell, who knew that by the time he had finished, Ashe would make a great deal more than $14,000 from his victory at Forest Hills.

'The price is one million and you have to take Charlie Pasarell and Bob Lutz as well.' It was Dell speaking as he shared a taxi back into Manhattan with Lamar Hunt. The boss of World Championship Tennis nearly fell out of his seat. Hunt was rich and was quite prepared to pump a lot of money into the organization Dave Dixon had bequeathed him, but one million dollars for a tennis player in the sixties was an unheard-of sum.

'Arthur's worth it, you'll see,' said Dell. 'When you agree, get back to me.'

It took a year, but Dell was right. Hunt got back to him and duly agreed to the million dollars, to be paid over a period of years. It was great for Ashe as well as, of course, for Dell. But sometimes I think it might have been better for this self-confident young man if he hadn't been proved quite so correct quite so early in his career. Down the line, a lot of people suffered from being subjected to Donald's terse demands in later years as a result of his having been so successful with the most outrageous price he ever put on a player's head.

6

WCT AND BOLOGNA

In Cologne, in between practising his flute in the hotel lift where, he insisted, the acoustics were better, Jeff Borowiak spent meal-times trying to persuade Fred Stolle that Ken Rosewall played tennis like Brahms. Not all Borowiak's thoughtful dissertations were easy to grasp first time around and, in the restaurant of the Esso Motor Lodge, only Torben Ulrich, nodding sagely behind his heavy beard, really understood what the young Californian was on about. Ulrich, who was to become Borowiak's guru as the tour progressed, was himself an accomplished jazz clarinettist and, at home in Denmark, used to hang out with a big black man called Dexter Gordon; around midnight, of course.

Cologne was the 15th stop on the 19-tournament circuit organized by World Championship Tennis (WCT) in 1971 and Borowiak was the new boy on the tour. Very tall and very dark and handsome, Jeff would have made an impact no matter what because, quite apart from his strange theories and bizarre musical habits, he was a dreamy, contrary sort of fellow who insisted on bringing his own health-food cereal down to breakfast. In 1971 this was considered very avant-garde. But then Borowiak was from Berkeley so what could one expect from a San Francisco flower child?

But if Jeff had delicate tastes, the players on the tour had to make hasty revisions in their notions about any supposed delicacy in his game. To a greater extent than his results showed over the years, Borowiak was an extremely fine tennis player, and he announced his arrival in the professional ranks by reaching the final of that tournament in Cologne with victories over Andres Gimeno and Cliff Drysdale.

Borowiak provided just the kind of colouring the tour needed in the autumn of its year. It had been in February in Philadelphia that John Newcombe had kicked the whole thing into motion with the first WCT title of 1971, and since then approximately the same group of athletes had moved through the seasons from a passionate Roman spring to the sticky summer heat of Boston, Toronto and Fort Worth and then, just prior to Cologne, to the cooling breezes of Vancouver in October. Jochen Grosse's event was housed in Cologne's exhibition hall but outside our hotel the trees surrounding the little lake were turning to russet-brown and gold and the ducks were preparing for a long, cold winter. Professional tennis was to face many of those in the years that lay ahead, not to mention an occasional explosive summer, but now, looking back over a myriad of matches and a thousand landings around the world, I cannot remember a more enjoyable period or one in which the bond of rivalry and competition, so often a fractious influence nowadays, combined to produce such wonderful tennis or such lasting friendships. There was a sense of adventure because we were, indeed, setting out on one. Professional tennis as we have come to know it today was in its infancy and while Jack Kramer had, with his Grand Prix format, been plotting a course in uncharted seas, so too had one of his former pros, Mike Davies, who had been hired by Hunt to replace Bob Briner as WCT's Executive Director. It came as no surprise to me that Davies should reach such a position, nor that he would immediately put into effect visionary schemes for the advancement of the professional game. Ten years before, when he was but a stripling amongst the Gonzales, Hoad and Trabert-led giants of the Kramer tour, Davies had bought me a beer at one of those stalls that line the concourse of what used to be called the Wembley Empire Pool and had spoken with Welsh passion about his hopes and aspirations, not for his own career, but for the role of the professional in the game's future. Despite a stunted conventional education that had stopped a long way short of the levels attained by the oil tycoons he would eventually be dealing with in Dallas, there was nothing stunted about Davies' mind, and the fact that he remained in a position of power and influence over a multimillion-dollar industry for 13 years as Hunt's chief tennis executive says all that needs to be said about his abilities.

The plans he had devised for WCT were basically a refinement of the ideas that had poured forth when we spoke at Wembley. The world's best players would be signed to contracts for a certain number of tournaments each year, and those events would be linked by a points system that would lead the leaders to a big showdown in Dallas. This was a Texas-based tour and Mike, metaphorically at least, did not shy away from wearing his ten-gallon hat — an image that served only to frighten the establishment still further. Davies had always been something of a rebel in his days as an emotional and hot-tempered British No. 1 and now, for heaven's sake, he was behaving like Jesse James. Or so the establishment liked to think. In reality he hadn't needed to rob a bank. Lamar had simply handed him the money so that he could show the world how a professional circuit should be run. If everyone had acted with greater maturity, the trail Davies blazed on behalf of WCT could have merged with the pot-holed path of amateurism. Then, with everyone putting their weight behind the steamroller, a beautiful new highway to Utopia could have opened up. Oh, yes, let us dream.

But if the dreams Davies had taken out into the world from his modest upbringing in the Welsh valleys were never completely fulfilled, he came a great deal nearer than most people do to turning his reveries into reality. Much had happened in the year following the experiments in Kansas City. Dixon had quit, Briner had been fired and Davies had started to put together a pro tour that was worthy of the name, even if some of the title names still belonged to never-never land. Pancho Gonzales, for instance, won the Howard Hughes Invitational in Las Vegas before the group hit the road to Morocco. You don't see the connection? Don't worry. Not even Bob Hope's best gag-writer could have come up with a line linking the two. Las Vegas and Casablanca just happened to be two cities that answered WCT's call while Davies was trying to lay the foundations of a tour that, the following year, would make greater sense. Then there would be points and a final in Dallas.

The European segments of the tour were being put together from a new tennis office with its headquarters at the premises of Hunt Oil on Sloane Street. The man in charge was a diminutive New Zealander called John MacDonald, who had become a familiar figure in British tennis circles. He was now destined to become a controversial one, too. Members of the All England Club were not supposed to get their hands dirty by organizing events that could, in any way, conflict with the well-ordered rhythm of a British summer. This was not at all what had been envisaged during those headstrong days of revolution in 1968. It was all right that MacDonald worked in the motor trade and was rumoured to be a dab hand on the drums in a few clubs most members had never heard of, but working for Lamar Hunt was quite another matter. MacDonald's infectious humour was put under considerable strain when he realized that he was being treated like a leper by certain members of the establishment.

That, however, should not have come as too much of a shock after the way Hunt had been treated when he came to Wimbledon in an attempt to work out a deal with the All England Club. For Hunt 'doing a deal' was legitimate business. But in Britain hypocrisy still had too strong a hold on people's attitudes for anyone to admit that a British sporting institution would lower itself to such behaviour. As a result Hunt was treated with appalling rudeness, not only by members of the All England committee, still headed by Herman David, who had appeared so enlightened a few years before, but also by the majority of my colleagues on the British press, who were determined to portray the quiet, courteous Hunt as a power-crazed Texan who was hell-bent on taking over the game and buying up Wimbledon in the process, if need be.

Hunt never wanted to buy the game but he did want a legitimate slice of it, a slice Davies was beginning to carve for him with the best possible cutting edge — well-run professional events offering world-class tennis to a truly international list of venues. By the time I had witnessed 11 of the 19 tournaments featured in that 1971 tour, there was at least one reporter — David Gray and Rex Bellamy were others — who needed no further convincing. With Open Tennis still trying to crawl out of its nappies, the game desperately needed the professional discipline of a well co-ordinated tour and that, without question, Hunt and Davies were providing.

They were lucky, of course, to have an exceptional bunch of guys headed by two players of such stature and such unimpeachable character that no one seriously thought of questioning the standards they set. Rod Laver and Ken Rosewall were not merely revered for their court craft and respected for their sportsmanship, but popular as people, too. It is true that Ken was one of the most reserved and private members of the tour, but he was never aloof and was even spotted in a couple of night-clubs by the end of the year. It was, of course, so much easier for players to form friendships in those days. Apart from MacDonald and a couple of other WCT staffers, plus the occasional hanger-on like me, they had no one to turn to for company except one another. A few were married, but not all the wives travelled. The occasional girlfriend joined for a week or two, such as the Jamaican beauty Nancy Burke who came to see Arthur Ashe in Cologne, but for the most part players shared rooms, meals and transport together and then tried to put it all out of their minds for a couple of hours each day on court. They succeeded remarkably well.

It would have been a great deal more difficult had not Laver, the great superstar figure who was even getting recognized at airports in the States following his Grand Slam triumph a couple of years before, not been so ready to muck in and behave like one of the boys. It was the Australian way, of course. If any Aussie tried to climb on his high horse there was always a bunch of his mates, who had probably achieved just as much, ready to haul him out of the saddle and fill him full of beer.

It was in Stockholm, after we had flown down to Barcelona from Cologne and then trekked back up north again, that Rod 'Rocket'

Laver got filled with a bit more fuel than usual even by Australian standards. It wasn't beer, either, but that deadly concoction called schnapps that the Swedes use as internal warming fluid to ward off pneumonia on those endless Nordic nights. We had been taken to a party outside the city and, almost inevitably, found that snacks from a table of smorgasbord were being washed down with small but rapidly replenished glasses of schnapps. 'Skoal!' roared our hosts. 'Scholl, mate!' replied a chorus of largely Australian accents. It had been snowing when we arrived and soon the garden was a glistening blanket all the way down to the water's edge.

By the time we staggered out in search of our cars, the whole scene was too much of a temptation for Roy Emerson, Ray Ruffels and a few of the other players. Deciding that Rod would make a perfect snowman — you didn't after all have to worry about adding a big, red nose — they started to pack the great Grand Slammer with snow from top to toe as he stood there in his overcoat. The funny thing was that he did just stand there, his mild protestations of 'Hey, come on fellas, that's not nice' dissipated by his happy schnapps-induced grin. In the end he made a very good snowman, did Rodney George Laver. We could have stuck a pipe in his mouth and left him there till morning with little danger. The combination of liquor and body heat underneath the protective layer of snow would have preserved him, if not quite until spring, then at least until his next match.

But Emmo wasn't going to risk being without a doubles partner, so our snowman was dusted off rather inexpertly and bundled into the front seat of this beautifully warm Volvo. Given our condition everything seemed twice as hilarious as it probably was, but I shall not readily forget the ride back into Stockholm, punctuated by little mutterings of complaint from the passenger seat as another splodge of snow melted and trickled down Rocket's neck. 'Getting a bit chilly in here, wouldn't you say, Emmo?' Laver would ask with a shiver.

'No, mate, reckon you're just catching a chill,' Emmo would reply with a straight face from the back. 'Have to fix you up with a nice beer when we get home.'

It was a bit of a soggy snowman that wandered into the lobby of the Grand Hotel in the early hours but the night porter had probably seen worse in his day. Rod Laver has also probably felt better than he did next morning. But he didn't catch a chill.

Laver was in better shape at other stops along the way on that tour, winning three singles titles to finish just behind Rosewall and John Newcombe who won four each. But significantly Rocket came through when the heat was on in every sense — when the crowds were large and noisy, the conditions demanding and everyone was playing at the top of their form. Rod was 33 at the time and neither mind nor body could cope with the level of commitment required to win week after week, but he responded to the big occasion and once the adrenalin pump was switched on, the genius flowed.

There had been no shortage of adrenalin at the Foro Italico in May when WCT's John MacDonald and Gianfranco Cameli of the Italian Federation joined forces to ensure that the Italian Open would get an infusion of new blood and excitement. Unlike most of the other events on the tour, the Italian event was one for which WCT wisely agreed to allow the draw to expand to its normal 64-man size, thus allowing non-WCT pros and local Italian players to compete. This was also the case later in the year at the Count Godo Cup in Barcelona, where a young left-hander called Manolo Orantes put a dent in WCT's pride by beating Bob Lutz in the final. But that was later. For a couple of days in Rome, too, it seemed as if an 'outsider' might upset the form-book. The top half-dozen Italians had been practising feverishly on their own red-clay courts at the Foro Italico for a full week before the WCT pros straggled into town from the Rawlings Classic in Dallas and, with partisan crowds screaming their support, they launched into the invaders with a vengeance. Half a dozen WCT pros failed to make it past the second round, and in one memorable encounter Newcombe, who had won in Dallas a couple of days before and was still trying to discover where he was, found himself match point down against Vincenzo Franchitti, the 12th-ranked Italian who seemed to have attracted half of Rome to Court Three. People were literally hanging out of the pine trees that line the outside courts of the Foro Italico as Newk bravely fought his way out of trouble, but that match and numerous others set the place alight, and when Laver eventually came through to beat Jan Kodes in the final (no mean achievement considering the Czech was in the midst of his two-year domination of the Stade Roland Garros at the time) the 1971 Italian Open was stored away as one of the most memorable in the championship's history.

As we headed for Paris, it would have been difficult to believe that another, very different Italian setting would provide a week of even greater thrills and higher skills before the year was out.

Bologna may have given its name to a spaghetti sauce but, as a city, it actually has a great deal more to recommend it. Culinary art is certainly one of its attractions because it is reputed to have more top-quality restaurants than any other town in Italy, but the colonnades that offer protection from sun and rain along many of the main streets are but part of a general architectural design that creates an atmosphere of faded grandeur. None of this, of course, has anything to do with the fact that, after more than 25 years of watching tennis in every corner of the globe, I remember Bologna primarily because it provided the best single week of sustained top-quality tennis that I have ever seen.

A number of factors contributed to this phenomenon. During the preceding weeks in Cologne, Barcelona and Stockholm I had sensed a fusion of forces and a honing of basic skills that subconsciously led to everyone's playing better. There were technical reasons for this but primarily it had to do with the personalities involved. As I have said this was a special group of people. Apart from the Australian contingent, players such as Arthur Ashe, Cliff Drysdale, Marty Riessen, Dennis Ralston, Bob Lutz, and Charlie Pasarell have gone on to prove themselves in life as men of substance and considerable achievement. After the better part of a year in one another's company it is highly probable that an average group of ultra-competitive young athletes playing, remember, an individual sport rather than a team game, would start picking on differences and exacerbating the inevitable contrast in personalities. But although we were far from being short on personalities — apart from Borowiak and Ulrich, there was Bob 'Nailbags' Carmichael, the one-time carpenter from Melbourne, Nikki Pilic, the chauvinistic Yugoslav and Tom Okker, the Flying Dutchman whose feet rarely touched the ground — the better they all got to know one another the better they got on. By the end of the year, everyone knew each other so well that there wasn't much left to prove, even on court. I am not suggesting that this diluted the competitive juices. Far from it. The money at stake may seem paltry by today's standards — each tournament offered a total pot of $50,000, with the singles winner taking $10,000 — but it was big enough in 1971 and, in any case, pride of performance remained undiminished. The top half-dozen knew they were the best in the world — with the possible exceptions of Ilie Nastase, Stan Smith and Jan Kodes who were playing the Grand Prix tour — and felt free, as a result, to go out and play their best tennis — keenly but without fear.

The technical aspects also played an important part in raising the level of tennis to such memorable heights. The previous week in Stockholm, the tournament, won by Ashe, had been played on those incredibly fast tiles that used to be a unique feature of the Kunglihallen. Scheduling was far from perfect in those days and the tournament in Barcelona, played, of course, on clay, had been sandwiched in between two indoor events. The players hadn't found that too amusing so it came as a relief to find conditions of such a neutral nature at the Palazzo dello Sport in Bologna. The indoor carpet was a rubberized composition called Uniturf which is no longer used on the pro tour but which gave a player the option of coming in to the net or staying back, much like Greenset and Supreme which are so widely used today. Although too heavy for constant use, the Pirelli balls enabled everyone to go for their shots without fear of the ball flying out of court. As a result the conditions suited just about everyone and the results were spectacular.

Bob Lutz, the burly Californian with the Robert Mitchum chest and laconic humour to match, was always a more naturally gifted player than his long-time doubles partner Stan Smith and, with due respect to Stan, I do not think it was a coincidence that Bob played some of his best singles when he was travelling alone, free of Smith's dominating presence. Lutz had won Cologne and then effected the kind of rapid surface-switch that only the truly talented can handle to reach the Barcelona final the following week. Now even the sight of Laver across the net did not phase him and, unlocking his full range of explosive strokes, he continued to hit the ball as hard as he had done in the first two rounds when he met the Australian in the quarter-final. Lutz lost, but it was a blockbuster of a match and the crowds, who were already warming to the standard of tennis the WCT pros were serving up, loved it.

Other quarter-final matches saw Okker, who tended to get blown away by Ashe on most faster surfaces, push the American to a first-set tie-break before going down 3–6 in the second, while Pasarell started to look ominously confident as he scored a rare straight-set win over Drysdale.

But the match of the quarter-final round was undoubtedly that between Rosewall and Riessen. Both had come through exciting second-round matches that helped set the mood for the whole week. A young lad called Adriano Panatta, of whom great things were expected, put up a very creditable performance against the little Australian maestro who had to work quite hard to win in straight sets, but Riessen, the former basketball star from Northwestern University, Illinois, who had used his great athletic prowess to become one of the fittest players on the tour, was in much greater danger against the left-handed British No. 1, Roger Taylor. It was the fifth time they had met that year and the rivalry was becoming a little intense. Both Riessen and Taylor were establishing themselves as the kind of players who could elbow their way past the tour leaders and grab the odd title or two if the stars were not on their toes. Twelve months previously Taylor had won his first WCT title in Midland, Texas a week before Riessen won in Tucson, Arizona. Then in May of 1971, Marty had won Tehran, refusing to be unnerved by the two-hour wait before his final against John Alexander — a delay caused by the fact that the Shah was meeting King Faisal of Saudi Arabia and had 'asked' that everyone wait for him to arrive. Four thousand spectators and two tennis players did — without a murmur.

The crowd did more than murmur in Bologna as Riessen and Taylor stretched each other as only players who know each other's game so well can. The athleticism and power of both men was examined to the full during some wonderful rallies, and Roger was probably a little unlucky in losing the match in the third set when Marty's running forehand clipped the net on match point, jumped over Taylor's racket and fell right on the line.

But Riessen had been playing well and went into his match with Rosewall with more confidence than usual. That was not particularly difficult because Rosewall was one of those players whom Riessen usually found incredibly awkward to play. Conversely Riessen had far less trouble with Laver whom he beat frequently, once actually holding a winning record over the Grand Slam winner. Rod was always a little bewildered by it. 'I just don't know what it is about Marty's game,' Rod would say, 'but often I find it very difficult to pick his shots.'

There were other cases of top players having constant difficulty with opponents ranked below them. Carmichael, who was not really in the same league, was a rarity on the tour in that he quite enjoyed playing Rosewall, almost always played well against him and even won a couple of times. But for Riessen, as for most of his colleagues, Kenny was a major problem.

In an attempt to alleviate it by at least trying something different, Marty decided to adopt a new strategy. After five straight defeats, he felt it was the least he could do! 'I decided I would chip my service returns and rush the net when he served and try to concentrate on accuracy rather than power with my own delivery,' Riessen said.

Great idea! Or so it seemed at the time. At 6–0, 1–0 to Rosewall it seemed rather different. Talking about it afterwards, Marty gave one of his short little laughs. 'So I chucked all those brilliant ideas out the window and resorted to all-out aggression. It was a desperation move, really, but amazingly it nearly worked!'

Indeed it did. From a one-sided match that had some of the crowd wandering off into the corridors in search of an espresso, it suddenly turned into a thrilling contest that required no caffeine boost to kick it into life. By acting on his decision to hit out on his returns, Riessen started to pierce Rosewall's defences and quickly snatched the second set 6–3. The American kept up the pressure in the third set and, at 6–5, found himself standing at match point on Kenny's serve — not bad after losing the first seven games of the match.

But with victory in his sights, Riessen went for a backhand cross-court winner and it was out by a foot. Chances against Rosewall are rare and Marty knew he might not get another. All the old insecurities about playing this great master of the game started to well up at the back of Riessen's mind. 'It's so frustrating to play him because he just appears out of nowhere,' Riessen explained. 'You never see him coming, you never even hear him and suddenly he's there, perfectly positioned for a shot you felt sure he could never reach.'

But to Riessen's credit, he did not panic and actually won the first three points of the deciding tie-break. He was still leading 5–4 when Rosewall stepped up to serve. 'I thought I was in a good position because just one of those Rosewall service points would have left me serving at match point,' said Riessen.

However, only people who have never tried to return Kenny's serve laugh at it. The delivery was, in fact, weightier than it looked and, keeping low, was tricky to handle. Rosewall duly won his two service points and, as the crowd hummed with excitement (the tie-breaker was still a relatively recent innovation in those days) Riessen undid all his great work by failing to put away an awkward smash and getting beaten by Rosewall's reply. Not for the first time that week, the Bolognese tennis fans rose to salute two players who had offered them such fabulous entertainment.

The match had been a physically demanding one and at the age of 36, as he was then, Rosewall was just a little stiff when he faced the lithe and fleet-footed Arthur Ashe in the semifinal. Even with the heavy balls, Ashe's rapier-like serve was still tough to handle and it was that weapon that dominated the match, helping Ashe to a straight-set victory.

There was, however nothing straightforward about the other semifinal which remains, to this day, one of the most dramatic encounters I have ever witnessed. Pasarell was appearing in the semifinal of a WCT event for the first time and his confidence was riding high. No matter that it was Rod Laver on the other side of the net. Pasarell, after all those great duels at Wimbledon, was experienced enough to ignore a man's reputation — at least at the start of a match before the nerve-racking big points arrived — as he launched himself at the Australian left-hander hammer and tongs. That big serve and even bigger volley carried him through to win the first set before Laver's incredible ability to absorb punishment and strike back to catch opponents off balance allowed Pasarell only three games in the next two sets.

But, with a best-of-five-set format adopted for the last two rounds, Pasarell still had time to gather his wits and soldier on. The noise started to build up as the lanky Puerto Rican halted Laver's rush towards victory in a stadium that was packed to the rafters with some 6000 people. The air-conditioning was not very modern and I remember the heat rising and the cigarette smoke hanging hazily in the air as the tempo of the match increased to a fevered pitch. Laver was playing well but I could not remember having seen Pasarell play better — not even against Gonzales at Wimbledon.

Taking risks at the net that few people would have even considered against a player of Laver's calibre, Pasarell pushed the fourth set to a tie-break and scrambled home to level the score at two sets all. Break points came and went all through the fifth and by the time another tie-break arrived the whole place was steaming with tension.

Fighting back exhaustion, Pasarell kept charging into the net behind his serve and his courage almost paid off when he reached match point, with his own serve to follow, no less than three times in the decisive tie-breaker. But Laver cracked the whip and that muscled left arm replied with devastating returns that forced Charlie into errors on the volley. Then it was Laver's turn to reach match point — once, twice and then three times. But he, too, was beaten back from the brink of victory by an inspired opponent who was producing shots that had spectators literally screaming in ecstasy and amazement.

Eleven points all. Tie-break. Fifth set. WCT points and big prize money on the line. The crowd could not have been more involved had Nikki Pietrangeli been playing for Italy in the Davis Cup. The drama and the excellence of the tennis superseded partisan feelings. And now, at the final climax, the standard of play remained just as high. Tilting backwards to recover from a Laver lob, lunging for a wide volley, trying to cover more yards of the court than even his long legs would allow, Pasarell fought desperately to hang on to the vision of victory that had loomed so clearly before his eyes. But Laver was equal to it all and, after two agonizing rallies that did full justice to everything that had gone before, the Australian clinched it by 13 points to 11 to score a truly memorable victory by 4–6, 6–0, 6–3, 6–7, 7–6.

After that the final was inevitably something of an anticlimax, especially as Ashe was never at his best against Laver — a man whom, until then, he had never beaten. Nevertheless Ashe was rarely dull, and a few whiplash backhands caught Laver on the hop to liven up an otherwise one-sided duel that eventually went to Rod 6–3, 6–4, 6–4.

And so ended a truly remarkable week in which some of the greatest players to have graced the game in the past 20 years all hit top form together and offered a standard of entertainment that would be difficult for any sport to surpass.

7

ROSEWALL AND LAVER IN TEXAS

Bologna had left everyone elated but, for the top eight points winners after the year-long odyssey, there was little time to savour the memories. The first WCT finals were due to start within two days — not in Dallas but at the Hofheinz Pavilion in Houston, where all four quarter-finals were to be played. The four semifinalists would then move on to the old Memorial Auditorium in downtown Dallas for a rendezvous with the man from the moon, astronaut Neil Armstrong. Lamar Hunt, who had a cheque for $50,000 waiting for Armstrong to present to the winner, along with a special gold signet ring and the use of a Lincoln Continental for a year, was determined to give the game a little pizazz even if he himself remained a very low-key, though conscientious, host. While his wife Norma, a dazzling blonde with a prodigious memory, set about learning a whole new list of names to fit to faces (the oilmen, footballers and soccer players were already locked into Norma's immediate recall system), Lamar was not above wandering around the stadium with a hammer on the eve of the finals, adding the odd nail to a sponsor's banner or reorganizing a piece of bunting. Detail is what makes sporting events a success and, as Davies had already discovered, very little escaped Lamar's hawkish eye.

It would be difficult for the present generation to appreciate just how much all this high-powered organization and media exposure meant to some of the older pros on the tour. The whole group realized that new standards were being set and that tennis was finally getting the kind of recognition it deserved, but to those who had known the dismal days just prior to the arrival of Dixon and MacCall in the mid 1960s when mere survival was the name of the game, Dallas represented the end of a rainbow few of them had thought they would ever see. At last they could be proud of their profession, and if one realizes just how much pride goes into the make-up of a true champion in any sport, the depth of their feelings will become clear. Even the younger players had tasted the haunting fear of failure at the start of the WCT enterprise. Few of the tournaments immediately following Kansas City were sufficiently successful to instil much faith in the future of a pro tour in America and, had Dixon not been clever enough to draw Hunt into the game so that he could bequeath those early money-losers to someone who could afford them, the whole thing would have ended in a total disaster as opposed to just localized disasters like Shreveport, Louisiana. It was there that the court failed to arrive, leaving the matches to be played on a bare concrete floor, and the handful of fans who did show up were let in free. Promoters have been known to shoot themselves at more successful events than that.

But Lamar Hunt is not the suicidal type. Behind the spectacles and the high forehead, there lies an obsessively determined brain. Having accepted the tattered remnants of Dixon's dreams, not to mention the legacy of all those tough years when Kramer's pros had doggedly kept the professional game alive against considerable odds, nothing was going to divert him from the challenge that lay ahead.

'Lamar is a very difficult man to dislodge,' said Davies, who has now gone full circle, through a period as Executive Director of the ATP to become Marketing Manager for the ITF. 'But he is also a very decent man. Through the 13 years I worked for him, he never reneged on a promise.'

To the best of his ability Hunt had laid the groundwork for a successful finale to his world-wide tour, and preparations were already under way for a switch to a more suitable arena, called Moody Coliseum, on the Southern Methodist University campus for the 1972 finals just seven months later. The first finals were played in November, but Lamar knew that the real ball game in American sport was television and there were too many other more established attractions competing for the networks' time at the end of the year. May would be much better and it was with this understanding in mind that the NBC, in the person of its wonderfully humorous and supportive Sports Director, Dick Auerbach, had come aboard. Hunt had the location, the time-slot, the network coverage and the cast. All he needed now were a couple of matches to fire the public imagination. Bologna had shown what his players were capable of but what were the odds on the right players producing the right kind of match when it mattered most? And at this particular time in the history of tennis, believe me, it really mattered. Tennis was still one of the best-kept secrets in American sport as far as the public at large was concerned. Although Laver might get the odd request for an autograph at an airport, Pancho Gonzales and possibly Arthur Ashe, because he was black and because he had won Forest Hills, were the only other names your average sporting Joe would have recognized.

But there was one other thing that would have seeped into the fans' consciousness. Generally, the best tennis players were Australian. Hopman's Davis Cup triumphs had made sure of that. So, as far as making a public impact was concerned, these inaugural WCT finals not only had to be dramatic matches but would have to feature two from a very small pool, comprising Laver, Ashe and Rosewall.

Maybe somebody up there loved Lamar or maybe St Peter felt he was getting too many harps and too few tennis rackets in Heaven. The more down to earth will call it fate and the carping cynics who think honest sportsmen exist only in fairy-tales will call it a fix. But professional tennis matches in legitimate tournaments are not fixed and never have been. So it was merely a blessing of some kind or another that took Laver and Rosewall into the final round of both events and, once there, helped them produce the very best tennis of their lives. In a way it is a shame that the magnificent duel they staged in the November final has been almost totally obscured by the utter brilliance of the second, which followed so soon afterwards. But no matter. Both matches did the game of tennis an immeasurable service, whetting the public's appetite for more and giving the burgeoning tennis boom that was spreading across America just the boost it needed.

After watching Rosewall stun Laver the first time to win the inaugural WCT crown 6–4, 1–6, 7–6, 7–6, Rex Bellamy, sucking thoughtfully on his pipe in the makeshift press room, was moved to write for *The Times*, 'The three-hour match was so thrilling that the strain of watching it — never mind playing it — became almost unendurable'.

In fact Rosewall had been a little fortunate to finish the match at all, because it was he who had been stunned in the literal sense when a hard return from Laver flew off the edge of his aluminium frame and hit him violently in the eye. The first person at his side was Laver himself but after a few minutes' attention, Ken was able to continue and recovered so well that he won 21 of the next 29 points. 'I guess I hit him in the wrong eye,' quipped Rod, bravely hiding the disappointment of losing to the man he had beaten so many times in the past. But that was to prove Laver's fate in Dallas, a city he could never conquer. Oddly, Laver ended his career as frustrated by the two great play-off finals of the pro tour as Rosewall was at his failure to win any of his four Wimbledon finals. Although Rocket's losses in Dallas are well documented it is sometimes forgotten that the Masters title also eluded him. In fact, largely because of his WCT commitments, the great left-hander played only enough Grand Prix tournaments to qualify for the very first Masters, held in Tokyo in

December 1970 and, after the six-man round-robin format had been completed, he was tied with Stan Smith with an identical record of four wins and one defeat. But the American took the title because he had beaten Laver in the opening match. The Rocket always did take a little time to get his after-burners to ignite and, in that perishingly cold stadium, it cost him the title. But it was close — just as it would prove to be in a rather more dramatic fashion when WCT moved into Moody Coliseum 18 months later.

For the only time in the history of the WCT finals — possibly as a result of the truncated period of time between the '71 and '72 events — the same eight players qualified: Rosewall, Laver, Ashe, Newcombe, Drysdale, Okker, Riessen and Lutz. All the matches were now being played in one hall in one city and everyone agreed it was an improvement. In fact it would have been difficult to improve on Moody Coliseum as an arena for tennis, and Nancy Jeffett, Lamar's counterpart as the city's equally dedicated promoter of the women's game, never lost any sleep over WCT's eventual move to the cavernous spaces of Reunion Arena in 1980. Nancy has continued to run her Virginia Slims tournament in the cosy confines of Moody where the Southern Methodist University stadium still manages to pack 9000 people into a double-tiered proximity to the court. Players respond to the feel of a crowd and I have no doubt that Moody itself must share some of the credit for the glorious tennis we have witnessed there over the years.

In 1972 the semifinals maintained the high standards the WCT pros had been setting all over the world, even though one of the matches was a touch one-sided. Little Rosewall, looking so lost and forlorn between points, still managed to muffle Ashe's cannon of a serve to such good effect that he won 6–4, 6–3, 7–6. It was a classic demonstration of how to use touch and timing to dismantle an opponent's power and by the end everyone had been reminded that no one needed to feel sorry for Kenny even if he was 37!

Laver, however, did seem to be in need of a little sympathy when he trailed by two sets to love in the other semifinal. His opponent was the man who enjoyed playing him so much, Marty Riessen. At that stage it seemed as if Riessen was heading for the final because he had totally outplayed Rod for those two opening sets. Marty is not a man given to exaggeration and when he said in his post-match assessment that he had 'killed' Laver for two sets he was, in tennis terms, perfectly correct. But Riessen, who had been the victim of some poor scheduling — he was playing the night after beating Drysdale in a gruelling quarter-final, whereas Laver had been given a day's rest — eventually started to tire and lost the sting in his wide, swinging serve that had been giving Rod's backhand so much trouble in the deuce court. In the end, Laver was more than a little relieved to close it out 6–0 in the fifth.

And so for the second time in seven months it was to be Rosewall versus Laver and, despite the previous result, the smart money was still going on The Rocket. But what no one had dared to predict was the kind of match one waits a lifetime to see — a nerve-racking, blood-tingling epic between two of the greatest players the game has ever known. By the time the match had reached 6–6 in the fifth set, we had seen both men's hopes ride the roller-coaster of fate. Rocket had roared away to a deceptive 5–1 lead in the first set, only to lose his service rhythm and see Kenny win the second 6–0 and the third 6–3 to lead by two sets to one.

By then Laver was perplexed. 'I wasn't sure what to do,' he said afterwards. 'I wasn't serving well at that stage of the match but then sometimes, strange as it may seem, it is better not to serve too well against Ken. The harder you serve at him with a flattish first serve, the harder the ball comes back at you! You just don't have time to set yourself for a good volley because his returns are so deadly accurate all the time. And if you feed him pace to go with that accuracy well . . . you're a goner.'

Although he was struggling, Laver fought his way back into the match from 1–3 down in the fourth set and, with the crowd starting to become involved in the duel as the intensity and the levels of skill heightened, the left-hander levelled the match by winning the tie-break 7–3.

So as another tie-break loomed it had all come down to the wire — the last stride, the last gasp and, for Rosewall, possibly the Last Hurrah. The television lights glaring down on to the court — were they really hotter in those days or did it just seem that way? — made the heat almost unbearable in the seemingly airless arena and, at 37 years of age, Kenny was beginning to show inevitable signs of exhaustion after nearly three and a half hours of gruelling tennis. But Rosewall's exhaustion was always something of a deception, too. Naturally he must have been tired. But not quite as tired as he looked in between points. As soon as the ball was in play, the drooping head and trailing racket would instantly perk up and there was never anything that smacked of exhaustion as he darted about the court after the most acutely angled balls Laver could conjure up.

The NBC network, nearing completion of its fourth hour of continuous live nationwide coverage, pre-empted three regularly scheduled programmes to stay with the action — something that had never been done on American television because of a tennis match before.

By the end, a record tennis audience of 23 million had tuned in as fans of others sports flicked their dials and became caught in the spell, riveted by the sight of these two extraordinary Australians exhibiting their skills in a finish too fantastic for fiction. Just as Hunt and Davies had hoped, it was turning into the greatest possible advertisement for the game.

Laver led 3–1 in the fifth-set tie-break after Rosewall had missed a match-point opportunity at five games to four when he hoisted a lob long. Laver, looking more and more confident as Rosewall dragged his tired body along the base-line in between points, moved on to a 5–3 lead. The crowd waited breathlessly for the end. Laver fans shouted encouragement. The atmosphere was thick with tension.

But, just two points from losing his crown, Rosewall produced a backhand to grab another precious point, making it 4–5, but then it was Rod's turn to serve and he needed just two good ones for the $50,000, the diamond ring, the gold cup, the Lincoln Continental and, probably most important of all to Laver, the pride and glory. It was, after all, the only title worth talking about that had eluded him.

Two good serves might have been good enough against most players but not against Kenneth R. Rosewall. Moving into a solid first delivery, Kenny swept his cross-court return off that incredible backhand, way down low to Laver's forehand side. Rod saw it coming, as he had seen thousands of them coming off Rosewall's racket in the past, and from the moment Kenny hit it he must have known it was hopeless. He streaked after it, a blue-clad blur topped with streaming copper-coloured hair, and thrust his racket towards the ball as it flashed towards the carpet. But he couldn't control the volley and it sailed out of court. Five all.

Again Laver attacked Rosewall's lethal backhand ('I would serve there again if I had to do the whole thing over,' he insisted afterwards) and cracked in a good first serve, and again the legendary stroke did everything its master asked of it. Taking the ball on the rise, Rosewall hit it straight and true for an outright winner. Laver, stranded in mid court, could do nothing but stand and watch. At 6–5 Rosewall was back at match point, and the end came almost before the crowd could grasp what had happened. Ken served, Rob blooped a return into the net and the WCT champion was still this man called K.R. Rosewall — master of his craft.

'Tennis was the real winner today,' Mike Davies told the crowd as he watched Rosewall clasping the huge gold trophy to the sweat-stained orange shirt he had worn through both of his victories in Dallas. 'That was the greatest match I have ever seen.'

No one was about to challenge that assessment of a duel that will be remembered for so much more than just being an exciting final of a big tournament. I have stressed already the effect it had on the game's popularity in America, but it was the personalities and talents of the two men themselves that gave the occasion its lustre. Rosewall's twin triumphs in Dallas would not have been half as glorious or as personally satisfying had his great and worthy rival not been on the other side of the net. For that alone, Rod had to temper his disappointment and take his full share of the credit. But one needed only to look at Rosewall's face to understand what this meant to him. He had been overwhelmed at his first victory the previous November but now it was springtime in Texas and he was still the champion; still able to use his wonderful skills to hold back the advancing years; still capable of doing what he enjoyed most in life and proving he could do it better than anyone else. Any illusions he might have harboured about the world or his chosen profession had been stripped away since those distant days of teenage triumph in Australia's Davis Cup colours. The road had been long and sometimes painful. Rumour had it that Ken had even had to dip into his own carefully zippered pocket to pay his colleagues' prize money after winning a tournament on the bankrupt pro tour after Kramer had left. But all that desperation and uncertainty seemed a world away now as the nation's television cameras picked up his shy little grin and a packed arena of affluent and influential fans clapped and hollered and called his name. Ken Rosewall. I do believe the man was crying. But then who would deny a 37-year-old a few tears of joy?

8

SECRET MEETINGS AND PUBLIC WARFARE

World Championship Tennis was, of course, becoming too successful. Having let the wolf into the chicken-coop, all those old ILTF hens were running around squawking about having their best chicks carried off into the night. By clinging desperately to absurd distinctions between various types of player, the ILTF were seeing more and more of their precious authorized players signing contracts with Hunt, who had 32 of them under lock and key by the autumn of 1971. By then war had broken out again because, at their meeting at Stresa, Italy in July, the ILTF, unable to cope with the brave new world, had passed a resolution banning the WCT pros from all their tournaments as from January 1972.

Everyone should have seen it coming, of course. As Davies pointed out, Hunt's ideas of free enterprise and team ownership — a concept he had become used to in American sport where he owned the Kansas City Chiefs — mixed no better with the conservative practices of the ILTF than oil with water. They were convinced Hunt wanted to own the whole game, which was ridiculous, and they could never understand how lucky they were that the wolf who had appeared was as reasonable and civilized as Lamar. It could have been someone like the boxing world's Don King. Hah! A black wolf with his hair standing on end? What would they have done then?

Maybe it was Hunt's conventional appearance that made them so afraid. Here was this man, with his short back and sides and dark suits that looked as if they could have been bought off the peg at Burtons, talking quietly and coherently about television rights and sponsorship deals and sums of money they just didn't understand. If he had arrived in his stetson hat and cowboy boots they could have laughed him out of the room. But they didn't dare laugh at Hunt because they had a nasty feeling he was a serious man who needed to be taken seriously. So they simply stopped talking to him.

At this stage of the proceedings it must be admitted that Mike Davies didn't help. The hierarchy at Barons Court in London and even his old confidant and fellow Welshman Herman David were aghast that the young firebrand they used to rake over the coals for not playing the game in the prescribed manner should now arrive on their doorstep with an expensive looking briefcase and an even more expensive brief from one of the richest men in the world. Davies had never been the LTA's favourite son and it was almost impossible to avoid a feeling that old scores were being settled when Davies started talking in terms of a 13 per cent cut of the Wimbledon gate receipts and total control over television rights. Ben Barnett, who was a better wicket-keeper for Australia than he was a President of the ILTF, found the whole thing preposterous and, along with the majority of his colleagues on the management committee, seemed quite content to banish the likes of Rod Laver and John Newcombe from the world's great tournaments all over again and walk away from the problem. So once more it fell to certain enlightened elements in the British game to maintain some kind of communication. Derek Penman and Derek Hardwick were the only ILTF officials of any stature who recognized the need for dialogue but, until Gerald Williams came up with an inspired idea, initiating any kind of contact between Barons Court and Dallas had not proved easy.

Williams, who had devised the highly successful Dewar Indoor Circuit which became so much a part of the winter tennis scene in Britain during the early 1970s, suggested that Ted Tinling act as mediator for a round of secret talks between Penman and Hardwick and the WCT representatives. Tinling is barely in need of introduction in this story. Anyone who has been near a tennis tournament during the past 65 years can hardly have failed to notice this 6 ft 6″ giant of a man, who began his life-long love-affair with the game as Suzanne Lenglen's personally designated umpire for over a hundred of her matches on the Riviera in the 1920s. As I wrote in the foreword to his fascinating book *Sixty Years in Tennis*: 'The man is stamped, sealed and delivered from above as one of a kind. There has never been a head that shape, encompassing a mind that sharp, a wit that witty or an eye so perceptive that it can analyse and strip bare the human condition at a glance. Anyone who leaves a conversation with Ted Tinling not knowing more than when he entered into it has to be deaf, because he could not possibly be that dumb.'

There were many people in British tennis at the time who were either horrified or plain embarrassed by Tinling's flamboyant appearance and personality, but Gerry Williams was much too bright to be one of them. A Welshman whose own personality was capable of orchestrating the full Celtic range of passion, fire and humour that emanates from the Welsh valleys, Williams had been tennis correspondent on the *Daily Mail* for many years before taking on the much-needed job of Promotions Officer for the LTA. Apart from the success of the Dewar Circuit, Williams' time there was one of frustration.

Having finally done justice to his talents at Wimbledon where he and Desmond Lynam have teamed up so successfully with their late-night 'Des and Gerry Show' on the BBC, Williams can look back with greater detachment at that period of his life.

'I was having an awful time trying to make any headway at the LTA,' Williams remembered. 'For a start they weren't quite sure whether they even wanted a Promotions Officer and when I got there I realized they were just paying lip-service to Open Tennis. Basically the two Dereks and Stanley Hawkins were the only people who had really believed in the concept in the first place. The rest had just gone along with it in '68 because Herman David had given them an ultimatum and they knew Wimbledon held the purse strings. And in any case, most of them were loath to do anything to upset Wimbledon because they all harboured the hope that one day they might get invited to be a member of the club.'

Williams chuckled wickedly at the memory. But he was right, of course. The vast majority of LTA councillors had absolutely no idea of what was happening to the game in the big wide world outside Barons Court and basically wished that Lamar Hunt and all those nasty professionals would go away. But if the LTA's offices at Barons Court used to sit like a sentinel at the entrance to the Queen's Club, quite a few enlightened people were in the habit of slipping past to indulge in the dubious pleasure of a Queen's Club lunch. With the headquarters of his fashion business nearby, Tinling was one of them and it was over lunch one day in October 1970 that Gerry suggested Ted put down his needle and thread for a minute and utilize one of his other great talents, that as communicator.

'A lot of people thought I was mad but that was nothing new,' Gerry laughed. 'But Ted, of course, was terrific. He was one of the few people around who understood the facts of life and, in the meetings I attended, was completely lucid and even-handed.'

Williams' idea of Tinling chairing a round of secret talks in an attempt to break the impasse that had developed between the two sides was implemented when Penman phoned Ted and said, 'I hear you are the only person who can reach Mike Davies'.

Tinling had, in fact, been one of the few people whom Davies felt he could turn to when his own Welsh temper had riled the establishment during his days as a Davis Cup player, and it did not take long for Mr Communicator to set up a meeting at a hotel near Olympia. Davies had insisted John MacDonald join him and, with Williams in attendance, the other side was represented as ever by Penman and Hardwick. The gathering never had the intention of achieving anything far-reaching or concrete. It was merely an imaginative attempt to create a new dialogue and keep the flickering flame of Open Tennis alive. But it was inevitably going to cause a stir when the secret became known. In an attempt to anticipate the press reaction, Tinling gathered a few trusted advisers such as John Barrett, David Gray and myself about him at Wembley to discuss tactics. But there was never going to be a way of calming the suspicions that were lodged so deeply in many writers' minds about the real intentions of Hunt and his men. J.L. Manning, one of the most brilliant columnists of his era, was predictably scornful.

'How sick can a game be when it needs a dress-designer to solve its problems?' Manning wrote. And when commenting on the fact that Hardwick, as a result of the Tinling talks, had been designated the sole spokesman for the ILTF in any further negotiations with WCT, Manning remarked, 'Hardwick will speak, so it is intended, for Babel in its cause against Mammon'.

But there was no doubting the sincerity of the two Dereks, to whom the game in general owes more than has readily been acknowledged. In a press statement issued at the time, Penman said, 'We are determined that if there is to be [a] collision, it must not be the result of a lack of communication between the two sides. We are ready and eager to talk through the night, days on end, to explore the most slender possibility, while there is still any hope that a collision can be averted.'

Going on to praise Tinling's efforts, Penman said, 'You will have some idea of the headway we all made under Mr Tinling's astute chairmanship when I tell you that even at our first meeting, which lasted three and a half hours, we agreed that the following be recorded — that, subject to financial and administrative problems not being insurmountable, it was in the best interests of global lawn tennis that World Championship Tennis and ILTF should co-operate in working together towards a single world-wide competition'.

It was a brave attempt, as Barrett wrote in the *Financial Times*, 'to break the ideological deadlock that has threatened to return the game to a new dark age'. In fact the lights went out quite literally during the Embassy Championships at Wembley, leaving everyone to wonder who they were bumping into along those subterranean passages. With a sense of timing that hardly augured well for the future, the incoming ILTF President, Allan Heyman, chose to give a press conference at that very moment. His most memorable statement was that he felt Lamar Hunt 'did not have anything to give to the game'.

It is quite extraordinary how blind some amateur officials can be. Heyman a Danish lawyer based in London, was either totally unaware of the unprecedented standards of professionalism WCT had set at the majority of their tournaments in the preceding months or he was merely revealing the pig-headed nature that did so much to ruin consecutive Wimbledons in 1972 and 1973.

'Isn't it amazing how amateur officials never learn?' Gerry Williams said when we were reminiscing recently. 'Look at athletics. In the mid eighties they are now in exactly the same situation as tennis was 15 years ago, but do you think they would ever ask tennis for a word of advice so that they could avoid some of the problems we faced? Not a chance.'

In fact Heyman and his more reactionary colleagues were not worried so much about what Hunt had to give the game as about what he wanted out of it. As Hunt's alias was not Santa Claus, despite evidence to the contrary, he was indeed wanting something in return for his investment. Thirteen per cent of the gate at Grand Slam championships and the right to negotiate television contracts was obviously too much for Wimbledon or the ILTF to stomach in an era when the total profit that the All England Club was able to turn over to the LTA for the development of the game in Britain was no more than £40,000. Thanks to the persistence of the visionaries, the bloody-minded refusal of Hunt to walk away and pour his millions into some more congenial and receptive sport, and the professional marketing expertise of Mark McCormack, Wimbledon handed the LTA a cheque for more than seven million pounds just 16 years later. But the Heymans and, sadly, even the Davids of this world could not see the riches that lay ahead. To them professionalism was just a dirty word.

The Tinling talks kept the door ajar for over a year but the smugness with which so many administrators viewed the whole situation ensured that it would be a long time before anyone walked through it. The ILTF ban on WCT pros duly went into effect on 1 January 1972 and in the March issue of *World Tennis* magazine, in 'The Roving Eye' — a regular column I used to write for Gladys Heldman's publication — I was raving on about the stupidity of tennis politics. Extracts reveal the state of play at the time:

'The complacency of people who talk blithely of no settlement for a couple of years was possibly the most appalling aspect of the mood prevailing at the Royal Albert Hall during the Rothmans International in London. This was the first big gathering of the world tennis community since the ILTF's ban went into effect. One had expected a feeling of horror that this absurd war had actually been allowed to begin, coupled with a determination to end it as soon as possible.

'This indeed was the mood amongst people who really have the game's interests at heart. For they know that a prolonged separation of the two groups endangers the whole structure of the sport. Not only does the bidding for players that is going on at the moment bring about inflationary price values but it cheats the public by offering them tournaments containing only half the world's best players.

'At the time of the Albert Hall, however, Lamar Hunt was showing considerable restraint with his cheque book. Not one of the many players approached by WCT — they included Ilie Nastase, Zeljko Franulovic, Ion Tiriac, Adriano Panatta, Manuel Orantes and Gerald Battrick — was offered guarantees larger than they could reasonably expect to earn as Independent Pros. I doubt if it is a position Hunt will be able to maintain very long. With four players — Andres Gimeno, Torben Ulrich, Frew McMillan and Dick Crealy — already out of his 32-man group, he is in need of players and, in the artificial situation that exists at present, he is going to be forced to pay over the odds to get them. . .

'Meanwhile certain ILTF officials strutted around the Albert Hall chuckling about defections from Hunt's camp and talking about how they were going to win the war. The ILTF President, Allan Heyman, a man by the way who rigorously opposed Open Tennis in 1967, was quoted publicly during the week as saying that he foresaw no settlement until 1973 while privately, I understand he was making it plain that he was not interested in a settlement because he was still certain that Hunt could be run out of the game. By this stage I am not sure whether the mood is any less militant or any more realistic in Dallas. . .'

Although they were not guilty of trying to prolong the war themselves, the players were the great beneficiaries of a divided game. With two powerful elements in a tug-of-war for their services the only certain outcome was that the prices would go up. With hindsight it is amazing to realize that the whole thing happened again 10 years later — the ban on WCT, this time by the Pro Council, the separation of the circuits and players hopping from one to another making a fortune. In 1982 Ivan Lendl raked in a staggering $2,028,000 in prize money — a figure that still has not been exceeded in a single year — while even Tomas Smid, who has never been ranked in the world's top eight, won a couple of the $100,000 top prizes on offer from WCT and finished with well over half a million dollars for the year.

The reason why the pickings, for players who were prepared to work for them, were so exceptionally rich in 1982 — apart, of course, from the natural inflationary spiral in the world economy and the game itself — was that exclusivity contracts no longer existed. By and large, players had become free agents. Back in 1972 this was not the case and my comrade-in-arms, Eugene Scott, who has since gone on to create his own publication, *Tennis Week*, was matching my own pitch in indignation in the columns of *World Tennis*. The following snippets offer some idea of the passions the dispute had unleashed. Scott wrote: 'Periodically this column is devoted to blind rage. This month objectivity is out the window. The author has a conflict of interest, an axe to grind and is generally not to be trusted . . . It is also a call to arms for every player to protest the conduct of World Championship Tennis in abetting the disappearing act of Rod Laver, Ken Rosewall, Fred Stolle, Cliff Drysdale, Roy Emerson and Andres Gimeno from the US Open. The mass pull-out was an act of disloyalty similar to a horse biting its rider.

'In sympathy for the players involved, they had been through a long season and, without a two-week lay-off at Forest Hills, would have had to play through eight more weeks of WCT events. But justification ends there, for the players owe high allegiance to an event that spawned them as professionals. Wimbledon and Forest Hills are monuments to Open Tennis and representative of the permanent security for every responsible professional.'

Scott, a former Forest Hills semifinalist and one of the finest all-round athletes ever to come out of Yale, was right to declare his conflict of interest because Forest Hills was naturally very dear to his heart. He might also have pointed out in his column that the players mentioned probably felt less inclined to support the US Open after the ILTF had decreed that they would not be allowed to play there the following year. Nevertheless Scott, despite his patrician background, was never an establishment man, which makes his stance in this instance all the more pertinent. And, in conclusion, he hit the nuts and bolts of the matter:

'The real problem seems to be the existence of contractual relationships. Normally it is impossible for two tennis people to agree on anything from gut gauge to high ILTF policies. However all dissenters agree that there should be no contracts. Professional golfers show up for the prize-money with no guarantees* — above or below the table. Let tennis do the same and have the entrepreneurs

---

* Golf, unlike tennis, now permits above-the-table guarantees at tournaments outside the United States.

make their living from the promotion of events. Oh, yes, there is one dissenter from this otherwise unheard of consensus: Lamar Hunt — the only contract-holder. Lamar ? ? ?'

Lamar's answer to that was 'the sooner the better'. He had told me enough times that the huge guarantees he was having to pay players was a burden he could do without but, considering the state of mistrust that existed on both sides, he felt he had no option.

While the politicians spent much of the early part of 1972 sitting around talking amongst themselves, the players were earning an increasingly good living playing tennis. But they were talking, too, and the subject of their frequent locker-room conversations was something that scared the ILTF even more than Lamar Hunt. It was called player power.

The Federation administrators knew the concept existed because some of us had been writing about it. One of the pieces I had written for *World Tennis* the previous autumn had been headlined 'Player Power?' Note the question mark. It was still a very iffy proposition at the time and the officials, in their usual way, just hoped that tennis players would go on being silly little tennis players and that the whole thing would blow over. But anyone who realized that the tennis pros were as intelligent and educated as any group of athletes in the world realized, too, that the age of revolution was settling over tennis and that Allan Heyman, Basil Reay and the rest of them were going to have about as much say in the changes that were in the wind as Marie Antoinette.

'The players could end the war any time they wanted if they just got together and acted as one body,' Arthur Ashe was to remark at the US Pro Indoors in Philadelphia in February 1972. It was not an original statement but I quoted him anyway just to frighten people. They should have been equally frightened about what had been going on at the Los Angeles Tennis Club the previous September. As I wrote in *World Tennis*, 'Player power emerged briefly but ominously during the Pacific Southwest. One had sensed a new mood of militancy amongst the players for some time and one did not have to look very far for the cause. At a time when the game's administrators find it impossible to agree on anything; when respected leadership is virtually non-existent; when rules are bent, broken and then torn up, it is hardly surprising that the players become anxious, wary and finally hostile to anything or anybody who threatens to cloud their primrose path.

'It is no use telling them that they are selfish, spoiled and that, money-wise, they have never had it so good. They know that. What the Independent Pros in particular are asking is that their affluent world be run by a set of fair, coherent rules.'

The problem that put the players on the war-path in a club that used to be run by Perry Jones, one of the most autocratic administrators the game has ever known, revolved around the event up at Berkeley the following week. In a well-intentioned attempt to wed the two circuits, the Redwood Bank International was to expand its draw to 64 and offer both WCT and Grand Prix points. Then things fell apart. Many Independents were told they would have to qualify whereas all WCT pros were admitted directly into the draw — this, of course, being in the age before the computer rankings — and then it was learned that there would be no first-round losers' prize money.

When all this emerged the WCT boys were obviously more relaxed that their less secure Independent colleagues, and Roger Taylor started teasing Pierre Barthes about how the Independents could never get anything organized.

The big Frenchman had suddenly had enough. 'I get mad and I think, OK I will show 'eem,' said Barthes, and, as it turned out it was no idle threat. Ray Moore, who was to take charge of the movement, and Jaime Fillol, the soft-spoken Chilean who would eventually precede Moore as one of the early presidents of the ATP, quickly rounded up a group of 20 players who agreed to draft a letter to Berkeley tournament director Barry MacKay, himself an old Kramer pro, in which they would threaten to boycott the tournament unless he agreed to certain demands. Eventually concessions were made, but the outcome of this little dispute is not important. What matters is that the players were starting to think as a group and that one person, in particular, discovered just what player power could achieve. Moore was still attired as a sixties refugee from the King's Road complete with droopy moustache and shoulder-length hair at the time, but he never forgot what he learned at the LA Tennis Club and he never let tennis forget it either. Perry Jones, who once refused to allow a little girl called Billie Jean to join in a group photograph at his club because she was wearing shorts and not a 'proper' skirt, would have turned in his grave. But times were changing and changing faster than anyone dreamed possible.

By the early spring of 1972 Hunt and Heyman had met and decided enough was enough. At a meeting in Copenhagen on 17 April it was agreed that, in 1973, the first quarter of the year would be given over to WCT for their circuit, ending with the Dallas finals in May, with the Grand Prix filling the rest of the calendar. Additionally Hunt would not sign any more players to contracts and not renew those that still existed. Wonderful. So now everyone could get back to playing tennis and the poor old tennis fan could see all his favourite stars competing in the big championships. At least that is what any logical, impartial lover of the game would have assumed. But since when has the great bureaucratic mind ever given logic a fair crack of the whip?

What transpired really told you all you needed to know about how much the administrators of the era truly loved the game. Although the agreement had been signed more than a month before the start of the French Championships, none of the WCT pros was allowed to play there, nor indeed were they allowed to play at Wimbledon two weeks after that. The rules, you see, stated that no player was eligible to compete in an ILTF event while still under contract to WCT, and Heyman was not prepared to bend that rule until the Annual General Meeting of the ILTF had rubber-stamped the agreement. And the ILTF AGM was not until July — four days after Wimbledon.

Of course the date of the meeting could not be changed. Heavens, no. Too much administrative work for the Honorary Secretary of the ILTF, Basil Reay, who was known to have admitted to friends that he didn't much care for the game and gave credence to that theory by almost never watching it. Meetings could be arranged in a hurry only when there was a panic on, such as when Herman David threatened to let professionals play at Wimbledon in 1968. Oh, they came running then all right. Emergency meetings all over the place. But not now. 'No point, old boy,' I heard Reay mutter to someone at Queen's, behind the back of his hand. 'Everything will be arranged in due course and nobody around here cares whether the Hunt pros play or not.'

Reay actually had that habit of talking behind the back of his hand while imparting some juicy titbit to an ally in the press. He was a whisperer and a stirrer and no friend of tennis players. When he died last year the *Times* Obituary Editor phoned me up to get me to fill in some details of Reay's accomplishments. Reay had several, but I tried to make it plain to the editor that he had come to the wrong person if he wanted an unbiased view of Basil Reay.

Heyman thought Reay was terrific and wrote a long letter to *World Tennis* complaining about a piece I had written about his secretary, but the fact was that Reay's considerable administrative skills had impeded open-minded progress for too long and they were doing so again now.

To be fair, he was probably right in his view that some people didn't care whether the WCT pros played or not. Hunt had not had a good press in Britain and the WCT players had done their image in France no good at all in 1971 by not playing the French Open. Philippe Chatrier, who had worked so hard to modernize the game in France and to attempt to build bridges of communication with the players was naturally furious and rightly so. But there again Davies had not been very diplomatic with his scheduling and there is no doubt that his players' absence from Stade Roland Garros precipitated the split that followed.

But now that there was a chance to get everyone back in action again, nothing was being done. One player in particular felt himself hard done by because, as reigning Wimbledon champion he had the greatest prize in tennis to lose — his Wimbledon crown. John Newcombe, being no one's fool, had seen it all coming and, alone amongst the WCT pros, had insisted that a clause be inserted into his contract to the effect that World Championship Tennis would not stand in his way if it became possible for him to play Wimbledon.

But Hunt was being as intransigent over this issue as Heyman. While the war was still on, a tournament had been arranged in St Louis for the first week of Wimbledon, and Lamar wanted Newcombe to play there. Even though the local promoter was prepared to change the dates as soon as the settlement became known, no one was inclined to go to the bother. The apathy, on everyone's part except Newcombe's, was extraordinary. In the 'Roving Eye' column, written in July for the September issue of *World Tennis*, I had this to say:

'People whose minds have become conditioned by the ponderous workings of a bureaucracy and all the red tape it involves seemed to accept [the post-Wimbledon date of the ILTF AGM] as if it offered sufficient justification of depriving Wimbledon of its champion — not to mention about 28 other top players. The public, who had bought enough tickets anyway, could lump it. And the player? Why should the player have any say in the matter? Wasn't he just there to perform like a puppet on a string and serve his board-room bosses?

'A rich puppet, you say? Certainly and about time, too. But the funny thing is that there are many I know who are willing to spend some of their well-earned riches on a large pair of scissors with which to cut the puppeteers' strings.

'The officials who have run tennis for the past several decades still scoff at the talk of a players' association but I firmly believe that they are in for a nasty shock in the not too distant future. And if the players turn out to more militant and more demanding than good sense would allow once they are properly organized, officialdom should sit down and contemplate its own navel for a while before deciding who is to blame.'

I wish I could have been so accurate in all my predictions over the past 30 odd years, but that one was proved correct sooner than I had dared hope. The Association of Tennis Professionals was formed at Forest Hills in September of that year.

9

THE ATP BOYCOTT

The funniest thing about the formation of the Association of Tennis Professionals, which signalled the beginning of the end for the amateur officials who liked to think they ran the game, was that it was those very same officials who instigated it. I am including Lamar Hunt in that. Hunt and Heyman — they forced the ATP into existence.

As soon as the ILTF and WCT signed that agreement in April 1972, the alarm bells rang in every locker-room on the tour. The Independent Pros had seen how the ILTF was coping with the brash new world of Open Tennis and they were not impressed. But, as long as Hunt was signing contracts, there was an escape route; somewhere to run and hide from the clutches of their own national association and the long arm of its parent body. On the other side of the fence, the WCT pros were content, by and large, because they were in control of their own destiny. They chose whether or not they would sign with Hunt and had a say in the terms of the contract. (Even if, as in Newcombe's case, it didn't always do them much good.)

But now Hunt and Heyman were in cahoots. No more contracts would be signed by WCT so what would happen to Rod Laver and Cliff Drysdale and Marty Riessen when their contracts expired? Back they would go under the jurisdiction of the ILTF. As soon as that realization hit home, everyone knew it was time to stop fooling around with ideas about a players' association and get something done.

The idle chat had been going on for years. When Jack Kramer divested himself of his own group of touring pros in the early 1960s, Tony Trabert set up shop in Paris and, with the help of Butch Buchholz and Ken Rosewall, ran a professional players' association. But the break-up of the group, the formation of WCT and the advent of Open Tennis made it redundant. There had been one other attempt in the intervening years. It began, Charlie Pasarell was telling me the other day, in a discothèque in Rome, probably Jackie O's just off the Via Veneto which was one of our hang-outs during the Italian Open. But after a while all discothèques tend to merge into one throbbing blur and Charlie wasn't sure.

At any rate, he had a perfect recollection of a conversation he had had with Newcombe over the blare of the rock music. Idly watching some lithe Roman beauty gyrate to the hypnotic beat, Charlie yelled over the table at his companion, 'This is the life, Newk! It should never end! No matter how long we go on playing tennis, we should celebrate moments like this; Rome one week, Paris the next. We should have reunions and meetings and things like that.'

Pasarell's vocabulary usually ran out of specifics before his imagination did. Charlie's imagination could be called expansive (and if you want to know what it can produce, go take a look at the vast Grand Champions' Resort at Indian Wells in the Californian desert. That's where an imagination can lead you).

But at Jackie O's, Charlie was just thinking about tennis players and the times they had and what a great life it was. Newk, having done with the beers, was into a little Scotch by this time and thought so, too. The conversation planted a grain of an idea in both their minds and by the time the tour reached Bristol a few weeks later, it had gelled into the formation of a players' association. Newcombe was elected Chairman, Pasarell Secretary and it was called the ITPA — International Tennis Players' Association.

'I really got into it,' recalled Pasarell who is an all-or-nothing man. 'I started putting together bios of all the players and we met with Marilyn Fernberger who promised to designate her Philadelphia tournament the official ITPA Championships.'

But there was someone else coming out with big ideas, too. His name was Bill Riordan and he came from a small town in Maryland called Salisbury which he very nearly succeeded in making famous. Not many people have been to Salisbury, Maryland but Jimmy Connors and Ilie Nastase have and that is entirely due to Bill Riordan.

I have to say that I think perhaps Riordan was in the wrong sport. Boxing would have been perfect for him. All that hype and all that baloney; Bill would have done well with that. There are many people who would tell you that he did well with tennis too, and they would be right. It took a strong, determined man to create something worthwhile within the confines of the USLTA in the early seventies, but Bill managed it with what soon became known simply as the Riordan Circuit. It was actually the USLTA Indoor circuit, but Riordan ran it his way and made it his own.

Running it his way meant arbitrarily choosing which players he wanted in his draw and saying 'Tough luck, kid' to a player who had travelled across the country to accept a Riordan invitation only to be told on arrival that he would have to qualify. That happened once to Ray Moore. If Riordan didn't stick around long enough to regret it, there are probably a lot of tennis administrators today who are regretting it on Bill's behalf. You can never be sure what a long-haired 20-year-old athlete can turn into.

Riordan, who had ears like a telegraph wire, didn't take long to hear about the ITPA and came along to the new association's meeting during the 1970 US Open. 'Bill had told us he represented all the players who were not represented by Dell or McCormack,' said Pasarell. 'But you know what he was like. After a long meeting it became obvious we were not on the same wavelength so the whole thing sort of fell apart.'

A year later Frank Froehling, the 6ft 5" beanpole who carried his lanky stride on to court on behalf of the US Davis Cup team for a number of years, tried to use his own considerable intellectual powers to revive the idea, but he found divergent forces pulling him in a dozen different directions at once and, after a bit, he gave up.

Marty Riessen was proving just how much he enjoyed playing Rod Laver by beating the great Grand Slammer in Quebec City when news of the peace deal between the ILTF and WCT came through in April 1972. Although Heyman and Hunt got most of the credit for it, the deal had been hammered into shape by Jack Kramer and Donald Dell in another of their behind-the-scenes blitzes that kept on reshaping the destiny of tennis in those formative years. As soon as the word reached Canada, the tour politicians such as Drysdale, Newcombe, Pasarell and Mark Cox, who chaired the Quebec meeting, started talking all over again about the need to present a united front to the amateur officials who, in their spare time, thought that they could rule the lives of more than 50 professional athletes in a booming, expanding, million-dollar business.

Appropriately, perhaps, it was amidst the dollar-laden world of Las Vegas that the first serious player meetings took place three weeks later. Alan King was staging the first of his tournaments at Caesar's Palace — a world of glitter and glitz where the mauve-carpeted bedrooms have mirrors on the ceilings and the coffee shop is called the Noshorium and the legs of the cocktail waitresses go on forever. In true Las Vegas style there is a fruit machine or a blackjack table barring every entry and every exit so that temptation is forever leering over your shoulder.

Even the losers always had a great time at Caesar's Palace because Alan King was a wonderful host and the players were treated the way kings and Caesars should be treated. I first set eyes on Alan King when he was the supporting act for Judy Garland at the Dominion in Tottenham Court Road way back in the fifties. But I never saw him in his element until he had assembled a couple of dozen of the world's best tennis players for an audience. After the day's play he would stand at one of the bars and unload his best comedy routines on Newk or Emmo or anyone else who was still standing after hours on court in the desert heat. Most of the guys still were, because the adrenalin kept you going and there was always Tom Jones or Diana Ross coming on in the Big Room at midnight. If anyone could recognize midnight when it came. There are no clocks in Las Vegas. As a considered policy, the hoteliers hope their guests will forget to go to bed and forget to leave.

But in 1972 the players were not forgetting the predicament they were in and, just in case any did, Donald Dell flew into town to remind them. Dell, with his law partner Frank Craighill at his side, was his usual forceful self and spelled out the terms of the Hunt-Heyman peace agreement, the burning necessity for the players to have an organization of their own and how to go about it. Craighill had the by-laws all ready.

Dell, who was, even then, a controversial figure because of his close relationship with the group of American stars he managed, received some surprising endorsement from the floor. Cliff Richey, the rough-and-ready Texan who was not in the Dell stable, supported the idea of Donald becoming the legal adviser to the would-be association and Ray Ruffels, one of the more irreverent Aussies who is now a somewhat reformed and hard-working chief coach at the Australian Sports Institute, also stood up long enough to tell everyone that Dell was really not such a bad guy. It later transpired that 'Hesh' as Ruffels was known to everyone (all Australians have to have a nickname, some being obscurer than others) not only had been fortified by a couple of beers but had been playing golf all afternoon with Lutz and Pasarell, two supporters of Dell.

But that was fair enough. Any way one wanted to look at it, Dell was the best-qualified man for a job very few people knew anything about. But an even bigger role would be taken by the association's executive director.

'We knew it would have to be someone of stature because we were already starting to get pushed around and over-tennissed,' said Riessen. 'Names like Jack Kramer, Bob Briner who had been doing a lot of backroom paper work for us and John Barrett of Slazenger were all mentioned as possible choices as was Dell himself.'

Few players had any doubt that Kramer was the outstanding candidate. His appointment would give the association instant clout and credibility and by the time everyone had assembled at Forest Hills the only question that remained was whether Jack would accept. After Dell had worked on him for the better part of an entire night 'practically bringing tears to my eyes' as Kramer laughingly put it later, the man whose name was still synonymous with professional tennis agreed on two conditions — that the players' vote would be unanimous and that he would work for no pay.

In his book *My Forty Years in Tennis*, Kramer explained: 'I felt it would help convince people that I wasn't taking the position just for the power. I felt that if Kramer were a pro's volunteer, then an amateur's volunteer like Herman David would be more inclined to accept me and my organization.'

So while the WCT and Independent Pros were united in battle once again inside the great concrete bowl at the West Side Tennis Club at Forest Hills, just a few yards away, underneath the stand itself in an area designated the Open Club, a group of players met to form the Association of Tennis Professionals and elect Kramer as their leader. On court, a wild Romanian called Ilie Nastase was in the process of scoring one of the greatest victories of a largely unfulfilled career as he battled back from two sets to one down in the final against Arthur Ashe to win the US Open title on grass, after Ashe had defeated the new Wimbledon champion Stan Smith in the quarter-finals. Everyone talks of Smith's victory over Nastase in the Wimbledon final as one of the finest matches of the era, but for sheer drama the Nastase–Ashe duel came close to matching it. However, neither encounter had as lasting an impact on the sport as the decisions that were being taken in the Open Club. As soon as the ATP was formed, the cliché became reality. The game would never be the same again.

It is certain, however, that none of the players elected to the first ATP Board of Directors had an inkling of the momentous part in the game's history that they would be called upon to play in so short a time. Cliff Drysdale was elected the ATP's first President, an inspired choice as it turned out because the role into which the players' leader would be forced at Wimbledon the following year required more tact, courage and political savvy than even Cliff realized he possessed until he had to prove it. Apart from Kramer, the other members of the original 11-man board were Arthur Ashe, Mark Cox, Stan Smith, Jim McManus, Jaime Fillol, Ismail El Shafei, Nikki Pilic, whose name would become a byword for boycott before the next summer was out, John Barrett and Pierre Darmon, the former French No. 1 who agreed to look after the association's affairs in Europe and open a Paris office.

Kramer, for his part, would turn the little office he used for his own business in Los Angeles into the ATP headquarters until something better could be organized. And that was obviously not going to be for some time because money was tight. Just over 40 players signed up there and then at Forest Hills and each came up with $500 in membership dues, but that would hardly cover the cost of a secretary's salary and Jack's phone bills. So Donald was asked to go out and find some endorsements. It was the Adidas deal, through the good offices of the late Horst Dassler, that kept the ATP financially afloat during those early years and even through the set-backs that followed. Dell did good work. But right from the outset those players who were not managed by his Washington office were wary of the amount of power and influence he exerted on the association. And their concern would openly grow as the years wore on.

Ever since his Grand Prix concept had been adopted by the ILTF, Kramer had been on good terms with administrators, who prior to the days of Open Tennis had viewed him as a pariah. So, during the winter months of '72-'73, Jack, often with Donald at his side, jetted round the world talking to the amateur officials in an attempt to explain the ATP's motives and to make it clear that they wanted everyone to work together. With a weaker ILTF president than Allan Heyman in office and a less devious honorary secretary sitting at Barons Court than Basil Reay, the explosion might never have occurred. In Paris, Philippe Chatrier was, after all, one of Kramer's closest allies and genuinely wanted the players to assume a powerful role in the administration of the game. But Chatrier was still completing his own revolution inside French tennis and had not had time to exert his influence on the international scene. In the meantime Heyman, lacking Chatrier's vision but matching his ambition, was determined that his amateur federation would continue to run the professional game.

But in reality the whole thing was a tinder-box, and although few were prepared to admit it at the time, it needed only one spark to set the whole game alight. As is so often the case, the match was lit in an unlikely place. More serious conflicts have been started in that part of the world now known as Yugoslavia but, as far as a sporting war was concerned, this one did nicely. It quickly became known as the Pilic Affair and, in origin at least, was really the Pilic Family Affair. The head of the Yugoslav Tennis

Federation was the uncle of Nikki's wife. 'Uncle' not unnaturally wanted Nikki to play for Yugoslavia against New Zealand in the Davis Cup in the first week of May, particularly as a new player of talent, Zeljko Franulovic — a French Open finalist in 1970 — had emerged to give Pilic support and enhance Yugoslavia's chances of real success. 'Uncle' said that Nikki agreed categorically to play. But when he did not play, thus pouring all the fat on the fire, Nikki was quick to say, in whatever language people were prepared to listen to, 'Hey, not so much of the categorical!'

That was the crux of the matter. Had Pilic given his unconditional promise to play for Yugoslavia? If he had done and then reneged, the ATP would not have supported him. But the letter Drysdale showed to me in Rome, after it had been translated from Croatian by some apparently reliable linguist in London, was shot through with so many 'ifs' and 'but's that no translation could have concealed the extent of Nikki's conditions. He would play *if* Franulovic had recovered from a shoulder injury, otherwise there would be no point. More importantly, he would play *if* he and Allan Stone of Australia did not earn enough WCT points to qualify for the doubles play-offs in Montreal which were scheduled for the same week as the Davis Cup. They did qualify and it was hard to argue — conditions or no conditions — where Pilic's real obligations lay. He was under a legally binding contract to play the WCT events he qualified for and, had he pulled out, he would have failed in his professional obligation to Stone who would have been deprived of several thousand dollars in prize money. But no matter what kind of peace agreement he had signed with Hunt, Allan Heyman was not interested in professional obligations between professional tennis players. As the Yugoslav Federation reported Pilic for not playing the Davis Cup, the issue fell like manna from Heaven into Heyman's lap and he proceeded to make the most of it.

'Uncle', who went by the imposing title of General Korac, had got a little carried away with his idea of military discipline and had suspended Pilic for nine months. Under the letter of the law, the ILTF were supposed to uphold this ban but, under pressure from Chatrier and Dell, Heyman agreed to allow the player to compete in the French Open while he and two other ILTF officials, Robert Abdesselam of France and Walter Elcock of the United States, reviewed the matter.

The hearing was held in Paris where Kramer had arrived in a hurry after a phone call from Chatrier who, with an understatement that would have been worthy of the British, had asid, 'Jack, we have a little problem here'.

Pilic was called to give evidence on his own behalf and he did so flanked by the two heavies from his new players' association, Kramer and Dell. Everyone listened politely and the ATP officials, having seen documented evidence that Pilic's commitment had been strictly conditional, were convinced he would get off. But what better opportunity for Heyman to prove that the ATP were paper tigers and that the ILTF still ruled the roost? With a great show of magnanimity, the ILTF panel reduced Pilic's suspension from nine months to one month — a suspension that ended right slap bang in the middle of Wimbledon. Which meant, of course, that Pilic would not be allowed to play in the world's premier tournament. That would be a test of everyone's resolve and no one was more aware of it than Heyman.

For the record, Pilic and Stone lost in the first round of the Montreal WCT doubles to the eventual winners, Stan Smith and Bob Lutz and, even though Franulovic was able to play for Yugoslavia and beat New Zealand's Brian Fairlie on the first day in Zagreb, he went down to Onny Parun in the fourth rubber and the home side lost 2–3. That, of course did nothing for General Korac's humour. What Heyman did not know was that there would be a third loser in the Pilic Affair and it would be not Nikki but the ILTF.

The fact that the players were prepared to stand four square behind Nikki Pilic over a matter of principle said a great deal more about the principle than it did about Pilic. The tall left-hander with the lop-sided gait was far from being the most popular player on the tour. He exuded a superior air of self-confidence which rivalled that of Charles de Gaulle. The comparison would have been apt in Nikki's eyes. He was fond of telling everyone about the Mercedes he kept at home in Split. Far from embracing the socialist doctrine Pilic's politics would have made Margaret Thatcher look decidedly wet. The term 'male chauvinist pig' could have been invented for him — 'The wife, she is to serve husband' he used to remind us — and, apart from a thorough distaste for flower children and the length of Jeff Borowiak's hair, he had a fairly straightforward solution to the drug problem: shoot the pushers.

Actually Nikki was quite fun to have around because he stood up well to an unmerciful amount of leg-pulling and he did stimulate some wonderful arguments over dinner. But he was no fool and was probably more surprised than anyone when he realized that his entire peer group was prepared to boycott Wimbledon unless he was allowed to play. The enormity of that proposition took a little while to sink in.

When the issue flared up just before the French Open, Cliff Drysdale was also surprised by the alacrity with which the rank and file sprang to Nikki's defence. But, on reflection, he realized that it was, in fact, the perfect issue for members of a new players' union. It was precisely because they were afraid of this sort of thing happening to them that they had joined. In the early 1960s the Europeans were constantly being told what to do and where to play by their national associations, and the Australians and Americans needed no reminding of how their immediate predecessors had been forced to ask permission before they could even leave the country to play abroad. Instead of congratulatory telegrams from home after winning titles in Australian colours, players like Bob Howe and Ken Fletcher used to receive ultimatums saying 'Your expenses overdue. Either supply or return home at once'. They were bitter memories, and Heyman's great mistake was in failing to realize how fresh they remained in the players' minds. It was not greed as so many British papers tried to make out. Money had nothing to do with it. It was simply never discussed nor even thought of. It was purely a revolt by professionals against amateurs who thought they could run a professional athlete's career as a part-time hobby. On that point they were adamant and, by the time the tour moved on to Rome for the Italian Open, which used to follow Paris in those days, Drysdale realized he had a real live bunch of revolutionaries on his hands.

'The press tried to blame Kramer but, as I soon found out by canvassing the members, they didn't need Jack to tell them what to do,' Drysdale told me recently. 'It was the players' revolt, not Kramer's, although he was certainly with us all the way.'

Being President of the ATP had suddenly become such a time-consuming job that it was amazing Drysdale found time to get on court. Sitting on his bed at the Holiday Inn, I helped him record, word by word, the translation of the Pilic letter as it was read over the phone from Barons Court. It included the sentence 'I wish to play Davis Cup but there are three or four obstacles. . .'.

'There's no way that constitutes an unqualified promise to play,' Cliff said after reading it through a couple of times. The next day he canvassed ATP members at the Foro Italico and found over 40 of them more than willing to sign a statement to the effect that they would boycott any tournament, including Wimbledon, in which Pilic was not allowed to play. At Tony Pickard's tournament in Nottingham the following week another 20 signatures were added, and from Hamburg, where Newcombe and Fillol were sounding out opinion at the West German Open, there came the most militant reaction of all. More than 20 other players signed a statement saying they wanted to enter Wimbledon and then stage a walk-out at 2.00 pm on the first Monday to dramatize the depth of their feelings. But the ATP had no quarrel with Herman David and the All England Club, and the Board of Directors refused to entertain the suggestion.

Drysdale, in fact, was doing his best to keep the most militant members of his organization out of the public eye and had pointedly refrained from making any inflammatory statements to the large group of reporters who had been hounding him in Rome and Nottingham. Still trying to find a way out of the impasse, Drysdale phoned Heyman three times to suggest that the ILTF President appoint an independent arbitrator to look into the case, and promised that the ATP would abide by the outcome. Three times Heyman refused.

Kramer, jetting into London after a quick trip back to Los Angeles, met with the Danish lawyer — a man with whom he had worked amicably in the past — and found him immovable.

'After 10 minutes I got the impression Allan wanted me to get up and leave,' a puzzled Kramer told me. 'He kept on repeating that the ILTF had made their decision and it was final. I think he wants a showdown.'

There was evidence to suggest that Kramer was correct. Before leaving Boston to fly over to Wimbledon, the USLTA President, Walter Elcock, told Dennis Ralston of a phone call he had received from Heyman. Apparently Heyman had told Elcock not to worry because 'the players will never boycott Wimbledon'. It was a feeling held by many who were out of touch with the mood of the new tennis professional. At the Queen's Club, Basil Reay's cronies, who included certain members of the British press, were crowding round the bar and telling each other, 'We've got them over a barrel. They might boycott a lot of tournaments but not Wimbledon. They need it too much.'

But the days were ticking by and neither side was moving an inch even though Kramer and Drysdale, with Barrett acting as the obvious link-man between the two sides, were doing their best to find a solution. You would never have known it by reading the majority of the British papers, however. The campaign against Kramer was hotting up and getting nasty. 'Kramer Should Resign!' exclaimed a large headline in the *Daily Express*. In the *Sunday Express*, Alan Hoby, who really should have known better, wrote that Jack Kramer, 'the hero of 1947, is a heel'.

Worse was to come, but Hoby's comment was indicative of the British attitude to the whole affair. Kramer was a hero in 1947 because he won Wimbledon. Wimbledon was sacrosanct. Anyone who revered Wimbledon and worshipped at the altar of the All England Club was a hero and a jolly good sport, while anyone who even suggested it was anything less than wonderful was definitely suspect. Although it is less true today, in 1973 Britain viewed tennis through the narrow prism of Wimbledon. Nothing else really mattered. Players who competed at Wimbledon were better known in England than anywhere else in the world because the British public truly loved them. Returning after a 12-month absence, Marty Riessen who, after all, wasn't the biggest star in the game, would be recognized in London restaurants. One year, at the party that Simpsons of Piccadilly used to throw for the players, a large lady in an even larger hat came bouncing up to Tom Okker and said. 'Oh, Mr Okker, so good to see you again. Tell me, do you get the chance to play a little tennis in between Wimbledons?'

Okker had a big enough sense of humour to be able to laugh at that, but it was this attitude that 'proper' tennis began and ended at the gates of the All England Club that was helping to fuel the campaign of hatred that was being built up in the press. The players were trying to hurt Wimbledon. How could they! How dare they!

What made it so desperately sad was that the players were not trying to do anything of the sort. It was Allan Heyman who had chosen Wimbledon as the battleground, not the players. And it was Heyman who was making sure that Herman David reversed his role of 1968 and stayed firmly in the ILTF camp. For John Barrett, the former British Davis Cup captain who, as an executive of Slazenger was responsible for providing Wimbledon with the balls and other equipment, the conflict was particularly embarrassing and painful. But, with a week to go he still felt there was time for a compromise. After meeting Kramer off the plane at Heathrow, Barrett ushered the ATP leader into a pre-arranged early morning conference with Heyman and David.

But although they were nearly 30 minutes early, the ATP representatives were not, according to Kramer, early enough. 'They were already in a pre-meeting and David, who had never been a friend of the ILTF and its hypocrisy, was getting the full powers of persuasion from Heyman,' Kramer related. Echoing Drysdale's plea, Kramer asked once again that Heyman hand the problem over to independent arbitration. Heyman replied that Pilic had broken an

ILTF rule and that the matter was therefore out of his hands.

Outside on the streets of London, the placards, reflecting the headline in the *Evening Standard*, read 'Mr Kramer, I must find you Discredited!'

Kramer was the obvious target, of course. The Fleet Street editors, sensing a great emotional story, knew that it would be very difficult to sell Ken Rosewall, Rod Laver, Stan Smith and John Newcombe as villains. Not only had they proved themselves to be great sporting heroes but the public had been told time and again, with commendable accuracy, that they were great people, too. Not even Fleet Street could slap black hats on their heads overnight. It was much simpler to sell the whole story as a Kramer-led plot to prise more money out of Wimbledon.

The story was becoming bigger and bigger news as every day passed. Meetings between members of the ATP hierarchy went on virtually non-stop at the Westbury Hotel in Mayfair. The Westbury had always been the Americans' headquarters in London during Wimbledon but, with the kind of timing that PR people dream about, the new Gloucester Hotel had come to an arrangement with the ATP to open the doors of the hotel two weeks early so that the main body of Wimbledon players could stay there at vastly reduced rates. As soon as the first players started checking in, the lobby was besieged by reporters and television cameras from every news-gathering outfit on earth. The Gloucester had suddenly become one of the most publicized hotels in the world and it wasn't even open! Since then it has remained the official Wimbledon hotel but the rates have never been quite so good again.

However, it was at the Westbury that most of the drama was being enacted. One evening I dropped by to catch up on the latest developments in the situation and when I called Kramer's room, he said, 'Come on up'. The tall, athletic frame was wrapped in a big white bathrobe when I walked in but apart from a few creases across the brow, I remember thinking how little he had changed since the first time I'd ever met him, which had also been at the Westbury, just after he had signed the British No. 1 for his pro tour. Chap called Mike Davies. The game and its personalities had moved on quite a bit in the intervening 12 years but Jack was still his usual good-natured self; still able to crack a joke no matter what he might have been feeling inside.

'Welcome to public enemy No. 1, kid!' he laughed by way of a greeting. 'Have you got the evening papers? What names am I being called today?'

Criticism in the press was nothing new to Kramer. Generally he had maintained excellent relations with reporters during his career as the world's premier tennis promoter, but there had still been hostility on occasion, especially in Australia, where there was resentment at the regularity with which he kept signing up Harry Hopman stars. But it didn't get any easier to take and, by the time we met, he had already resigned himself to the fact that, if the players did boycott Wimbledon, he would not be very welcome in his usual position alongside Dan Maskell in the BBC Television commentary box. Rather than embarrass anyone, he had already offered to stand down, and although the BBC chiefs made all the right noises initially ('No problem, old boy, you're our man' — that sort of thing), by the time the final decision had to be made, Jack found himself suddenly friendless at both Television Centre and the All England Club. He was, indeed, public enemy No. 1. My colleagues on the press had seen to that.

So, I wanted to know as he disappeared into the bathroom to shave, what was the next move?

'We are being advised by a lot of apparently knowledgeable people that we should get Pilic to take an injunction out against the ILTF,' Kramer replied from behind a layer of lather. 'That'll throw it into the courts and, providing the injunction is granted, it will get us through Wimbledon. The case would never get heard in under a couple of weeks and until a judge rules, the ILTF would not be able to prevent Nikki playing.'

Tactically, that turned out to be the ATP's worst move of the summer. If Heyman had been truly interested in saving Wimbledon he could have let the injunction go through and continued the battle afterwards. But the evidence was piling up. Heyman was using Wimbledon deliberately. And the sad thing was that Herman David was not objecting. So Heyman, using all his legal skills, fought the injunction and a meeting was called on the Monday of Queen's, just a week before the start of Wimbledon, in the High Court chambers of Mr Justice Forbes. Heyman, David, Kramer, Drysdale and the increasingly embarrassed Pilic were present. Mr Justice Forbes read painstakingly through each ILTF rule and cross-questioned counsel at length. And three days later he announced he was rejecting Pilic's application for an injunction on the grounds that the ILTF were within their rights to suspend the player. He added, however, that it would be wrong for a British court to start passing judgement on a case that had been tried abroad and had involved a foreign association.

'Player's Case Thrown Out of Court!' screamed the headlines, and editorial after editorial lectured Drysdale's union on how they were now honour bound to fulfil their commitment to Wimbledon.

They had lost in one court so now they had to play in another. Hah, hah. But it wasn't that simple or that funny. They had not, in fact, been able to get as far as a law court and although Mr Justice Forbes' summation had *implied* that he would have come down on the side of the ILTF if the injunction had been granted, he had not, in fact, ruled on whether or not Pilic was guilty as charged. As a result the ATP Board did not feel bound to abide by a decision that had not been clearly stated.

By this time the dispute had reached Government level and the Sports Minister, Eldon Griffiths, invited Drysdale and Heyman to meet with him separately at his Westminster apartment. Unlike some of the people involved, Griffiths knew all about the press and how things worked in America because, although Welsh by birth, he had risen to the very top of American journalism during a long career in the States as a columnist for *Newsweek*. He attempted to put a little transatlantic knowhow to work on the issue and, after talking to both sides, invited Drysdale and Heyman to return together for another session the following day. It was, however, the same old story. Drysdale agreed. Heyman declined.

The extent of the ILTF President's willingness to solve the problem was a promise to sit down with the ATP *after* Wimbledon and work on the revision of some outdated rules. In other words he was asking the players to trust him and it was too late for that. It was not Heyman personally; it was the whole structure of the establishment he represented that the players could not trust. The game's hierarchy had treated the players like workers for too long. Now the players were acting like workers and implementing their right to strike.

It is so difficult, even today, for the public to understand that for professional athletes, the game is their life, their livelihood, the means by which they put bread on the table for themselves and their families. People who trudge off to the office on some dreary suburban train every morning quite understandably want to live vicariously through the exploits of their idols in the sporting arena. The day will look a little less grey if David Gower has just taken a hundred off the Australians at the Gabba or if John Barnes has weaved his way through another mesmerized defence to score for Liverpool. Commuters don't want to be bothered about Barnes' contract. Although they know it is not possible, they wish their sporting idols were playing purely for the love of the game.

In 1973 this attitude was even more prevalent as far as Wimbledon was concerned. If they forced themselves to think about it, the public realized that tennis players had to eat and that some of them had

For Jack Kramer this was the beginning — the 1947 Wimbledon Cup presented to him in the Royal Box by His Majesty King George VI and Queen Elizabeth. Looking back Jack may think winning Wimbledon was the easy part. *Photo: Acme Photos*

Even the camel looks proud to have Lew Hoad and Ken Rosewall aboard as coach Harry Hopman leads two of his greatest protégés around the pyramids on an early visit to Cairo in the 1950s.
Photo: L. Hoad private collection

Chatting with one of the great
Musketeers Jean Borotra or
attending a black-tie dinner
are familiar poses for ITF
President Philippe Chatrier.
Borotra Photo: Ed Fernberger,
Black tie: Michael Cole

Donald Dell caught in a more aggressive pose by one of the game's most aggressive photographers, Art Seitz.

'Please Mr Chairman, after you!' Donald Dell in one of his most solicitous moods as he ushers former Philip Morris Chairman Joe Cullman onto the court for a presentation ceremony at Forest Hills. *Photo: Linda Pentz*

Donald Dell has had many roles in tennis but acting as a linesman for Pancho Gonzales was not one of the most frequent! But the proof is here in this photo taken at the Los Angeles Tennis Club during the Pacific Southwest Championships in the early 1970s. *Photo: R. Evans*

Party time at the Alan King Classic at Caesar's Palace in Las Vegas. Left to right standing, Marty Riessen, Geoff Masters, Jim McManus, Alan King, A. Gorilla, Stan Smith, John Newcombe, Charlie Pasarell. Kneeling, Colin Dibley, Roy Emerson, Rod Laver. *Photo: Todd Friedman*

A great big Billie Jean smile from Mrs King for Ann Jones and husband Pip as the Wimbledon Champion climbs the stairs to the old players tea room which has now been demolished. But in her prime it was the Billie Jean serve that did the demolishing.
Photo: R. Evans

Gladys Heldman, without whom there might not have been a Virginia Slims Circuit, and Ray Moore in his side-burn days. *Photo: Ed Fernberger*

Ted Tinling and the way women tennis players could look if there was anyone left in the business with Tinling's skills. Julie Heldman, Gladys' daughter is next to Ted and the Truman sisters, Christine and Nell are at the other end of the line in this shot taken, not in a Mexican Hacienda, but on the roof of a store in London's Kensington High Street. *Photo: Arthur Cole*

Spreading the word—Richard Russell, the Jamaican No 1 (facing camera) stages an exhibition on King Street in Kingston with Barry MacKay and Charlie Pasarell (in track suit) in 1971. *Photo: Susan Tyndale-Biscoe*

babies to feed, but basically they didn't want to know about that. Let them go off and earn all their filthy money somewhere else. Wimbledon wasn't about prize money. Wimbledon was about green grass and fresh strawberries and healthy young people playing a wonderful sport. Talk of politics and boycotts ruined the image and shattered the dream.

'Stupid! The Money-Mad Stars of Tennis!' That was yet another headline as the sense of crisis increased, and the *Evening News* editorial on which it was based was even more revealing. 'Now we have seen the unacceptable face of sport,' it read. 'And we hope we will not see it again — the face of Jack Kramer. It is time to go home Mr Kramer. Leave us to enjoy the game the way we like it. Clean.'

A copy of that example of sick journalistic expertise was lying around the lobby of the Westbury as the ATP meetings continued in the lower-ground-floor conference room. Pilic, humble at last, had offered to withdraw his name from the Wimbledon entry list and had flown home to Split to escape the pressure that was building up all around him. But the issue had left Nikki far behind. The players were fighting for their future and a gesture like the one Pilic had suggested would have been meaningless. Stan Smith understood that and he was the reigning champion — the man who would not be able to defend the most coveted crown in tennis if the boycott went into effect. John Newcombe understood it and John had been through what Smith was facing — the inability to defend his title the year before because of tennis politics. And now with the years slipping away he was going to miss out again. No one needed to remind Ken Rosewall about the passing years. The 38-year-old veteran had just flown in from Sydney, primed and ready to make what most people felt must be his last serious assault on the one major title that had evaded him throughout one of the longest and most distinguished careers the game has ever known. But Ken understood. To have accepted Pilic's offer and played, with no concrete gesture from the other side apart from a vague offer to talk after Wimbledon, would have wrecked the credibility of the ATP and put the players back in bondage; whipping boys for the whims of Basil Reay — 'Play here! You can't play there!' — and of the kind of Queen's Club official who, that very week, had started berating Arthur Ashe, of all people, in the most discourteous tones because the ATP Vice-President had dared stay on an authorized practice court for an extra quarter of an hour, even though no one else wanted it. All too often the players were confronted with that kind of petty-minded rudeness and they knew they had to face up to it once and for all. So, on the Thursday evening, the Board met and voted to boycott Wimbledon.

'We knew what we were doing,' Ashe told me many years later. 'In fact we were so conscious of the momentous decision we had taken that we all decided to go home and sleep on it and come back and have another vote the following day.'

So once again the athletes filed into the Westbury conference room and the reporters camped in the foyer and drank coffee, perched on the flight of stairs leading down to the little lobby area just outside. Drysdale had made two decisions in the intervening 24 hours. First, he would take a final suggestion of compromise into the meeting, and secondly, he would allow three non-board members to attend so as to broaden the discussion and allow more voices to be heard. The three players were Rosewall, Charlie Pasarell and Cliff Richey.

The compromise proposal asked that the ILTF recognize, in writing, that the ATP members owed their first allegiance to their own association and not to their national federations. If the ILTF would agree to that, the ATP would accept Pilic's offer to withdraw and play Wimbledon without him. The proposal was never passed and, in retrospect, it should have been. No one seriously thought that Heyman would agree to it because it hit at the very heart of what he was trying to prevent — loss of control — but, tactically, it would have thrown the ball back in his court, forced him to make the eleventh-hour decision of whether or not the players would play and pin-pointed for the public the real issue.

But the second meeting was more militant than the first. For a start, Newcombe, who was not a board member at the time, had phoned Kramer that evening and told him that he would be prepared to go along with whatever decision the Board came to regarding whether or not to play at Wimbledon.

'But if that decision is to cave in and play,' said Newk, 'I tell you this, Jack. I'll never have anything to do with a players' association again.'

So everyone knew where Newcombe stood and within a few minutes of the meeting getting under way, no one was in any doubt as to the feelings of Pasarell or Richey either. Compromise was not a word they wanted to hear and, along with Ashe and El Shafei, they became the driving force that killed off any chance of reversing the vote of the previous night.

'Looking back I am still not sure whether I was right or not to let Charlie and Cliff into that meeting,' Drysdale admitted recently.

'They were not board members so, of course, they couldn't vote, but they certainly made their presence felt and might well have influenced the others.'

A majority of those present was needed to overturn the boycott vote and this time Mark Cox aligned himself with the other Englishman, John Barrett, and Stan Smith. They voted to play. Kramer, Ashe and McManus voted for the boycott. Three all. Everyone turned to the President. 'I abstain,' said Drysdale.

Kramer nearly fell off his chair. 'It was brilliant!' Kramer was to write later. 'What a politician the kid turned out to be!'

'I just felt instinctively, as of that moment, that it was the right thing for me to do,' said Cliff. 'To an extent we had a divided association and as President I did not want to align myself on such a huge issue irrevocably with one side or the other. But I also knew that if we had reneged on our original stance and kowtowed to the establishment, at least 25 members would have walked out of the association next morning and the ATP would have been dead. You must remember we had been in existence only nine months and we all knew that it offered the one chance the players had of being able to direct their own careers.'

It was in the early hours of the morning that Drysdale eventually emerged to confront a tired and irritable press corps. Like most of the young athletes around him, he looked pale and haggard but, not for the first time that week, one could only be impressed by the way a 24-year-old with no previous experience in union leadership was handling himself. The majority of the reporters were hostile, if not to him personally, then certainly to his association, but he answered every question with dignity and quiet restraint before letting out a stream of oaths as he got into the car that would drive him back to the Gloucester through the deserted streets. He had not wanted this. All the players desperately wanted to play Wimbledon just because they were tennis players and this was their Mecca. 'But we've got no choice,' Drysdale kept muttering. 'We've got no goddamn choice.'

Once the decision had been made, the next task was to make it stick. There were 80 ATP members entered for Wimbledon and if more than a handful broke ranks and elected to play, the whole impact would be lost. Various anti-player factions in the press were predicting that no more than 70 per cent of the membership would remain solid, and immediately Roger Taylor was put under tremendous pressure to remain loyal to Wimbledon rather than to his international union. Ilie Nastase was wavering, too, pleading pressure from his own Romanian Federation who, he insisted, were ordering him to play. Ion Tiriac, who wasn't speaking to 'Nasty' at the time, said that was rubbish and that his one-time protégé was only trying to grab a Wimbledon title on the sly. The war of words was hotting up.

Drysdale knew that there was a danger of the other top European names being coerced into defying their union by the powerful national federations of such leading tennis nations as Italy and Spain. 'We've got to baby-sit Adriano and Manolo,' said Drysdale, marshalling his forces the following day. 'If we can keep them with us, the others will follow.'

Adriano Panatta was the new Italian heart-throb who, with his equally talented little doubles partner Paolo Bertolucci, would turn Italy into a powerful force in tennis for the next half-dozen years. Manolo Orantes, Santana's successor in Spain, was also emerging as a major talent, and his Davis Cup colleague Juan Gisbert was, despite his awkward style, a good enough competitor to offer Orantes valuable support. This quartet of Latin stars was vital to the ATP cause. Drysdale was right. If they defected, so would most of the other Europeans. But they didn't. In a show of solidarity that was quite remarkable considering the penalties they knew would be levied against them by their federations, they closed ranks and stayed loyal to the cause. With Jaime Fillol using his quiet powers of persuasion with the big South American contingent, that continent, too, was totally behind the ATP. With one exception there was no problem with either the Australians or the Americans, and when the names were sent to Wimbledon referee Captain Mike Gibson, who had delayed the draw until 11.00 am on the Saturday morning in the hope that there might be some last-minute change of heart, the list of withdrawals stunned the entire tennis world. Only three ATP members had not sent their names for withdrawal — Taylor, who was dithering up to the very last minute, Nastase and a low-ranking Australian called Ray Keldie who said he was too poor to miss out on the Wimbledon prize money. Heyman's gamble had failed. The players had called his bluff and boycotted the one tournament he felt sure was immune from such action. It was, as Heyman's enlightened successor Philippe Chatrier would admit to me 14 years later, a blow from which the ILTF never fully recovered.

But a war brings casualties to both sides and the ATP lost a good man when John Barrett resigned from the Board, in protest not just because of the decision to boycott Wimbledon but because of the kind of tactics being used by some of the more militant members.

'It started to get out of hand when some of the young firebrands like Pasarell and Richey began threatening John Lloyd and telling him he would be barred from all ATP events in the States if he played,' said Barrett. 'At that point they lost me. It was time for me to leave.'

Although the ATP was to squander the position it had earned for itself in later years, the battle had not, however, been fought in vain. From it grew the idea of a professional council to administer the world-wide sport, which was growing at such a rate and in so many different directions that the idea of Reay and a rotating part-time President trying to run it all from Barons Court was ludicrous.

When Donald Dell, who had craftily stayed out of the thick of things during the run-up to Wimbledon, finally flew in from Washington, he brought with him a proposal he and Kramer had worked out concerning the structure of just such a council. After a few days Heyman handed back a counter-proposal which was, in effect, a precise replica of the Dell-Kramer document except for two vital paragraphs. The ILTF wanted the right to appoint the chairman, rather than have the council members elect him themselves, and they wanted the council to consist of four ILTF members and three from the ATP. Kramer and Dell had suggested three ILTF, three ATP and three tournament directors — which is, in fact, precisely the make-up of the Men's International Professional Tennis Council as it stands today with the chairman being elected by the members.

Heyman was actually rejecting the ATP's proposal in favour of his own. Dell was fuming. 'How much fairer can we be?' he raged as he swept out of the Westbury for a final visit to Wimbledon. 'We are prepared to place ourselves under the total control of the council but we feel it is vital to have the tournament directors represented because they play such a vital part in the running of the professional game. If we are to be in a minority, we want the swing votes to be in the hands of knowledgeable people who have a real stake in the game. We cannot be expected to sit on a council that has four rigid ILTF officials and three of us. We will accept a lot but not a stacked deck.'

The facts, as I wrote in *World Tennis*, were no longer cloaked in the emotionalism of Wimbledon and were becoming embarrassingly transparent. The players wanted a democratic council with all facets of the pro game represented — they were even asking for the sponsors to be consulted — while the ILTF were primarily interested in retaining control. Heyman was not being coy about this, despite Reay's typical attempts to call a press conference without anyone knowing about it. Basil could be unbelievable. On the final Saturday of that sadly historic Wimbledon, Reay arranged a press conference for his President without passing the word around the press writing-room where over a hundred reporters were working. When seven carefully informed, friendly faces showed up, Reay suggested the conference begin.

Luckily a few more of us got to hear of it and were able to put a few pertinent questions. Heyman was perfectly straightforward when I asked him if his primary concern was to retain total control of the game for the ILTF. This is what he said:

'Yes, we do want to retain control. We have a responsibility to the smaller nations and the Communist countries who would never accept the major tournaments having so big a say in the running of the game. That is why we do not feel the tournament directors should sit on the pro council. We feel we must retain control because pro tennis is just the tip of the iceberg and we have to look after all those hundreds of thousands of amateurs as well as juniors. We realize, as our proposal says, that many of the present rules are out of date and we are willing to work with the ATP in a spirit of co-operation and harmony to get them changed. But we want a majority vote.'

So the irony and the tragedy of a month-long saga were complete. Allan Heyman, sitting in the All England Club two weeks after it had given him its support in one of the biggest crises the game has known, said, in effect, that he was more interested in ensuring that a body of part-time officials retain arbitrary control over professional athletes than in allowing Wimbledon a say in the running of the professional game. The players wanted Wimbledon's representatives on the council. The ILTF wanted them off. Poor Herman David could be excused for wondering who his friends were.

IO

GLADYS AND BILLIE JEAN

Gladys Heldman is one of the most remarkable people I have ever met. At first glance she comes across as a stylish, frail-looking sort of woman with quizzical eyes that stare at you from behind thick dark glasses. The gaze would be followed by a nervous laugh and some faintly idiotic remark about one of her cats. The first one I met was a white thing called Putty and it was quite the most arrogant animal I have ever come across. It used to sit on a ledge at the Heldmans' high-rise apartment in New York, staring down in superior fashion on to Gracie Mansion, the official residence of the Mayor.

By the time Gladys and her husband Julius moved to Houston in 1970, Putty had expired and had been replaced by not just one other white cat but two. Almost inevitably, knowing the way Gladys' mind worked, they were called Virginia and Slim. They were much more agreeable than Putty and they ran the house. The Heldmans' housekeeper Mrs Laura Haywood might have thought *she* did, but actually it was Virginia and Slim.

One night when a highly-strung young publishing lawyer from CBS Publications was visiting the lovely one-storey house at the end of Timberwilde — a residential street as attractive as its name — Gladys was called to the phone, and Julius, the lawyer and I sat around having a drink while Slim started shredding the upholstered legs of the settee with its claws.

'But Mr Heldman!' shrieked the lawyer, who was still pumping on all that artificial New York adrenalin. 'The cat's destroying the furniture. How can you let it do that?'

Julius, sound and sane man that he is, just sat there with a contented smile on his face, calmly sucking at his pipe. After a few seconds, he answered quietly, 'It's worth it'.

He was right. With Gladys it was always worth it. She may have been a little potty about Putty and some might have considered her difficult or even eccentric — and eccentricity is a trait viewed with far more suspicion in America than it is in England — but a blind devotion to a couple of cats did not have anything to do with the straight 'A's she got at Stanford University where Julius introduced her to tennis or with the fact that she eventually became one of the first women in America ever to be appointed to the Board of a bank. Or with the way she created, published and edited *World Tennis* magazine and finally sold it to CBS for two million dollars. Or, of course, with the battle she won to set up an independent women's tour and change the face of tennis for ever.

Gladys needed two people to help her transform the women's game into the attraction it is today. She needed a star like Billie Jean King and she needed a financial godfather like Joe Cullman. The story of how this dedicated trio took on the amateur establishment and created a professional game for women is, in many ways, even more dramatic than anything achieved by the men. It took a great deal of courage and an incredible amount of hard work, on the part of not only Gladys and Billie Jean but also the large majority of those female players who signed up with Mrs Heldman and then went out, not merely to play, but to sell themselves and their tour on television shows at the crack of dawn and on radio programmes in the dead of night, irrespective of what time they had to play the next day. They were pioneers and publicity agents and true professionals and, because they had such a barrier of prejudice to break down, they were always so much better at selling the game of tennis than the men.

It is for this reason that I get a little impatient with a star like Hana Mandlikova, who threw a childish fit at the 1987 US Open and tried to hide from the press in a women's lavatory, slamming the door of this public convenience in the face of women reporters and screaming at everyone in general to 'Screw off!' Later Hana wrote an article — in *World Tennis*, appropriately enough — apologizing for her behaviour, but she and all the other women who are earning millions today should not forget that, 15 years ago, it wasn't necessary to hide from the press. More often than not there wasn't any press to hide from.

Recognition of women's tennis as a worthwhile entity in its own right would have come sooner or later, but it needed, ironically enough, a really hard-nosed male chauvinist promoter like Jack Kramer to kick it into gear. It is hard to keep Kramer out of this story and that is as it should be, for even his negative moves turned out to be positive in the long run — even for the women. It was the fact that Jack was offering $12,500 to the men's singles winner of his Pacific Southwest Championships in 1970 and only $1,500 to the women's champion that incensed Billie Jean and her long-time doubles partner Rosie Casals to such a degree that they decided to do something about it. Instinctively they turned to Gladys Heldman.

Contrary to what many women players believe, Kramer never had anything against women's tennis. As a true lover of the sport he wanted to see all aspects of it flourish, but he was a realist and, in his experience, the post-war public paid to watch men play tennis not women.

So when Gladys approached him during the 1970 US Open at Forest Hills and told him there was talk of the women boycotting his event, Jack's response was, 'That's fine with me. I'll take the $7,500 we've set aside for the girls and throw it into the men's pot.'

Gladys realized that Kramer was reacting out of pique — he never carried out his threat — but, with two weeks to go before the tournament in Los Angeles, she knew it was now or never. She was moving her entire household to Houston 24 hours after Forest Hills finished that year and it was to Houston that she turned for a solution. A quick phone call to Paul Pearce, Secretary of the Houston Tennis Association, produced a positive response. Pearce contacted Dolores Hornberger of the Houston Racquet Club and Jim Hight, President of the Texas LTA, and, within three days, a prize-money total of $5,000 had been agreed, seating facilities had been rented and tickets were being sold. The tournament would be held in the same week as the Pacific Southwest. But, as only eight players would be involved, Kramer would still have plenty of entries for his own women's event.

Anyone who has had even peripheral contact with the running of a tennis tournament will understand just what kind of a miracle Mrs Heldman and her Houston cohorts were working. Something that needs a minimum of six months' preparation was being produced out of the hat in two weeks. And that was not all. As soon as word got out, the USLTA came down on the whole enterprise like a ton of bricks. In the first of many belligerent battles the establishment would fight with Gladys and her rebel women, USLTA committee-man Stan Malless, who has known finer hours during a lifetime's devoted service to the game, said he could not grant the new tournament a sanction if Kramer objected. Backed by his Southern California colleague Bob Kelleher, another man who had fought so hard for openness and honesty in the game, Kramer made his objection plain. As a result Malless told Mrs Heldman that not only would her tournament not receive USLTA approval, but any woman who played in it would be suspended.

It was at this stage that Gladys contacted Joe Cullman, Chairman of the Board of Philip Morris. They had been friends ever since they had started playing tennis together at the Century Club in upstate New York in the 1950s, and Cullman had been one of the businessmen who had answered her call in 1962 when this indomitable woman was personally trying to breathe life back into the ailing US

Championships. Gladys' scheme, which she carried out with great success, was to hire a plane and fly it from Amsterdam with 85 European men and women players who would not otherwise have travelled to New York because in those pre-Open days they simply could not afford it. Gladys' plane was going to cost $18,000 in those days, and after she had kicked in $1,800 out of her own pocket, she went after similar contributions from nine friends and received only one negative response from her first 10 calls. One of the first to put his cheque in the mail was Joe Cullman.

It was also through Cullman's influence that the Board of Philip Morris had agreed to sponsor the first US Open in 1968 and now, answering Gladys' call yet again, Joe made his most historic commitment to the game. It was financially a small one at first — an immediate agreement to add another $2,500 to the tournament in Houston in return for the right to call the event by the name of the cigarette brand that Philip Morris had marketed especially for women — Virginia Slims. When Madison Avenue dreamed up the slogan to go with the launch of the brand — 'You've Come a Long Way, Baby' — they had no idea how apt it would be or how far Virginia Slims and women tennis professionals would take a sport that, until then, most people in America had considered barely worth watching.

A deadline was approaching and everything was becoming a bit tense. The approval from the Texas LTA for the name to be changed to the Virginia Slims Invitation came at 10.00 am on the Tuesday, one day before the tournament was due to begin. At 4.00 pm that day, as Mrs Heldman related it later, Jim Hight got a sanction from Malless to run an *amateur* tournament. This would mean everybody being paid under the table, just as they had been in the bad old days of shamateurism. It would be unfair to pin the blame for this kind of hypocrisy on Malless, because he was only following the wishes of his own association, which mirrored the view of the ILTF — that it would be far better to let the players receive money in an underhand way than to lose control of them altogether. But once again amateur officials were underestimating the pride and determination of the players whose lives they sought to run. And they certainly underestimated Gladys Heldman.

At 1.30 pm on the Wednesday, two hours before play was due to start. Gladys, the tournament officials and nine players met in the conference room of the Houston Racquet Club and made another little piece of tennis history. Gladys asked them what they wanted to do. With the exception of Patti Hogan, who said she could not risk it because she was committed to a series of tournaments in

Britain the following month, the remaining eight women all said they were prepared to face the possibility of suspension and play for prize money rather than accept money under the table. That was a brave stance but it also involved the club, which would suffer similar penalties if it defied the USLTA. With the clock ticking, Gladys came up with her master-stroke. If all the players signed professional forms with an organization, say *World Tennis* magazine which she owned, they would become contract pros and the club would then be running an all-pro event which did not require a sanction because, just like WCT, it would be outside the auspices of the amateur governing body. A piece of paper was hurriedly typed and hurriedly signed. At 3.00 pm Billie Jean walked into a room full of waiting reporters and announced that the eight women who would play the event had just signed professional forms with *World Tennis* magazine, for a token fee of one dollar. A few minutes later, Gladys' daughter Julie Heldman, who was injured at the time, arrived at the club and added her name to the renegade list. Apart from Julie and Billie Jean, the other seven whose names deserve to be preserved for posterity were Peaches Bartkowicz, Rosie Casals, Kristy Pigeon, Nancy Richey and Val Ziegenfuss, all of the United States, plus two Australians, Judy Tegart Dalton and Kerry Melville Reid.

Within a matter of weeks Mary Ann Eisel — who had just married the British Davis Cup player Peter Curtis — and the eighth-ranking American, Denise Carter, also signed with Gladys. The movement was catching on, but even when Barry MacKay supported their cause by finding an additional sponsor for his San Francisco tournament, thus enabling him to increase the total prize money for the women to $11,000, it was still a very worrying time for Gladys and her team. They had put themselves out on a limb and even if Cullman had an outstretched hand, ready to break a fall, the pressure on the women to prove themselves was tremendous.

'It was a real risk,' Billie Jean told an admiring Ted Tinling some time later. 'We would have looked pretty silly if we had failed. If nobody had come to see us play we would have been dead. But they did come. The timing was right.'

The timing and the commitment. When Ann Jones — who had followed Angela Mortimer and preceded Virginia Wade as a British Wimbledon champion in 1969 — joined the tour, she worked as hard as Billie Jean and Rosie to sell the concept by giving innumerable interviews in cities across the nation.

Meanwhile back at home base Gladys was on the phone. For the next few months she was rarely off it. I was a frequent house-guest during that period and I shall never forget the sight of the publisher of *World Tennis* ensconced on her huge circular bed, surrounded by drafts of editorials, photographs, correspondence and paste-up boards, as she literally and figuratively put the magazine to bed while trying to put together an entire women's circuit through the telephone crooked in the pit of her shoulder.

Julius had long since given up reminding her that she had a perfectly good office a few blocks away and, in an effort to enjoy just a few hours' sleep a night, had retired to the camp-bed in his dressing-room next door. As a man of considerable accomplishments himself — he was a vice-president of Shell Oil — Heldman never felt threatened by his wife's manic endeavours and, whenever it all became a bit much, he used to take off into the night and drive down to the Gulf of Mexico to fish. But as man and wife their line of contact was never broken.

Contact with the tennis establishment, however, was another matter. Despite a truce early in 1971, called by the USLTA when they surprisingly lifted the suspension they had imposed on the players who had signed with Gladys, players found themselves under pressure not to enter the series of tournaments that the Heldman-Cullman partnership was putting together under the Virginia Slims banner. It was extraordinary how unrealistic the USLTA could be. They were trying to persuade professional athletes to enter their tournaments, where the prize money was seldom in excess of $5,000, in preference to Gladys' tour, where some events already had as much as $40,000 on offer. But the amateur body did have four cards up its sleeve and they were marked Roland Garros, Wimbledon, Forest Hills and Kooyong — the world's four premier championships. Time and again the USLTA used banishment from the Big Four as a stick with which to beat the pros over the head, and the next two years became a catalogue of threats, fights, suspensions and thinly veiled hints of legal action as the women battled to establish their own identity.

Chris Evert's parents were told that their 16-year-old daughter, already a semifinalist at Forest Hills, would be banned from playing for her country in the Wightman Cup and the Federation Cup if she joined the professional tour. The situation descended to the level of farce when the USLTA somehow got hold of a tentative schedule Mrs Heldman had drawn up for 1973 and then announced it was running a big-money tour of its own, based on the cities Gladys had lined up. Perched on that bed, Gladys reddened their faces for them by writing an editorial which revealed, in part, that: 'Dorothy Chewning picked up the Richmond morning paper and read that she was running a USLTA women's tournament in the first week of

January. She was furious (she is scheduled for a $25,000 tournament with *World Tennis* in March). Orlando was on the USLTA circuit but didn't know how or why. St Petersburg and Fort Lauderdale turned down the offer to go with the USLTA but were still listed on the USLTA release. . .' The list went on and on and Gladys finished off by observing bitingly, 'The only things this super $600,000 prize-money circuit announced by the USLTA lacks are players, cities and sponsors.'

Midway through this period of almost constant warfare, the USLTA had actually gone as far as inviting Gladys to take over as its official director of women's tennis. Suspiciously Mrs Heldman accepted but within six months, during the autumn of 1972, the USLTA suddenly announced that it was running its own tour and, having been told nothing about it, Gladys resigned. For the no less than the seventh time her players were threatened with suspension.

Despite all of these absurdities, the game was flourishing. Quite apart from the magnificent achievements of Margaret Court and Billie Jean King, who dominated Forest Hills during the early seventies, two fresh young talents had burst on to the scene — much as Steffi Graf and Gabriella Sabatini were to do towards the end of Martina Navratilova and Chris Evert's dominance in the mid eighties. One of them, of course, was Chrissie herself, which says all that needs to be said about her extraordinary staying-power as a primary force in the game. The other was the delightful Evonne Goolagong who, along with Maria Bueno, was the most graceful player I ever saw.

Evonne possesses one of those wonderful natures that allows many of life's stresses and strains to wash over her. Like a cloudless day in the Australian outback, she seems to radiate permanent sunshine, and tennis crowds around the world have become totally captivated by her charm. But it was her talent that made her a champion, and even though her triumphs in 1971 appeared effortless at times, her foster-parent and coach Vic Edwards must take a lot of credit for moulding her into such a memorable, if fleeting, winner. That year of 1971 saw Miss Goolagong beat Helen Gourlay in straight sets in the final of the French Open, execute a crushing 6–4, 6–1 defeat of Mrs Court to win the Wimbledon crown and fail to win her native Australian title only when Margaret beat her 7–6 in the third set of their final at Kooyong.

So when the draw decreed that Evonne should meet Chrissie in the semifinal at Wimbledon in 1972 it provided the kind of match that tennis fans dream about. At Wimbledon more than anywhere else in the world, the women's game has been accepted on an equal footing with the men's as far as the crowds are concerned, even if the prize-money ratio has never reflected the extent of the women's popularity. Chrissie, unknown at the time as a personality, was viewed simply as a cute little thing from America with a deadly two-handed backhand, while Evonne was already the Queen of Wimbledon — but the way Miss Evert had been playing, it was obvious her reign was not secure.

That much was borne out when Chris, trying to expose Evonne's inconsistency, played herself steadily into a 6–4, 3–0 lead, only for the Australian to seize control of the net with her beautifully timed volleys and run off a streak of six games. Even then Miss Evert led 3–2 in the third set before Miss Goolagong, having levelled at 4–4, swept through the last two games in that majestic manner of hers with the loss of only one point, to complete a memorable victory, 4–6, 6–3, 6–4.

Soon afterwards, the small, erect and proud figure of Chris Evert was to be found wending its way back to the players' tea-room through the labyrinth of passages and small backrooms that make up the vast stadium complex. Passing the BBC Radio control room, she came upon an even smaller area where engineers working on overseas television transmissions were sitting hunched over a couple of monitors. One was showing a replay of Chrissie's match and she stopped to stare intently at the flickering image of herself. Already she was such an established star that it came as a shock when she turned to me as I stood with her in the doorway and said, 'You know, I've hardly ever watched myself play on TV. You can learn a lot from watching what you did wrong.'

After a few minutes, she let out a little gasp. 'Look at that,' she exclaimed with a touch of horror and amusement in her voice. 'I look as if I'm about to cry!'

Standing there in person, Chris did not look as if she was about to cry. There had been no public tears since she had left the Centre Court. As she was to do so many times in the years that followed, she had conducted herself with great composure and dignity at the press conference, revealing an intelligence beyond her years.

As she stood there in the doorway of the monitor room, one of the engineers looked up and asked with a broad cockney accent, 'Were you very disappointed about losing, love?'

'Oh, a bit,' she replied quietly.

The replay reached four all in the third set. 'I don't think I want to watch any more,' Chris said suddenly. 'I'm not sure I'm ready for that bit yet. How do we get back to the tea-room?'

Very soon Chris no longer had to ask. She found her way around Wimbledon and the courts of the world with an aura of ever-increasing poise and stature to become a stabilizing force in a game that sometimes appeared to be tearing at its traditional moorings. Winning at least one Grand Slam title each year for 13 consecutive years from 1974 to 1986 was a phenomenal achievement that will probably never be equalled. But it was the manner of her triumphs that set her apart in an often chaotic age.

Like Miss Goolagong, Chris was a godsend to the women's game in America in the early seventies and although she did not join Gladys' group at the outset, her appearance in various tournaments that included most of the top women players only helped to heighten the growing interest in the new independent circuit.

One of the most successful events was run by the other strong personality in the women's game in America, Nancy Jeffett. Just as determined as Gladys, if a little less radical and irreverent, Mrs Jeffett began promoting tournaments in Dallas, and, less than a year after Little Mo died at such a tragically young age in June 1969, Nancy set up the Maureen Connolly Brinker foundation in her name. Tournaments, if properly run, would obviously provide a source of funding for the Foundation and in 1970 Billie-Jean, Rosie Casals, Ann Jones and Virginia Wade headed the first of Nancy's tournaments. But it was two years later that the event caught fire when, after much prodding from Gladys, it became the eighth stop on the Virginia Slims circuit. The tour had been boosted by unexpectedly large crowds at Fort Lauderdale and Washington DC in the preceding weeks, and when it was announced that the reigning Wimbledon champion Evonne Goolagong would be making her first appearance in America along with Chris Evert and all the top established pros, the PBS (Public Broadcasting Service), for whom Ann Jones and I were doing the commentary, decided to cover the finals live on over 200 of their local stations. This was the kind of exposure women's tennis desperately needed, and even though the long awaited clash between Chris and Evonne never materialized in Dallas, the level of excitement lived up to expectations. Evonne nearly gave Nancy Jeffett a heart-attack by falling behind 3–5 in the final set against her fellow Australian Wendy Gilchrist, but having won it 9–7 and cruised on into the semifinal, Miss Innocence was given a very quick lesson in what the women's tour in America was all about. Billie Jean King was delighted that tennis had an attractive new star but she also had no intention of allowing a fresh young newcomer to steal her thunder, Wimbledon champion or not. In a typically gutsy display Billie Jean weathered Evonne's irresistible opening and fought back to win 6–1 in the third set. As Billie Jean had already beaten Chris in the quarter-finals, that took care of the youth market, but in the final it was an equally determined Texan, Nancy Gunter — Cliff Richey's sister — who took care of Billie Jean, winning 7–6, 6–1 on the medium-paced Sportface carpet. Up in the commentary box I seem to remember that Ann Jones and I had an awful lot of air time to fill — probably because Billie Jean was due to play in the doubles final, too — but even with 25 minutes to ourselves, which is a long time in front of a television camera, there was plenty to talk about. In their different ways Gladys Heldman and Nancy Jeffett had made sure of that.

A LOOK ON THE INSIDE

By 1973, I had spent eight years fitting tennis reports into the kaleidoscopic career of a foreign correspondent; dodging snipers' bullets in Newark, New Jersey, getting hit over the head by a truncheon-wielding cop in Miami and watching a Cambodian armoured column try, unsuccessfully, to swat one nifty Vietcong machine-gunner in the Pich Nil Pass. I had also followed the caravanserais of two US presidential elections and watched the idealistic hopes of the 1960s trampled underfoot by Nixon's storm-troopers. At least, on moving to Paris, the twin ambassadorships of Britain's Christopher Soames and the USA's Sargent Shriver had enabled us to put a smile back on to the face of political writing.

But basically I had had enough. Unlike the political arena, which was awash with Watergate and the soaring price of oil, professional tennis was on the brink of a boom that would turn it into one of the great success stories of the decade. In a few short years it had grown 'from a backwater pastime into an industry that burst through the boundaries of a mere sport to become the fashion-leader of a life-style and a byword for excitement, fitness and consumer spending.

America, over the top as usual, made it the fad activity of the age. Equipment sales went through the roof and people who kept calling a rally a volley and couldn't hit a backhand to save their lives were to be seen strutting down Main Street, USA in their Fila gear with their Arthur Ashe Head Competition racket slung over their shoulder.

This was all very well but in the engine-room of the sport there was a job to be done — a job that had been delayed for far too long. Tennis, from the grass roots up, had to be modernized, streamlined and, at the top, professionalized. With the formation of the ATP there was, at last, an organization with the expertise to look after that latter task, and the strength they derived from the stand the players had taken at Wimbledon made them all the better equipped to deal with it. In the months following Wimbledon no one in the tennis world needed to be told that the ATP meant business. They were the new power in the game and although Heyman was still clinging on to what was left of the ILTF's influence, tournament directors, in particular, were realizing that the future success of their events was inextricably bound up with a solid working relationship with the ATP.

Suddenly everything seemed possible and when Kramer and Dell approached me at Forest Hills in September 1973 with the idea that I become the ATP's Press Officer I was happy to accept. The need for someone to handle the ATP's overall image had become painfully obvious at Wimbledon which, from the public relations point of view, had been a disaster for the players.

Happily, that year's US Open went some way towards re-establishing the credibility of the ATP pros in the eyes of the public. Everyone turned up, everyone played and most of the leading lights played well. Newcombe worked off some of the frustration he felt at having been forced to miss two consecutive Wimbledons by winning his second title there — although his first in the Open era. However, Newk had to struggle to do it, fighting back from two sets to one down in the final against none other than the man so many people had scorned as a devalued Wimbledon champion, Jan Kodes. As a non-ATP member, Kodes had seized the opportunity fate had offered him — an opportunity squandered by the likes of Nastase and Taylor — by beating Alex Metreveli of the Soviet Union in the only Wimbledon final then or since to have been contested between two players from the Eastern bloc.

Kodes, with his straight-backed style and tight-lipped demeanour, was not a popular figure and earned scant respect in the locker-rooms of the tour for his achievement — until Forest Hills. But by the time he had beaten Smith 7–5 in the fifth set to reach the final for the second time in three years — Smith himself had beaten the Czech in the 1971 final — even the players were forced to admit that Kodes' volley was nothing to be sneezed at and that he was a great deal more than just a clay-court specialist who could play a bit on grass. If one looks back at his record, Kodes was probably the most underrated player of his era.

Nevertheless, Kodes remained a hard sell as a pin-up boy for the game and, happily for the new ATP Press Officer, there were more charismatic characters one could present to the public that was now prepared to treat the tennis star as a fully-fledged celebrity. Although a young Swedish sensation called Bjorn Borg — beaten, ironically enough, by Nikki Pilic at Forest Hills that year — was emerging as the first real teeny-boppers' idol of the courts, it was the commanding figures of Newcombe and Smith who, through the sudden exposure the game was getting on American television, were starting to become the most recognizable exponents of this newly-popular sport.

Apart from fulfilling his role as legal adviser, Donald Dell had been hard at work selling sponsorship deals for an organization badly in need of cash — the ill-fated attempt at gaining an injunction for Pilic had left the ATP with an $18,000 bill — and one of his most successful coups was the creation of the players' first tournament of their own, to be called the American Airlines Tennis Games. Before moving on to the Palm Springs area, where it has undergone various changes of venue and sponsorship, it began life in Tucson, Arizona at the local Racquet Club where Fred Stolle was engaged as Tennis Director. Amongst other things, it offered me an early challenge as a new ATP official.

Public relations is a strange profession based largely on the ability to come up with pertinent and workable ideas. As a newcomer to the field I was a bit reluctant to start throwing my weight around when American Airlines sent down a couple of their supposedly high-powered and certainly highly paid PR men from New York, so for a couple of days I sat around and waited for them to suggest methods of creating extra publicity for the airline and the tournament. That, I thought, was the name of the game.

But when it became obvious that they didn't have an original idea between them, I thought it was about time somebody did something. We had been taken out to Old Tucson the day before to visit the studios where a large percentage of Hollywood's television westerns are made. It is the sort of place where you expect to see Gary Cooper arrive at High Noon. Better than that, I thought, what about John Newcombe and Stan Smith at High Noon? They had been trying to outdraw each other in numerous televized matches across the country in the preceding months, so what better than to dress them up in the full cowboy regalia and put a Colt 45 instead of a racket in their hands? Both were willing as, of course, was the peripatetic tennis photographer Russ Adams. We all thought Newk and Stan looked terrific as gunslingers and, judging by the huge number of newspapers who used the pictures, so did most of the nation's photo editors.

Then came the question of how to make sure that the American Airlines name and logo were visible when the eventual winner was climbing the steps up to the television commentary position to be interviewed. The PR pair sat around scratching their heads again, so I said, 'Those mobile stairways you use to get the passengers off your planes at Tucson Airport; they're transportable, aren't they?'

'Sure, they're motorized,' one of the PR men replied.

'Then take a measurement and see if they are the right height and if they are you'll have the winner walking up and down your own American Airlines flight steps.'

They both looked at me as if I'd just flown in on the wing of one of their 727s, but the height was right and it looked great on television when John Alexander went up for his interview.

My ideas which, unlike some others I have had, happened to work on that occasion, were not the inspiration of a PR genius but simply the result of applying myself with a little imagination to the task in hand. I mention them primarily to highlight the greatest single failing from which the game has suffered over the past 10 years — a total lack of positive public relations. Dressing tennis players up as cowboys is very seldom the answer, but since I left the ATP no one has seriously tried to come up with anything that shows off the players in a good-natured, light-hearted, appealing manner. Far from a positive approach to the problem being taken, there has not even been a proper defence offered whenever the players come under attack from various sections of the media. Like a certain Mr McEnroe, injustice makes my blood boil and it really hurts me to see players accused of things that are completely beyond their control. It is a subject I shall return to, but let me offer one example here that occurred during this period.

Stan Smith, a player of great stature and drawing power, had notified the ATP three weeks in advance that he was injured and would have to withdraw from a small tournament in the mid-western states. On this occasion the ATP informed the tournament director immediately, but nothing appeared in the local press. The tournament director went on selling tickets and only when Jack Kramer flew into town to make the draw was the announcement made. Kramer didn't feel inclined to make a public fool of the tournament director because the players needed his event, so who took the heat? The ATP and, in particular, Smith, who was accused in the local press of letting down the tournament at the eleventh hour. Irresponsible tennis players. Greedy, overpaid, uncaring. One reads about them all the time. Sorry, but close up, at first hand, the image just doesn't fit, as I was soon to discover.

I must have been doing something right other than giving Newk six shooters to play with, because after a few months I was asked to take over the Paris office as ATP's European Director. Pierre Darmon was starting up his own equipment business and didn't want the responsibility of running the ATP's affairs on a day-to-day basis, so the opening was there and, as I already had an apartment just across the Champs-Elysées from the Rue du Colisée office, the appointment made perfect sense.

I was delighted because it gave me the opportunity of getting on with the most important job of all — that of turning many of the old, traditionally-run European championships into modern professional events. Compared with the splendour of the tented villages that one sees today in Rome, Paris, Monte Carlo and Wimbledon, our operations were still in the Dark Ages. My initial task was not to sell a champagne brunch and gold-box seats to Mercedes or Gucci but simply to ensure that the players had decent locker-room accommodation and towels to shower with and that they didn't have to pay for their practice balls. We were talking about the basics.

Occasionally it took tact, occasionally a harsh word or two and sometimes just luck from an unexpected source — like the interview Wojtek Fibak gave to John Vinocur, now Managing Editor of the *International Herald Tribune*, who was then covering the Monte Carlo Open for the Associated Press. Fibak complained about being forced to eat outside on the terrace before his match on a chilly April day — the restaurant was reserved for club members — and of having to pay 10 francs for a towel and to change behind a curtained-off section of the main locker-room where 800 amateur players were milling around for the traditional Easter tennis festival. 'How could a professional be expected to perform under conditions like that?' asked Fibak, and Vinocur's article was given a prominent display in the *Herald Tribune* the next morning. The tournament committee were embarrassed, to say the least, but as soon as they got over their anger they went to work with commendable speed. Under the direction of Bernard Noat, sumptuous new locker-rooms were built especially for the pros and for the past several years Monte Carlo has provided top-class amenities.

But mostly it came down to the tournament director and me. 'Miguel, let me try to explain to you,' I found myself saying to the delightful Miguel Lerin at the Real Club de Barcelona one day. 'You must understand that even Jan Kodes has enough money not to go off and sell the practice balls after he has used them. Some might get lost but most of the players will return the balls and the towels. They are professionals. There will be towels wherever they play next week.'

I mentioned a few other things that could have used improvement in the otherwise beautiful surroundings of that famous and historic club and after a few minutes Miguel said, 'You have made me very cross, coming here and telling me how to run my tournament but I shall go and have a coffee and think about it.'

As usual there was a twinkle in his eye as he spoke and a little later, Miguel, who was one of life's gentlemen, came back and agreed to everything I asked for. It was not always that easy and whenever I return to Barcelona now I miss Miguel, who passed away a few years after he had come to terms with the game's brave new age.

One thing I would not tolerate was tournament officials treating the players like cattle. Just as I expected civility on the part of the pros, so I expected officials to speak to them in a polite manner. Frequently this was not the case and one old Italian referee, all done up in his blue blazer, started yelling at the young South African John Yuill to get back on court immediately for his doubles. Quite apart from the fact that Yuill was simply trying to gulp down a cup of tea after racing into the clubhouse direct from a three-hour singles, I didn't like the man's tone of voice, and told him so in very forceful terms. 'You will never talk to a tennis professional like that again,' I said. He couldn't have looked more surprised if Mussolini had just walked in through the door.

Generally, however, I found officials at most European tournaments totally co-operative and even rather relieved to have someone around who could handle the players. It made their life much easier, especially when I made a point of telling the ATP members to come to me with their complaints rather than go barging into the tournament director's office. Players are notorious complainers over trivia and I wanted to make sure that only the most serious problems reached the ears of those people who had worked so hard to make everything as comfortable as possible. I knew what I was letting myself in for and sure enough the list of messages back at the hotel every night was never short. (One of the current road managers is called Weller Evans and there are times, when we are both staying in the same hotel in Melbourne or Miami, when I will get a call at some ungodly hour and will know instinctively that it is a player calling from another continent wanting to know if his ranking would get him into the next week's tournament in Sydney or Orlando. 'Wrong room,' I say sleepily. 'Try Weller.')

The one saving grace when I was trying to cover the triple role of European Director, road manager and public relations officer was the computer. Without it life would have been impossible. Anyone who has read about tennis will have seen the complaints listed against the poor old ATP computer but, as one who helped programme it in its formative years, let me assure you that for every argument it creates, it stifles a thousand at birth.

Over the years various organizations, including the USTA and the Pro Council, have tried to get their hands on the computer, but as it doesn't concern anyone half as much as it concerns the players, whose very careers and bank balances are governed by it. I think it should remain just where it is — at the Fort Worth headquarters of the ATP in Texas. The players devised it and, first and foremost, it has to satisfy them. This, by and large, it has always done and whenever inconsistencies have arisen, changes have been made by the hawk-eyed computer expert Ray Moore and his committee.

The computer's basic function is to decide which players should gain direct entry into each tournament that is designated a Grand Prix or ATP event. Some years at Wimbledon, for instance, No. 109 will get straight into the main draw. In other years, because of injuries or higher-ranked players electing not to play, No. 115 will get lucky.

Briefly, the computer works like this: A certain number of points are awarded round by round, depending on the status of the tournament. The Grand Slam championships are awarded the most 'stars', which translate into the most points. The rest are graded according to the level of prize money and the size of the draw as well as the difficulty factor, i.e. how many of the top 10 or top 20 players are entered in any particular event. Additional points are awarded when a player beats someone ranked in the top 75. Originally, after I had come up with the first set of bonus points at a typically informal and argumentative meeting one afternoon in St Petersburg, Florida — Izzy El Shafei and Owen Davidson were doing most of the arguing, I seem to remember — a player beating anyone in the first eight on the computer received six extra points, scaling down to four points for the next eight and two for players ranked between 17 and 24. Now this has been extended considerably so that the incentives are there for anyone who can beat No. 34 or even No. 68. And this, of course, happens all the time because in terms of basic ability there is really nothing to choose between great blocks of players. Today you could throw everyone ranked between 20 and 70 into a hat and the winners would be determined by such factors as court surface, venue and whether someone was homesick or had a bad elbow.

This presents the most pertinent case for keeping the computer secret — at least from the press and the public. No, I would not seriously advocate such a move because, even if it were possible, I don't believe in obstructing the public's right to know. However, if a player could escape being branded the 27th best player in the world it would be an enormous advantage to the people who try and promote the game, because the public won't buy tickets to watch the 27th best tennis player in the world. The 27th best footballer is a crowd-pulling star playing in the colours of Real Madrid, Juventus or Arsenal. The same is true of a baseball player or a cricketer or a basketball star. But they are not labelled one, two or three. They are just stars on one of the top teams. The 27th best footballer in *England*, whoever he may be, is a star whom no one would dream of dismissing in the way the 27th best tennis player in the *world* is dismissed when he ends up as No. 1 seed at a Grand Prix tournament that has been hit by injuries.

So from a public relations point of view, that is the problem with the computer, which, to complete the technical explanation, works on a 52-week rotating basis. In other words, if the Belgian Open of 1987 was played in the 12th week of the year, by the time the 12th week of 1988 comes around, the points awarded for that week in the previous year will drop off, even if the tournament itself has moved its date.

The main complaints levelled against the computer usually come around the time of the French Open and Wimbledon when, at the players' request, the seeding committee accepts the computer rankings for seeding positions, irrespective of an individual player's ability on clay or grass. This obviously creates the odd nonsense but, until rankings for each surface are produced, the players would rather have it that way and who is affected, after all, apart from the players? It is their careers that are at stake.

But seedings are the concern only of the privileged few. From the moment any player in the world picks up a racket with the serious intention of making it on the international circuit he is after one thing above all else — an ATP computer point. And this is just as true for the women, who have a computer based on the same general idea, which is programmed by the Women's International Tennis Association (WITA). Without at least one point, no man or woman will have much chance of even getting into the qualifying rounds for a satellite circuit, let alone anything of a higher grade.

One of the best in-jokes perpetrated on a cinema audience occurred a few years ago when many Wimbledon players were invited to attend the Leicester Square Gala Première of the James Bond film *Octopussy*, in which Vijay Amritraj played Roger Moore's Indian sidekick. One of the players present was the red-headed Californian Bruce Kleege, one of those honest journeymen pros who was always battling on the periphery of the big tournaments. The qualifying rounds were due to start the next day at Roehampton, and Kleege — ranked, say, 114th — was next in line for the main draw should anyone drop out at the last minute. So when Vijay met a sticky end up there on the big wide screen, most of the audience were a little confused when a large American leapt to his feet and screamed, 'I'm in! I'm in!' Two rows of players on either side of Kleege practically fell out of their seats laughing.

The players may stop one pace short of murder for a computer point, but it remains the most valuable commodity a pro can own on today's circuit and, happily, it is immune to theft and argument. The players accept it without question and one shudders to think what it would be like trying to run the tour on the old basis of national rankings or of whether a tournament director thinks a certain player is a better draw card. The system has an in-built method of satisfying promoters in this respect, namely by awarding every tournament director a certain number of wild cards, depending on the size of the draw. The choice is entirely theirs, but the wise ones keep at least one wild card until the very last minute in case the phone rings and Yannick Noah says, 'Can I play?' If Noah had not entered through the ATP the stipulated number of weeks in advance, his only method of entry into a tournament he suddenly wanted to play would be through the wild-card system.

The ATP computer is completely separate from another ranking list that readers of the small print in the results sections of certain newspapers will see from time to time. The Nabisco Grand Prix points standings and the Virginia Slims tour points are awarded solely for events that come under the designated 'Grand Prix' or 'Virginia Slims' categories and are collated for one calendar year. Their function is to determine the distribution of the bonus pool money at the end of each year's play.

For the third consecutive year Ivan Lendl collected $800,000 for finishing top of the Nabisco table in 1987 but, much as he will value that achievement, occupying the No. 1 spot on the ATP computer remains the toughest nut to crack. If a player's winning Wimbledon or the US Open can be likened to a team's winning the FA Cup, being No. 1 on the computer is the achievement of a long-haul standard of excellence equivalent to winning the Football League. Since the computer was instituted in 1972, only six players have ever scaled the heights to the premier position in the men's game. The first No. 1 was Ilie Nastase, and he was quickly superseded by John Newcombe. But since 1974, only Jimmy Connors, who remained on top for the next four years, Bjorn Borg, John McEnroe and Ivan Lendl have managed it. The computer does not lie. These six are, without question, the pedigree, gold-plated champions of the Open era.

The same is true for the women. Since the WITA got rid of some teething troubles and started programming an equivalent computer ranking system in 1977, only Chris Evert, Martina Navratilova and, in 1987, Steffi Graf have made it to No. 1. More people have climbed Mount Everest.

It was not only the computer that was going through the growing-pains of youth in those early days of the ATP. By the time Ashe had taken over the presidency from Drysdale in 1974, the idea of a governing body for the men's game in the form of a nine-man council was taking shape. But although Heyman was losing his battle to retain control of the vote, the council had still not come into being and, in the meantime, the conscientious Ashe had set himself the task of writing a new set of rules to fit the pro game. Consulting a whole range of players from the top stars to lesser-known performers whose intellects tended to be sharper than their forehand volleys — the brothers-in-law Erik Van Dillen and Freddie McNair provided a good example (OK, Erik, so your forehand volley wasn't that bad, either) — Ashe laid the groundwork for the bulky book that now constitutes the Code of Conduct as laid down by the Pro Council.

Ashe turned up in my Paris office one day and we spent hours fiddling around with the sub-paragraphs of various rules and continued over lunch at the corner café. It was not the most scientific method of organizing a major sport but, until the politicians got their act together, someone had to do it and the ATP was fortunate to have a leader of Arthur's intelligence to get it started. We would have been more fortunate had we had a little more space to work in. Calling it, rather grandly, 'my Paris office' does not quite paint the true picture. Forget any ideas about banks of telephones, plush carpeting, plants in the corner and views of the Eiffel Tower. The ATP Paris 'office' was a tiny, windowless, partitioned-off section at the back of a wholesale women's ready-to-wear clothing depot. It belonged to a wonderfully volatile character called Benny Berthet; it was free and we were very grateful.

Benny had been a top player in France in his youth and had survived the revolution that had taken place in the French Federation in the late 1960s to emerge as one of Philippe Chatrier's most powerful supporters. He had a temper that would put McEnroe to shame and frequently, as I was trying to hear what some player was trying to tell me over the phone from Bologna or Bratislava, Berthet's bellowing would rattle the flimsy walls of my little 'office'. But with true French sang-froid, his army of women workers would go on carting dresses about and, when the storm had subsided, still professed to love him. Benny was, at heart, a very generous and lovable fellow and although my secretary and I worked in a sort of hole that was literally not big enough to take more than one visitor, he got the ATP out of one, too, financially.

Although it was to become a matter of dispute later on, I spent as little time as possible in the Rue du Colisée, not because of the cramped conditions, but because the most urgent work in the restructuring of the European game took place on site at the tournaments. But even Europe was not the limit of my domain. Back in Los Angeles Jack Kramer, with his assistant Bill Holmes, would take care of North and South American tournaments as well as those in Australia and the Pacific, while Africa and the Middle East were my responsibility.

Thanks to the tours Donald Dell organized for Ashe in 1970 and 1971 I had been able to take a quick, but fairly detailed, look at tennis in Africa, visiting six English-speaking nations the first year and six former French colonies the second. Stan Smith was Arthur's exhibition partner in 1970, but the next year Ashe and I set off with Marty Riessen and Tom Okker on what we quickly dubbed Charlie Pasarell's honeymoon for the simple reason that it was just that. He had married Shireen Fareed — the beautiful daughter of Dr Omar Fareed, who has looked after innumerable US Davis Cup squads — just a couple of days before our departure for Dakar. For some reason that maybe Shireen can explain, Charlie turned out to be the most successful player on the tour, which was not quite what we had expected!

It was on that trip that Arthur stopped to watch a gangling little 11-year-old hit some balls with his uncle at the tennis club in Yaoundé in the Cameroons. I will never forget the expression of wonder on Yannick Noah's face as he looked up at Arthur and accepted the offer of the gleaming silver Head Competition racket. Rushing back on to the insect-strewn court with it, Yannick hit a huge serve and followed it with a half-volley off his toes. No matter what kind of amazing feats of athletic skill he has produced on the world's courts since, those two shots were the most important he has played in his life. Arthur was so impressed that he spoke to the boy's father and, when we got back to Paris, to Chatrier, who arranged for him to be integrated into the French training system. For that alone, the trip was worthwhile.

Needless to say that whetted my appetite for Africa, and some of my most fascinating experiences in the game came about as a result of the tournaments I helped to set up or reorganize in Algiers, Cairo and Khartoum as well as on the island of Malta.

Quite apart from my efforts to spread the gospel and encourage the local officials to follow the stricter code of professionalism that was sweeping through the game, it was what the players taught me about loyalty and commitment that sticks in my mind from these forays into the Dark Continent.

Khartoum, the meeting point of the Blue and the White Niles and of the Negro and the Arab races, remains one of my favourite cities, but in the mid seventies it was not a modern one nor very accessible. The Meridien and the Hilton were the only twentieth-century hotels in town and we were not staying at either. And just to make life more complicated, East African Airways had seen fit to collapse about two weeks before we arrived. As any seasoned Africa-hand will confirm, it is easy to fly into Africa but almost impossible, even at the best of times, to fly within it. These were the worst of times. East African Airways had provided the main link down the eastern half of the vast continent and now, suddenly, the planes weren't flying and I had half a dozen players scheduled to come up from a tournament in Johannesburg. Forget the political niceties of the situation. We were down to the basics. Was it physically possible to fly from Johannesburg to Khartoum? The answer was: not very easily.

In fact the whole situation was so difficult that no one could have complained if the players had given up. The prize money in Khartoum was $12,000 for 16 players which, even in those days, was meagre pickings and there were no Grand Prix points to be gained. The tournament was nowhere near Grand Prix status. So why bother, right? Well, that was not the way four young Australians looked at it. They had a commitment to play in Khartoum and they were going to honour it. So Brad Drewett, John Bartlett, Charlie Fancutt and John Marks got on a plane to London and turned round and flew all the way back down to Khartoum. I never dared work out how many hours they spent in aeroplanes. I was just too grateful for what I still consider to be a wonderfully professional gesture.

Bob 'Nailbags' Carmichael chose another route. He got himself to Nairobi, spent the night on an airport bench, flew up to Cairo and then back down the Nile. That was no less of an effort but then it was the sort of thing one would expect from one of the game's tireless wandering minstrels. I had just got into bed when the phone rang in the early hours of the first day of the tournament.

'Richard? Huh, Nailbags here. What sort of place is this anyway?' One of the Australians' most endearing characteristics is that of calling themselves by their generally accepted nicknames in moments of dire stress and this one-time Melbourne carpenter was no exception. He was also, I knew, on the point of exhaustion.

'Listen. Nails, first of all thanks for coming,' I replied with as much understatement as I thought appropriate for a Brit in Gordon's old town. 'Now go and ask the fellow down there in the turban for a beer and don't worry about the smell. It tastes OK. Then get some sleep and I'll see you in the morning. Oh, by the way, you're playing at noon. You know, when the sun's up.'

I never understood how they did it — or still do for that matter. Even if you are young and fit, getting off a plane and producing something that passes for tennis in blistering heat after a journey like that would turn most people into a cripple. But, in tennis every bit as much as in show business, the show must go on, and our delightful hosts, who ran one of the best-organized small tournaments I was ever connected with, were very appreciative when all but one player showed up. Carmichael, incidentally, went on to reach the final and then lost to a West German called Rheinhart Probst who had never won an international tournament before and never did again. Nailbags had barely heard of him and wasn't impressed — especially as the tournament was played on just about the only strip of grass in the Sudan. Germans weren't supposed to be able to play on grass.

These pioneering events I created tended to come up with champions who were not frequent visitors to the winners' circle. Mike Estep had won Khartoum the previous year so at least he could look Martina in the eye as her coach and say, 'Yes, I, too, have won a tournament on grass', and in Algiers it was the tall Swedish farmer Birger Anderson, who always tended to look a little lost in big cities, who came through to win his only ATP title. But Algiers was not such an amusing experience.

It was a long drive from our sprawling modern hotel by the sea — pleasant, no doubt, in summer but freezing in February — to the club near the centre of town. The tournament assigned us minibuses with drivers who ranged from the competent to the suicidal. Midway through the week, I followed one bus that had left about 30 minutes before and, on turning a sharp bend in the road, found a small group of people standing around staring at what had been the bus. It was in a ditch with the passenger cabin crushed in. The players, I learned, had been taken to hospital.

I shall not readily forget the sight of the figure lying on the casualty table in its blood-stained, pale blue Adidas track suit when I reached the hospital. For a moment I thought we had a fatality on our hands because it was impossible to believe anyone in the passenger seat had survived. But although badly hurt, Myron Grunberg, a Canadian player who was never able to resume his career, was alive. He had a broken hip, several fractured ribs and other injuries. Over in a corner Tadeusz Nowicki, the Polish No. 1, was sitting, ashen-faced, with his arm in a sling, having dislocated his right shoulder. He recovered sufficiently to rejoin the tour, but was never as good again. The third player who had been in the bus was Robert Rheinberger, the tall Australian who is now back on the circuit as coach to West Germany's Claudia Kohde-Kilsch. Robert had been lucky. He had been sitting directly behind the driver, whereas Grunberg had been on the impacted side with Nowicki in the middle. Having seen how the driver handled the bus in the preceding days, all three players had refused to sit up front on that particular journey. The decision saved someone's life.

Once the doctors had assured us that Grunberg would not die of his injuries, the next thing to ensure was that he would not die of anything else. Myron was Jewish and we were in Algeria. In reality there was nothing much to worry about, apart from Myron's understandable apprehension at being left at the mercy of Algerian staff at a hospital that gave one the creeps just looking at it. Although the Canadian Embassy started to make immediate plans to have him air-lifted to Paris, it was obvious he would have to spend a couple of nights in the hospital. I took a few of the players up to his room to try and cheer him up but it was not easy. The paint was peeling off the walls, the floor was filthy and the wind was already blowing through the broken window pane. I was just starting to wonder if anyone could survive a night in a place like that when Nik Kelaidis offered to keep Myron company.

'I'll get the hotel to give us some extra blankets and we'll be OK, don't you worry,' said Kelaidis, who at the time was the top-ranked player in Greece and for the past several years has been coach to the Swiss Federation Cup team. It was a magnificent, selfless offer which, like the journey taken by Drewett, Bartlett, Fancutt and Marks, was above and beyond the call of duty. With Nik acting as nurse as well as companion, Myron made it through the night and on to the plane, but he needed a week or two in the American Hospital in Paris before he could be moved again. It had been a close call.

12

WORLD TEAM TENNIS

The idea belonged to Billie Jean King and her husband Larry and it deserved to be a great deal more successful than it was. Nevertheless it was hardly surprising that the very mention of this bastardized form of tennis which might have sprung from a Tom Wolfe novel turned the traditionalists apoplectic. One-two-three-four-bam-bam-and-thank-you-Mam scoring-on-technicolour-courts-laid-out-in-strips-of-green-and-blues-and-oh-my-God ORANGE can-you-stand-it,-cheer-leaders-and-mascots and-more-hyped-up-American-hoopla-than-Barnum-ever-thought-to-mention-to-Bailey. It all made WCT's initial efforts in Kansas City seem like Surbiton on a quiet afternoon.

It was called World Team Tennis and although it is still played for a few weeks every summer in America it has ceased to be a matter of concern to the game's governing fathers. Had a slightly eccentric Hollywood millionaire called Jerry Buss not lost interest and decided to buy Pickfair, Mary Pickford's old mansion, as a plaything instead, WTT might have survived its teething period and taken a permanent place in the tennis nursery. Buss was owner or part-owner of various teams at various times, including the Los Angeles Strings, the San Diego Friars and the Pittsburgh Something-or-others for whom Vitas Gerulaitis used to turn out, giving Steel Town, USA a kind of with-it, hey-man-it's-happening look that it doesn't often enjoy. But Vitas doesn't stay anywhere long and has probably forgotten the name of the team, too.

Yes, it is easy to be glib and flip about World Team Tennis and easy to see why people were so scared of it. I didn't like it much myself to start with because there was, given the incredible tennis boom in America at the time, just a small chance that it would catch fire and start making so much money that a majority of the world's best players would become permanently contracted to the league. That, of course, would have been a disaster, because the abbreviated ping-pong scoring system was even more detrimental to a player's ability to grow into a proper championship-match player than limited-overs cricket is to a prospective Test player.

And the threat was certainly there. Despite hasty pronouncements from the ATP in 1974 to the effect that it would back tournament tennis to the hilt, many of its leading members, including past President Cliff Drysdale, were signing WTT forms even as it spoke. Ilie Nastase joined, of course — the concept suited his style perfectly — but outwardly-conservative players like Mark Cox also signed up, and when Bjorn Borg's contract with the Cleveland Nets prevented him from playing in the French Open in 1977, fears that WTT's springtime schedule would cut through the traditional European clay-court season proved well-founded. But despite the sizeable sums of money on offer, in reality WTT should never have been a vehicle for the superstars of the 'proper' game. Once a team had established itself as part of a city's sporting scene, it was the team that fans would support, provided the players were of a good enough standard to win the team its fair share of matches. WTT would have been perfect for the star — such as Nastase in the mid seventies — who was just starting to decline from his peak, as well as for solid middle-ranked players who had never quite made it to the top.

I started to see the benefits of the concept for American audiences when I spent a couple of weeks trailing round with the LA Strings. I was doing a book about Nastase at the time, and after we had pitched camp in places like Fresno, California and Salt Lake City, Utah, as well as the Inglewood Forum near LA Airport — home base for the Strings — I realized that the average of three hours that it took to decide a WTT match provided a perfect evening's entertainment for the kind of sports fan who would not normally have gone near a traditional tennis tournament.

Even the Soviets got into the act. In a bizarre move that had a lot to do with the fact that the ATP had refused to go on paying out prize money to players who were still designated amateurs by their respective federations, Moscow did a fast deal with WTT so that it could replenish the supply of dollars that Alex Metreveli and Olga Morozova used to bring home from Grand Prix events. In the years following Metreveli's appearance in the 1973 Wimbledon final, both he and Miss Morozova were annually winning about $75,000 each on the pro tour and virtually all of it was going into the coffers of the Soviet Federation. But as soon as the ATP said 'No professional status, no prize money', Moscow mumbled something about their players not being allowed to enter tournaments that included South Africans and they were never seen again. The humbug and hypocrisy that goes on as soon as politics worms its way into sport is breathtaking.

So WTT provided a golden opportunity for the Soviets. Metreveli and Morozova became a sort of curiosity act for American audiences, especially in the Midwest where they still think Communists have a horn growing out of each nostril. Actually everyone had felt sorry for Alex and Olga for they were great people and very popular with their fellow players. But that, of course, did not mean they could escape Nasty's barbed sense of humour.

'It's OK Olga, you can smile now,' cried Ilie on seeing the Russian in Salt Lake City. 'I know you have to have permission from your Government to smile but I give you permission. It's OK Olga, come on now, let's have a smile!'

By that stage Olga was already in fits. Metreveli, a Georgian from Tbilisi, also had a sharply developed sense of humour and both of them were practising their own form of sporting *glasnost* before Gorbachev got near the Kremlin.

Nastase was definitely one of WTT's assets as well as being one of its embarrassments. Vijay Amritraj, who, with his talented brother Ashok, played on that same LA team when Ilie was player-coach, was full of praise for the way the Romanian looked after the team. 'All week he was a super guy to have around and very conscientious about his duties,' said Vijay. 'But within minutes of going on court he would turn into a different human being. Some of the things he said to opponents and people in the crowd who were cheering for the other team made my blood run cold. He became a maniac.'

I am sure that if McEnroe had played WTT, his colleagues would have been making precisely the same kind of observation. McEnroe, as his Davis Cup colleagues have discovered, thrives in the team atmosphere but the pressures of a match bring out a side of his character every bit as dark and impossible as Nasty's.

Nevertheless, Nastase only helped to popularize the LA team, as did its other great and temperamentally very different star, Chris Evert. In 1977 they were not having a very successful year, but even when they were bottom of their division, crowds averaging 7000 used to turn up at the Forum. Basketball didn't do much better than that, and in attracting above-average audiences for a losing team, the Strings had disproved the widely accepted belief that sports fans in blasé LA would support only successful sides.

So everything seemed to be on the up and up for Billie Jean's brain child until Chrissie started to make noises about not renewing her contract and Buss, in what looked very much like a fit of pique, sold his interest in three of the league's leading teams. WTT never recovered from that blow but it had served a purpose, primarily in showing just how far not to go in search of something modern and different. It gave a lot of lesser players some valuable extra income and provided them with memories that will stay with them for ever.

In an article she wrote for *World Tennis*, Jeanie Drysdale, a sweet, lovely lady who died far, far too young, used her descriptive talents to offer us some of the flavour of this strange tennis phenomenon. Jeanie's writing skills ran in the family (*A Handful of Summers* by her brother Gordon Forbes is about to be republished in America as a sporting classic), and I'll let her round off the story of WTT with a piece that will remind a lot of people of some crazy times when tennis players were told to go over the top and didn't find it as easy as they had imagined. Jeanie's piece began:

'"Ah, Pittsburgh," said Bill (W.W. for William Walter) Bowrey, taking a deep draught of ale to fortify himself. "You won't believe what happened in Pittsburgh. This is the all-time zinger! Are you ready for it?"

'We were at the Lakeway World of Tennis in Texas, reminiscing about WTT. "Don't tell the whole restaurant, Bill," said wife Lesley [née Turner, of course, and a former French champion].

'"The all-time zinger," said Bill firmly. "We arrive in Pittsburgh and go along to practise at this great new stadium, indoors. *Indoors*. Had a snack. Old W.W.'s got his bucket of popcorn to see him through the evening. And at 7.30 the girls go on for the first match — *indoors* — mark my words here. Wait for it. This is the zinger. In the middle of the first set we suddenly notice that the wind is blowing. Which is a funny thing to happen *indoors*. And then the girls on court start looking up, and we all look up, and the roof is leaving us. The whole bloody thing is rolling back and we can see the bloody stars, the moon, and what's more, there's a bloody wind blowing all over the court. Now suddenly we're no longer playing *indoors*, we're *outdoors*. And we're losing the match. No one has ever played *outdoors, indoors*!"

'There are a lot of good things about World Team Tennis. Things like more publicity for tennis, crowd participation, the excitement of a team sport, shared responsibility, fun and pressure. "The first WTT match we played was the most exciting tennis experience I've ever had," said Mark Cox. "We were down eight games and we came back to win the last game 27–26. It was a great feeling afterwards, all being part of a team and all winning."

'"The toughest thing to get used to is the pressure on every point because of the no-ad rules," said Cliff Drysdale. "There's no time to get into the game. It all goes so quickly."

'I was learning that WTT is good for tennis. That sports writers are being exposed to the game not only for one week a year but several times a week and are beginning to understand what it's all about. That, in Miami, the Florida Flamingos and tennis received more publicity in the first five weeks of the season than tournaments did there in the past six years.

'The first WTT match I saw was awful. I realized later that it had actually brought out all the worst things about Team Tennis. There were 5,000 people who had come to see Billie Jean but Maria Bueno was injured and Billie Jean had to play Laurie Fleming who looked like a junior martyr up against a pro lion.

'It is not surprising that all the efforts to put new life and team spirit into the old game fell sadly flat. The scoring system came out like an abridged version of Tennis for Idiots. The players turned their backs on opponents and walked off the court without shaking hands, looking confused and ungracious. Once Brian Fairlie actually waited for a spectator to sit down before serving. That was obviously ridiculous and everyone laughed. Even Brian had to laugh.

'The only cheering sight was Philadelphia's Fred Stolle looking like a tall, thin bell. He apologized. "Don't mind my gear. I only use it to play matches. I've lost seven pounds. Never been so fit in my life. Billie Jean has us on a strict schedule."

'The next match was a new day. The first welcome sight was Ann Haydon Jones playing as if she had never retired five years ago. There it was all over again, the big looping top-spin forehand which always appears to be going out and always drops just inside the base-line; the little sliced backhand that looks like nothing and does terrible things to your game. Ann made two unforced errors during the match and Betty Ann Grubb joined the long list of girls who wonder why they are hitting so many good shots and losing so many points. Good mark for WTT for enticing former Wimbledon champions back into the fold.

'Against the Boston Lobsters Gordon Fales, celebrated wife Donna's debut as a Flamingo by arriving with a live lobster on a leash to distract the team. But it must have distracted the linesmen. They made continuous bad calls all against the Lobsters. Player-coach Ion Tiriac raged up and down, registering complaint. For the first time the crowd sensed a worthy foe.

'"Animal!" they shouted.

'Tiriac shook his black locks and snarled through teeth that can grind up glass. Several cans fell on the court.

'"Now that," said the umpire with great dignity, "is the height of bad sportsmanship."'

Jeanie Drysdale had some more pertinent things to say about this ambitious experiment but you'll have got the picture. Like Dave Dixon's efforts at Kansas City, it was reaching too far, trying too hard and a little ahead of its time. But the point Jeanie made about how WTT generated more publicity for the game and improved the knowledge of local sports writers was an important one. Local papers search for stories with which their readers can identify and obviously a team as opposed to a bunch of individuals passing through town supplies that. I spent 10 days in San Francisco during the WTT season one year and there must have been at least half a dozen stories about the Gaters top stars Tom Okker and Frew McMillan during that period. Tom and Frew were a big deal in the Bay Area by then, whereas only the real tennis *aficionados* hacking away down on the courts at Gold Gate Park would have recognized their names before. In that respect WTT was terrific for tennis in America.

Because of the saturation coverage BBC Television gives Wimbledon every year and the continuously good coverage in most national newspapers, the British public are far better informed about tennis in general. But there were other reasons for a British form of team tennis to be instigated in Britain, and John Feaver, who is now putting a bit of life and imagination into the LTA's tournament operations, recognized them before anyone. In 1986 he started the Mortgage Corporation National League, with teams like the Heston Fiats, the Croydon Direct Liners and the Woking GTIs, and every ticket for every match was sold. You can't do any better than that with a new promotion and it proves that there *is* a place for some sort of team tennis — and very likely not only in America and Britain. All it requires is a sensible schedule that interferes minimally with the main Grand Prix calendar and rules that do not obliterate the spirit of the game. Which means that the courts do not necessarily have to be orange, nor the lobsters pink.

13

ASHE—CONNORS

In the big arenas of the world the cast was changing. For the first time, in 1974 two players who had been too young to take any part in the birth of Open Tennis swung out of the cot and grabbed hold of the greatest trophies the game had to offer. Bjorn Borg, a few days after his 18th birthday, succeeded Nastase as French Open champion by giving the left-handed Spaniard Manolo Orantes a two-set start and then sweeping him aside 6–0, 6–1, 6–1 in the last three sets. For Borg it was the first of six French titles in a commanding domination of Europe's premier clay-court championship that was interrupted only by his two-year absence in 1976 and 1977 with World Team Tennis.

Borg was a new breed, a superb, fleet-footed athlete who could run all day, and needed to, because his weapons were stamina, speed, concentration and top-spin. It was a style that did not delight the eye but which soon induced admiration and respect. He was also an instant role model for any parent who wanted to teach their child how to behave but, as the years passed, it became obvious the kids were taking to his two-handed top-spin backhand more readily than to his manners.

Borg's lasting appeal, which does not seem to have dimmed that much even now, six years after his retirement, may lie in the fact that throughout his playing career he remained resolutely his own man, conducting himself in a quiet professional style that was hardly in keeping with some of the irreverent punk attitudes of the early seventies and then, even when everyone got out the scissors, stubbornly sticking to the headband and the shoulder-length hair. But then Borg was Borg — something different, something apart from the loud life that danced around him, both on and off court. To an extent that was a façade, because Bjorn could be-bop with the best of them on certain nights at Jimmy'z in Monte Carlo or Régine's in Manhattan, but he was brilliant at playing the great, distinguished champion amidst the foul-mouthed adolescents who sprang up around him. In this and a few other ways Borg was blessed with a strange good fortune. Alone, amongst today's cast-list of look-a-like Swedes and Lendl,

Borg might have been branded boring. But Nastase, Connors and McEnroe made him look great.

No sooner had Borg heralded the arrival of a new age-group than we were given the most striking possible illustration of the generation gap when in 1974 Jimmy Connors, aged 23, defeated the 39-year-old Ken Rosewall, first in the final at Wimbledon, and then again two months later in the US Open final at Forest Hills. What a bittersweet summer that was! Connors, brash and vulgar and absurdly sure of himself, produced a brand of tennis in both matches that was quite breathtaking. This was power tennis personified and poor Kenny had no answer. Despite his immaculate timing and uncanny anticipation, there had always been a select group of big hitters like Gonzales and Hoad who could blow him off court when playing at their best. Now, at an age when most athletes have turned to gentler pastimes than trying to tame savage newcomers in Wimbledon finals, Rosewall found he had no answer and went down 6–1, 6–1, 6–4 at Wimbledon and, even more embarrassingly, 6–1, 6–0, 6–1 at Forest Hills. The tragedy of results like that — similar in a way to Sweden's rout of India in the 1987 Davis Cup final — is that people tend to forget just how much it took for the loser to have got that far.

Rosewall performed miracles at Wimbledon in 1974 which should be remembered long after the score in the final has been dismissed as an inevitable aberration. This little man with his poopy serve and ageing legs had beaten three of the biggest servers of the decade in successive rounds to get to the final — Roscoe Tanner, the young American whose devastating left-handed serve would carry him to the Wimbledon final five years later, Newcombe, who was still at the peak of his powers and, in a quite remarkable come-back for a man of any age, Smith in the semi-finals, after trailing by two sets to love. It was an astonishing performance which said more than any words can describe about the structural soundness of Rosewall's stroke-play 21 years after he had won his first brace of Grand Slam titles in Australia and France at the age of 18. Ironically the only man who has come close to enjoying such longevity in the game's upper echelons is Connors himself. But even Jimmy will be hard pressed to make it to a Wimbledon final in four years' time, when he, too, will have reached the age of 39.

At Forest Hills Rosewall sliced and cut his way through the field again, using brain instead of brawn as he beat Raul Ramirez, the clever Mexican; Vijay Amritraj, who with Borg and Connors was being hailed as part of the new ABC of tennis, and, once again, Newcombe, this time in the semifinal, after losing the first set. Kenny smiled sheepishly when the New York press fawned on him, but Connors had been playing like a tornado in the other half of the draw and although Rosewall saw the storm coming he was no better equipped to deal with it than he had been at Wimbledon. Jimmy was awesome in that final. Talking to Linda Pentz of *Tennis Week* after the 1987 Masters, Connors admitted, 'I was an animal early in my career. It was like I had that disease when you foam at the mouth, what's it called? Rabies. It was like I had rabies. I've bitten a lot of people along the way and that was the way I wanted it. Now I don't need to bite them any more.'

That will be small consolation to Rosewall after suffering at the hands of the wild dog, but even at the time he received sympathy from an unlikely source. Connors' great pal Ilie Nastase had been watching the final and afterwards in the old West Side clubhouse he said, 'Jimmy hits the ball so hard now. It's incredible, unbelievable.' Then, speaking from somewhere deep inside himself, he went on, 'You know, when you lose like that, you are like naked in front of the whole world.'

Everyone used to think Ilie was a buffoon, but lurking behind that manic personality there is a perceptive, sensitive mind. The same, of course, can be said of McEnroe although both men, in their different ways, do their level best to conceal it. But McEnroe was still a ball-boy at Forest Hills the year that Connors became the hottest ticket in town; a young firebrand who was going to sweep all before him around the world. He certainly made a pretty good job of it in 1974, adding Australia to his two other Grand Slam titles in a 12-month assault that had many of his contemporaries shaking in their shoes. 'He's practically unbeatable,' I heard players mutter in the locker-room. 'Jimmy will go on winning everything for years.'

That sort of talk is, of course, very dangerous because it affords the winner of the moment extra protection from defeat. As soon as his peers walk on court in awe of him, half the battle is won. I cannot remember the number of times I have seen a big name have an off-day, get himself into a losing position and then be allowed off the hook because his opponent suddenly realizes who he is playing. It is called winning by reputation, and Connors' reputation was suddenly big enough to win him the Grand Slam. Except for one problem. In that year of 1974, Connors had signed a contract with World Team Tennis and, although he made himself available for the French Open, Philippe Chatrier, acting in concert with the war the ILTF were now waging against this newest threat to the establishment game, banned Jimmy from competing at Stade Roland Garros.

Strangely, it only helped to increase Connors' image of invincibility. Had he played in Paris there is absolutely no evidence to suggest that he would have been able to win the French title, because in the ensuing years he never managed to win a singles title of any sort on red European clay. So the ban saved him from almost certain defeat and he finished the year as No. 1 on the computer with a staggering match record of 99 wins out of 103 played.

Chatrier's ban on Connors precipitated the next bitter political war that was to engulf the tennis community. Seizing the opportunity to thrust himself and his client into the limelight, Bill Riordan, acting as Connors' agent, convinced the player that it was in his best interests to sue the French Federation, the ATP and three particular individuals — Chatrier, Kramer and the man whom Connors found himself playing in the 1975 Wimbledon final, Arthur Ashe.

Riordan was livid that his own loudly trumpeted attempts to set up a rival players' association to the ATP had failed. Not content with running a highly successful indoor circuit on behalf of the USLTA, Riordan had been telling everyone that he had 30 or 40 players signed up, but when the ATP called his bluff he was able to produce a list of precisely three names — Connors, a lawyer in his home town of Salisbury, Maryland and Riordan himself. It was all a bit pathetic, but the lawsuit was serious enough and it added an unwanted backdrop of personal antagonism to the first, and hopefully the only, Wimbledon final featuring two players who were in litigation with each other.

No matter what was going to happen in the court of law, virtually all the experts were convinced they knew what was going to happen on the Centre Court. Although he had lost his Australian title to John Newcombe at Kooyong in January — losing a brilliantly played final 7–5 in the fourth set — Connors had looked as sharp as ever on the Riordan circuit during the early months of the year and only Vitas Gerulaitis, another of the rising young stars, had managed to beat him, during an indoor event in New York.

Everything pointed to the cocky young champion retaining his crown and there were probably only three people in the world who truly believed Ashe had a chance — Donald Dell, who remained Arthur's closest confidant and supporter; his Davis Cup coach Dennis Ralston, who had lost to Manolo Santana in the Wimbledon final nine years before, and Ashe himself. They formed a small but strangely confident group.

Connors' form through the early rounds of this sun-blessed Wimbledon only confirmed the experts' view that he was superior to everyone else in the draw, including Ashe whom he had beaten several times in the preceding months. Not that Ashe himself was playing badly. Having disposed of Bjorn Borg — thus becoming, little did we know it at the time, the last man to beat the Swede at Wimbledon until John McEnroe did so six years later — Ashe then went on to out-hit the stylish Tony Roche in a five-set semifinal.

Arthur looked sharp and fit in that encounter, giving ample proof of the hard work he had been putting himself through during the preceding months. He had set his mind on Wimbledon right at the start of the year, having worked out, with his customary cool logic, that he was the best grass-court player in the world who had never won Wimbledon. Therefore, Arthur reckoned, it was his turn. As long as he prepared properly. That was all very fine but after a couple of glances in the direction of Jimmy Connors whenever he took the court, one was left with a feeling of helplessness. How could any preparation, no matter how carefully and cleverly devised, make any difference against a player producing that brand of tennis? Against early-round opponents, the defending champion worked out whatever little kinks might have existed in his game, using the likes of John Lloyd and Vijay Amritraj as virtual guinea-pigs on his way to more important experiments. In the third round Mark Cox started to feel the full brunt of the brutal Connors power, and by the time Roscoe Tanner was lined up against him in the semifinal, Jimmy was primed and ready for one of the most awesome and terrifying displays of attacking tennis ever seen on the Centre Court.

Connors did things to a tennis ball in that match that made people wince. No matter how far he had to run, no matter how awkwardly the ball came to him, no matter how much off balance he was when he swung into his stroke, Connors belted ball after ball into Tanner's court with barely credible accuracy. The harder Tanner hit the ball, the better Connors liked it. He devoured power, swept it up inside him and then exhaled it like some dragon breathing fire.

Poor Roscoe simply got scorched. Pumped up and rolling like never before, 'Jimbo' only just stopped short of beating his breast like some miniature tennis Tarzan. But in fact this extravagant show of power-packed tennis was merely contributing to his ultimate downfall. Towelling off after his shower, Ashe was watching the match on BBC television. It only confirmed what he already knew. Feed Connors pace and you are dead. He had tried it. He knew. But everyone else knew that Arthur's whole game was based on power. How many times had we seen him go down hitting, seemingly unable to change the magical pattern of that beautiful flowing game of his. It was magical when it worked, but anything that allowed so little margin for error was liable to come apart at the seams and Ashe's game had often done just that. The way Connors took the ball early and stepped into those howitzer drives of Ashe's spelt doom for the black American and there didn't seem to be anything Arthur could do about it.

At least that was what everyone believed. But Ashe, as he sat watching Connors' incredible display, believed otherwise. That night he phoned Dennis Ralston, who was back in the States, and in consultation with Donald Dell they worked out a strategic plan, a plan that would ask Ashe to do the most difficult thing you can ask of any skilled athlete on a big occasion. Briefly, the plan demanded that Ashe go out and play Jimmy Connors in the Wimbledon final — his first Wimbledon final — in a way that was totally foreign to his nature, to play in a way he had never played before in his life. It was an incredible thing to try and a seemingly impossible one to execute.

It was a warm, overcast day when at 2.00 pm precisely the two players walked out on to the Centre Court, turned to bow towards the Royal Box and then opened up a match that was more eagerly awaited by the crowd than almost any other I can remember witnessing at Wimbledon. The political background to the confrontation had obviously added spice to the occasion, but even without that the match would have attracted an unusual amount of interest, because Ashe had already established himself as one of the most articulate and popular athletes in the world while Connors was the perfect anti-hero — brash, vulgar and threatening.

This match, which turned out to be so extraordinary, started in routine fashion with both men holding serve and Connors moving ahead 40–15 on his serve in the third game. Then Ashe produced a marvellous chipped cross-court return to Jimmy's forehand and the defending champion sent the ball into the net. It started right there. From that moment on, we began witnessing things out there on the Centre Court that many of us found hard to believe. Ashe pulled back to deuce with a smash off a short Connors lob and then, very gently, stroked a ball deep on to the base-line, and Connors again put the return into the net. Although the call came late, Connors' overhead shot on the next point was definitely long, and suddenly Ashe was ahead 2–1 with a service break.

Ashe held serve with ease to make it 3–1 and then, as an amazed crowd looked on, first in bewilderment and then in growing appreciation of the miracle that was unfolding before them, Arthur proceeded to dismantle the powerfully welded structure of Connors' game as a skilled engineer might defuse a bomb. More gentle, floated chips to Jimmy's forehand made the champion lunge and miss. A double fault put Connors behind 0–40 and then a superb, spinning lob gave Ashe his second break.

At 1–5, Connors lost control of a backhand to go 0–30 down and then found himself playing mouse to this cool, black cat. Ashe lofted two lobs over his head, which Connors only just managed to reach, and then calmly sent passing shots down the line. Could it be that easy? A 6–1 set did not guarantee victory in any match; most certainly not in a Wimbledon final with a man of Connors' calibre across the net. Could Ashe continue in this vein of calm, unhurried authority? Twenty minutes later we had our answer. The second set had gone to Ashe, also by 6–1.

At that point I remember the former Swedish No. 1 Ingrid Bentzer turning round to grin at me in helpless amazement. 'I know,' I said, responding to her expression. 'I'm not sure I believe what I am seeing, either.'

We had both watched Arthur play all over the world more times than we could count in the previous eight or nine years and neither of us had ever seen him play this way before. It was alien to his style, alien to his nature, alien to everything he had ever learned about tennis.

But unless something radically different took place, it was going to win him the Wimbledon crown. Something nearly did. Ashe almost lost control of the carefully woven web he had wrapped around his frustrated and bewildered opponent. Up until that moment Ashe's tactics had been bewitchingly simple. Yet given the occasion and the opposition he was facing, they were also incredibly difficult to achieve. In a nutshell, they were based on making no errors. Gone from Ashe's game were the wild, slashing winners. Gone was the power and the do-or-die glory. One of the game's hardest hitters was denying Connors the thing he craved most — pace.

Everyone knows that now. But before Ashe walked on to that Centre Court at Wimbledon that year, no one had tried it. Certainly no one had taken it to the extremes Ashe was taking it to now. Only his first serve stung. Every other shot he played was either a delicately placed chip or a gently rolled groundstroke. Even with his volleys he concentrated more on placement than on power and suddenly his one chronic weakness — his forehand volley — became a shot of authority and strength.

However, Jimmy Connors had never been known to lie down without a fight and when Ashe made a rare error on an overhead to lose a serve at 2–3 in the third set, the match suddenly changed complexion. Slapping his thigh and grunting with effort, Connors hurled himself back into the fray and momentarily seized command. Two superb service returns when Jimmy was leading 6–5 deprived Ashe of his serve a second time and gave Connors the set. In a flash

Jimmy had jumped to a 3–0 lead in the fourth. Now what price for Ashe's brave tactics? Would Arthur's nerve hold? Would he continue with the pre-match plan to slow-ball Connors into oblivion or would he find, as danger loomed, the wholly natural desire to resort to type and play his normal game too tempting?

At change-overs, Ashe was still sitting motionless in his chair, eyes closed like some meditating Buddha, letting his whole body and mind sink into a state of complete relaxation for 30 seconds. It must have been an infuriating sight for the hyped-up, fidgety Connors who, despite his recovery, was still looking perplexed by what had been happening.

In the fifth game of the fourth set, Ashe, a player who had never been too secure with the lob, suddenly produced a perfect lob and then, two points later, swept a beautiful forehand down the line to grab the break back. The answer was clear. Ashe was not going to be diverted from his premeditated path. He would continue to spin his web, secure in the knowledge that Connors would, once again, become entangled in it. And so it proved.

Ashe continued serenely on his way, chipping and stroking, lobbing and dinking until, in the ninth game, he let rip with a backhand down the line and then nailed his man with a cross-court backhand on the next point. Like a boxer who had softened up his man, Arthur had decided it was time for the big one-two.

At 5–4, Ashe was serving for the Championship, for the fulfilment of a life's ambition. He did not falter. Swinging yet another serve wide to Connors' backhand from the deuce court, he blocked out the premature roars of the crowd as Jimmy's desperate return floated towards him, and put away the final forehand volley. Only then did he turn towards the players' enclosure and, with a clenched fist raised in salute, allow a shy but deeply satisfied smile to cross his face.

Afterwards, while facing an incredulous press corps, Ashe said quietly, 'When I walked on court I thought I was going to win. I felt it was my destiny.'

If so, it was a destiny richly deserved. It was also a triumph that spread happiness and satisfaction throughout the sporting world because it turned a good man and fine sportsman into a great champion. It had been a victory in which intellect and character had called the shots and reaped a just reward.

But if the plan itself had been brilliant, it was its execution — not so much initially, but after Connors had worked his way back into the match — that stamped Arthur Ashe as an immensely impressive performer, a man who had the strength of mind not to panic under pressure but to stick with a difficult and wholly unaccustomed style of play in the sure knowledge that he could make the tactics work. That, for me, was what made this match so utterly absorbing from a technical point of view.

But on a personal level, the joy Arthur's victory brought to me and to all those who knew and respected him was something quite different and very special. It would have been quite unthinkable for Ashe's career to have ended without his having a Wimbledon title to his name.

In bearing and stature and skill, he was every inch a Wimbledon champion, and the fact that he was also the first black man ever to wear the tennis world's most coveted crown only made the occasion more memorable and more significant.

Yet now, in retrospect, looking back down the years, I am aware that it was the *manner* of his victory that was so unbelievable. Arthur never played that way again. Not ever. It was all biff and bang and glorious technicolour winners for the rest of his career. But not that day on the Centre Court. That was the day Arthur Ashe, at the age of 31, proved he could set himself an extraordinarily difficult task and pull it off. It was a very sweet victory indeed.

14

A CHANGE OF LEADERSHIP

By the mid seventies the game was starting to change at a breathless pace. The arrival of Bjorn Borg and Chris Evert had given it a teenage face; the pending formation of the Men's International Professional Tennis Council (MIPTC) would give the men a totally new governing body, and while the politicians, agents and entrepreneurs continued to jockey for position, money was pouring into everyone's pockets in defiance of an ailing world economy.

Arthur Ashe may have won only £10,000 for his triumph over Jimmy Connors at Wimbledon in 1975 — as opposed to the £130,000 Boris Becker would collect 10 years later — but by the end of that year Ashe had earned $326,750 in prize money for his year's work, a one-third increase over Ilie Nastase's total two years before. Even Ross Case, the 14th highest prize-money winner of the year, finished with $104,900 but, as usual, 'Snake', as Case was known, got lucky. The cherub-faced little Aussie who was always slipping into the best situations — hence his nickname — played one of the best matches of the year while losing to Roscoe Tanner in the final of the Alan King Classic at Caesar's Palace. Possibly because he smiled so sweetly when he went up to receive the loser's cheque, the President of Caesar's Palace decided to make one of those gestures for which Las Vegas has become famous. Having just given Tanner a cheque for $30,000, he said, 'That was such a great match, no one deserved to lose so I think we'll give Ross 30 thousand, too!'

That was $15,000 more than the stipulated loser's prize money and, not for the first time, the chorus went up amongst the players, 'It could only happen to Snake!'

But Case was lucky in other ways, too. On arriving at Denver Airport one year, he was met by a very attractive young lady from the tournament's housing committee. 'You asked for private housing and you've been allocated to me,' she said, not quite spelling out the fact that it was she who had done the allocating. Despite the hint, Case still expected to be taken to the typical affluent middle-class home that players were accustomed to staying in during the American segments of the tour. The girl, Case thought, would be the daughter of some local businessman. She might have been, but Snake never found out. Instead of the family home he was driven straight to the girl's apartment and her first words as she opened the door were, 'I hope you don't mind, but there's only one bed.'

Ross Case enjoyed Denver and once again the players were heard to mutter in disbelief, 'It could only happen to Snake!'

But it was not all fun and games. Predictably enough the Riordan lawsuit was settled out of court, but only after Kramer had counter-sued Riordan and Connors for three million dollars. Jimmy eventually got fed up with signing depositions and opted out but his relationship with the other players had been permanently scarred. Nothing good came out of it, just as nothing good came out of the other needless lawsuits that were subsequently to hit the game, in the early 1980s. But in his book Kramer was big enough to admit that he had been on the wrong side of that particular dispute in so far as the French and Italian Championships had been wrong to ban the World Team Tennis contract players from competing in Paris and Rome. 'My whole life, I've fought to open up the game for the players and this one time I got caught on the side that was trying to keep the players out,' Kramer wrote. 'As much as I dislike contract players, they were the lesser of two evils in this case.'

Typically, Jack omitted to mention in his book that his personal bill from his own lawyer amounted to $25,000 which, considering he was working for no salary and had already lost his job with the BBC at Wimbledon as a result of the boycott, made his role as Executive Director of the ATP rather expensive. He could afford it of course — every Wilson 'Jack Kramer Autograph' racket sold was earning him 50 cents and they had been the industry leader in America for years — but it merely contributed to the general weariness and disenchantment Jack was beginning to feel with the job. The real reasons for wanting to step down had much more to do with the heat he was getting from Gloria for being constantly away from home and, more importantly still, with his own deeply-felt disgust at the way several senior ATP players had rushed off and signed WTT contracts so soon after pledging their support to the tournament game. Kramer was even more intransigent about WTT than he was about Lamar Hunt, which was saying something, but although I understood his fear, the whole issue could have been handled with a little more common sense and a little less panic than it was.

People sitting behind large desks, with secure salaried jobs and a pension plan as long as their driveway, call it greed when athletes readily accept the next large sum of money that is dangled in front of them. Kramer, after all, had been in the business of doing the dangling himself for enough years to know how difficult it is to refuse. The Grand Prix, funded at the time by one of its best sponsors, Commercial Union, was starting to offer more and more players an extremely good living, but neither Kramer, Dell nor Commercial Union's tennis manager Geoff Mullis could guarantee that the concept would survive forever. Nor could anyone guarantee that Cliff Drysdale, Bjorn Borg, Mark Cox, Roger Taylor, Vijay Amritraj or anyone else would not make a false turn chasing a lob in their next match and suffer the kind of catastrophe that befell Peter McNamara a few years later when his career came to an abrupt end one evening in Rotterdam. If you have not put enough money in the bank by the time your knee ligaments are shattered, who pays the bills? That is what is always lurking at the back of an athlete's mind and so when WTT owners started waving contracts in the players' faces for just three months' work, it was hardly surprising so many accepted.

The tournament directors were, of course, scared stiff — hence the hasty and costly ban — but Kramer was merely weary and disgusted. He had been at it a long time and he was fed up with trying to tell tennis players to whom they owed their loyalty and allegiance.

We were talking about it at Wimbledon in 1975 after one of the ATP Board meetings, which as European Director I always attended as a non-voting member.

'The new kids coming through have no idea what Kenny and Rod and the guys went through to keep pro tennis alive,' Jack was saying.

'You're right,' I replied, 'And they never will until someone tells them.'

At the Longwood Cricket Club in Boston two months later, we tried to tell them. Or at least Jack and I got as far as talking to Borg and Orantes at the motel across the street on a couple of afternoons in an attempt to set in motion the germ of an idea which flickered very briefly and died — primarily because, within a year, neither Kramer nor I was there to carry it forward. Tragically for the ATP and the game as a whole, the idea, which has far bigger implications than chatting informally to a couple of young tennis stars, has never been implemented to this day.

Basically it involves one word — education. As I suggested to Kramer's successor, Bob Briner, the ATP should set up schools in America and Europe for aspiring tennis pros between the ages of 16 and 18 — and possibly younger in special cases — not merely to give them some top-level coaching but, more importantly, to prepare them for the life that a tennis professional is forced to lead.

Apart from the glamour, which does exist to an extent, it is a hard, demanding and difficult life and, over the years, I have seen several talented young players fall by the wayside because they were quite unable to cope with it.

A series of seminars conducted by famous players to whom the kids would listen would go a long way towards preparing them for what lay ahead and giving them a chance of deciding whether it was really the life they wanted. And the history of the game would form a part of the curriculum, which was what Jack and I had been trying to relate to Borg in Boston.

Both of us were worried by the way the young Swedish sensation was being led to the trough of dollars that were his for the taking by Mark McCormack's agents at the International Management Group. Bud Stanner — who also looked after John Newcombe — and some of the other IMG people were nice guys and, within certain parameters, good at their job. But their job was making money. They were not about to tell a teenager who had left school at the age of 13 that he should play a Grand Prix tournament with a top prize of $20,000 because he owed it to the game when there was an exhibition on offer that would guarantee him $50,000 win or lose. The IMG did not see it as their job to do that, and I felt very strongly that it was the ATP's job to show the young players that there was another side of the coin. In my view quick bucks had to be balanced with a longer, broader view of what was good for everybody. Bjorn never learned that, and earned a reputation inside the game of always being more interested in adding the next million to his fortune than in becoming involved in ways to improve the lot of the tennis professional.

As I have told Mark McCormack, I blame the IMG more than I blame Bjorn, because we are all products of the way we were raised and from the age of 15 Borg was taught by his money managers that making money was the first, second and third most important thing in life. They taught him well and, as he and they have admitted, it took Borg a long time to realize that maybe a few other values counted, too. Given the way it has all turned out, it is hard to say that the IMG were wholly wrong, but a slightly different emphasis would have been helpful to those of us who were trying to balance a player's perception of life and career in those early days.

Very soon, in the latter half of the 1970s, Connors, Borg and the powerful Argentine left-hander Guillermo Vilas would be dominating the tour, but unfortunately they did not feel inclined to take over the leadership role from their predecessors. I sensed at the time that we were going to lose a whole generation as far as a genuine commitment and a feeling for the future of the sport were concerned and I was right. Borg and Connors were simply not interested, but Vilas was disappointing because he had the capacity to contribute a great deal. Guillermo was, at his own request, totally controlled by Ion Tiriac. It amazed me to see how a man of such intelligence and imagination could put himself so completely under the sway of another person. 'Here's how much I want to play; here's how much I want to make; don't bother me with the details.' Those were the orders Vilas gave Tiriac at the start of every year and from then on he virtually turned himself into the Romanian's slave. Tiriac used to tell him when to get up, when to practise, when and what to eat and what shots to hit. Guillermo said it freed his mind to write poetry but the life he led was more akin to that of a stevedore than to that of a poet. The harder Tiriac worked him the better he liked it. Unfortunately one of the aspects of the game that Ion led him away from was any involvement with the ATP.

I don't think this worried Vilas too much because there was a very strong, self-centred streak in his character and sitting around at board meetings worrying about other people's problems would not have amused him. But Tiriac was on the Board himself for a time and, although he disagreed with just about every subject supported by the majority, he was a refreshing and enlightening influence to have around. One thing you could always count on with Ion — he would tell you what he thought and, despite a limited vocabulary and the occasional lapse in grammar, there was never the slightest doubt as to his meaning.

A crisis blew up between Tiriac and the Board in Tucson in 1975. The actual incident that precipitated the row escapes me but it ended up with Tiriac announcing that he was willing to accept the request for his resignation if that was what the Board wanted.

'But first,' he said, raising a stubby finger in front of that great droopy moustache, 'first I want to tell you all what I think of each and every one of you so everyone knows exactly where we stand.'

I remember the scene to this day. There were about 10 of us sitting around a room in the clubhouse at the Tucson Racket Club — six or seven players, Kramer, Dell and myself. The atmosphere was heavy with anticipation.

'Jack, I start with you,' Tiriac began. 'You were a great player, a great champion, but like most great champions you can be a shit. You don't understand what today's players think and you try to stop them signing for World Team Tennis for no good reason just to preserve your precious Grand Prix.

'And now Donald. You are an even bigger shit than Jack because you only want to make more and more money for yourself and your own group of players. But you are clever so you are very dangerous ...'

Tiriac went on round the room and thankfully lost interest before he got to me. Having completed his blunt analysis, he lifted his great bulk out of his chair and said with solemn dignity, 'And now, gentlemen, you know what I think and you are free to make up your minds. Please let me know your decision.' And with that he walked out into the warm desert air.

'Wow! I never knew ATP board meetings could be such fun,' exclaimed Newcombe, who had not fared much better than Kramer and Dell. 'You've got to hand it to Tiri, he doesn't let his English get in the way of what he means!'

On the principle that it is best to have the tiger in bed with you, where you might at least have the chance of tickling his tummy, rather than ready to pounce outside the window with dripping fangs, the Board were big enough and far-sighted enough not to insist on Tiriac's resignation and he remained, outspoken and fascinating as ever, for another couple of years.

There was no question that Tiriac cared, but none either that he viewed life from a very different point of view from that of most of the conservative middle-class Americans he was dealing with. That was hardly surprising as his Balkan upbringing had begun in the mountain town of Brasov and continued through the University of Bucharest and various pugilistic forays all the way to the Romanian Olympic ice-hockey team, where ethics are probably not quite the same as those expected from a Davis Cup player. Hence the resentment felt by members of the United States team who suffered, but still won, when Tiriac used a variety of ungentlemanly tactics in the 1972 Davis Cup final in Bucharest. Ralston, Smith, Gorman and Van Dillen were amongst those who swore they would never speak to Tiriac again.

Despite the devious tactics he used on behalf of his country, Tiriac is as honest as the day is long and I have had enough serious business dealings with him now to be satisfied on that score. The ATP needed someone of his calibre during those early days of its existence because Dell's influence was becoming a problem and, when Kramer departed, the problem would only grow.

Looking back now with hindsight, it is my opinion that the ATP began to become less united the moment Bob Briner took over from Kramer. I am not going to pretend that I objected to Briner before his appointment became a *fait accompli* because I didn't. I was not very happy about the way the appointment was made because Bob was obviously being foisted on us by the Dell group, with Ashe the leading pro-Briner spokesman amongst the players, but basically Briner seemed a perfectly logical choice.

The problem of who was to be Jack's successor was discussed at that same board meeting in Tucson and I remember Drysdale and Newcombe both pointing out that Briner had left World Championship Tennis in a financial mess back in 1968 just before Mike Davies took over.

'Hunt had the money to clean it up but we don't,' Drysdale pointed out with unhappy foreboding.

None the less nobody put up a strong enough case to dissuade Briner's supporters. Bob was a vast, soft-spoken Texan who had done a great deal of conscientious staff-work on behalf of the ATP during its first two or three years and was generally well-liked by everyone. There was no question, however, that he had become Dell's man.

The discussions continued, inconclusively, through Wimbledon, but at the board meeting that was held in Kramer's Bel Air home during the Pacific Southwest in September, Ashe was suddenly talking about 'When Bob takes over...'. I had missed one ATP meeting during the US summer circuit, but other board members assured me no final vote on the Executive Director's position had been taken. Yet suddenly it was just accepted that it would be Briner. We were very wrong in allowing that to happen.

By the time of the Stockholm Open in November it had become official, and it was in his room at the Sheraton Hotel that Briner said to me, 'I hope you will continue as a member of the team. I want to have you and I'll need your support.'

It was at that meeting that I came up with my idea for an ATP school and a few other things I wanted to pursue and Briner seemed enthusiastic. At the time I really thought we could work together. By April of 1976 I realized I had completely misread Briner. What he should have told me at that meeting was that I could stay on as European Director if I was prepared to surrender every piece of decision-making to him and become a kind of superior office boy, while he ran the entire tennis world not merely from Texas but from a place called Garland, wherever that was.

Personality clashes within an organization are essentially boring but I will offer just one example of why I found him impossible to work for. In those days before MIPTC designations it was my job in Paris to handle the entries for European tournaments and to try to ensure that the big-name players were spread equally between those events taking place in the same week.

In Düsseldorf, a bright young promoter called Horst Kloster-kemper, who would later devise the highly successful World Team Cup, was running the Agfa Cup, a regular Grand Prix tournament, against the Italian Open. Bjorn Borg and Manolo Orantes had both agreed to play Düsseldorf, which did not please the Italians too much but, as they still had Guillermo Vilas, John Newcombe, Brian Gottfried, Raul Ramirez, who was the reigning champion, and their own burgeoning star Adriano Panatta, I felt the balance was about right.

Then, a couple of days after we had held a European tournament directors' meeting in Nice, the phone rang at midnight in my Paris apartment. It was Klosterkemper and he was irate. 'Why have you taken Orantes away from me?' Horst wanted to know. The problem was that I hadn't taken Orantes away from him and, immediately suspecting who had, I wanted to know why as well. All I could do was apologize and, feeling like a fool, promise to get back to him.

'Yes,' said Briner when I phoned him next morning. 'I decided to switch Orantes to Rome because the Italians were very unhappy when I spoke to them in Nice.'

Of course the Italians were unhappy. Every tournament director in the world is unhappy until the very moment he sees all top 10 players in the world walk through his front gate. In my view, Briner was being rather naïve in falling for a little act that would have done credit to Marcello Mastroianni, but worse than that he created an incredible mess that ended up confusing and annoying one of the ATP's most pleasant and co-operative members, enraging two tournaments and totally undermining the reputation of his European Director. Bravo Briner!

It took more than a week to sort out. When I saw him in Madrid, Orantes said, 'I don't care where I play but just let me know soon, OK?' That was a more than reasonable reaction, but as the Italian Open had already released Manolo's name as an additional top attraction for the championships, it was going to cause a major disturbance in Rome when I reversed Briner's decision. That I felt I had to do, partly because Rome had no need of another big name and partly to keep faith with Klosterkemper. Having created the problem in the first place, Briner allowed his attention to be diverted to some more pressing problem back in America and when I insisted on putting Orantes back in the Düsseldorf draw, he raised no objection. But by then I knew it was not going to be an easy summer.

For me personally it became impossible. An inkling of the extent to which Briner was out of step with his Board over the way Europe was being run came within the space of 24 hours at the start of the

French Open. The first thing Arthur Ashe said to me when we ran into each other in the newly-renovated locker-room at Stade Roland Garros was, 'Hello, Richard, everyone's been telling me what a good job you're doing over here.'

The very next day a somewhat embarrassed Ashe and Jaime Fillol were sitting down with Briner and myself while Bob explained that he was unhappy about the way things were going in Europe, that I was not spending enough time in the office and that my role was under review.

Another contentious issue had arisen when I put my name forward as a candidate for the Pro Council, which was finally about to be formed. Briner was furious. 'None of my staff shall be allowed to run for the Council,' he decreed, referring to myself and the small group of nice young men he had gathered about him in Texas. As they knew rather less about the world at large than Briner did himself and had been in the game little more than five minutes it was hardly likely that they would bother. But I was another matter. Briner knew that the European players were unhappy at the way more and more decisions were being taken in Texas, but as he was quite incapable of walking into a locker-room and talking to them about it, the divisions were growing and Briner was rightly frightened of the problem escalating into a power play between him and me.

Briner's inherent shyness and inability to converse with the rank and file of the membership were his greatest failings as boss of the ATP. How can you have a players' leader who doesn't want to spend time with the players? Worse than that Briner kept putting himself in the role of adversary to certain members. In February of that year Briner had written an editorial in the ATP's *International Tennis Weekly* that was severely critical of the way a group of French players was 'suing the French Federation' over a problem that had arisen concerning endorsement badges worn during the French National Championships. For a start the French Nationals were nothing to do with the ATP and secondly he had got his facts wrong. In the 16 April 1976 issue of *ITW* the players concerned, Patrick Proisy and Georges Goven, wrote a rebuttal, pointing out that it was the club and not they themselves who were taking legal action and finished a detailed explanation by saying, 'It's very bizarre that somebody like you, who is supposed to work for the players, didn't check your information and didn't ask "the group of players" what they thought about this case.'

I feel this was another example of Briner interfering in European matters that he didn't understand. The subject of Briner, Evans and Europe became a locker-room topic and when the news came out that I was not being allowed to put my name forward for the Council elections, some players decided to get up a petition on my behalf. Oddly, it was a Texan, Mike Estep, who organized it but Mike, apart from enjoying a good political battle, had known Briner since his days with the Dallas Chapparells basketball team and, to put it mildly, was not his biggest fan.

While Estep was collecting over 70 signatures on my behalf, I was organizing a couple of meetings with the Europeans playing in the French Open, in an effort to find out what they wanted to do about the growing US–Europe divide. In doing so I made a tactical mistake. Pierre Darmon, who still had control of the Paris office finances and was the senior voting ATP board member for Europe, had aligned himself very clearly with Briner and was one of the official ATP candidates for the Pro Council. Apart from the fact that he was always rushing about doing Briner's bidding, I had no particular quarrel with Pierre and did not want to start holding meetings at Roland Garros behind his back. So I asked Jim McManus, the Californian who quickly carved out a career for himself as a salaried member of the ATP staff, to tell Darmon what was going on. Jim, I thought, was a friend but that did not turn out to be wholly true. I am not sure what McManus told Darmon, but he must have at least intimated that I was hatching a plot that would damage the Frenchman's position because Pierre took the meetings as a personal affront and aligned himself very firmly with the Briner camp in the events that followed.

With Benny Berthet's permission, I called a meeting in the new offices Chatrier had built underneath the Centre Court. Adriano Panatta, Paolo Bertolucci, Patrick Proisy, Georges Goven, Rolf Thung of the Netherlands and the voluble Austrian Hans Kary were amongst those who showed up. In particular I appreciated Panatta's support because he was in the middle of the most successful streak of his career. The previous week he had survived 11 match points against Australia's Kim Warwick in the first round of the Italian Open before going on to win his national title. On arriving in Paris he had to save another first-round match point — diving goalkeeper-style to make an incredible backhand volley off the wood — before beating the Czech Pavel Hutka and then, in the quarter-finals, was to become the last man ever to beat Borg in Paris with a victory earned in the fourth-set tie-break.

Panatta knew he had a great chance of winning the French title as well — which he eventually did, beating Harold Solomon in the final — but he still found time to come and talk about matters he felt were important to the future of European tennis. I was grateful for that and grateful, too, for the support the Europeans were giving me. But solutions to our problem were hard to find unless one was prepared to contemplate the most drastic of measures — a breakaway move that would split the ATP in two. Given the mood of the players at the time, I think we would have had enough support to go through with it but I never put it to the test and it was never seriously discussed at any length. But it was in the back of the players' minds and in the forefront of mine.

Talking about it a long time later, Proisy said he felt that the players would have gone along with the idea of forming an independent arm of the ATP, totally divorced from the jurisdiction of Briner's Texas office. We shall never know because, after a couple of sleepless nights, I opted out of the responsibility of trying. Given a few more months to organize it, I might have felt better prepared but, apart from the awesome task it would have dumped in my lap, something else stopped me, too. I just didn't feel it was right. I have always been something of an internationalist and, through incessant travel, have come to think in global terms. The idea that professional athletes from every corner of the world could live and compete in some kind of harmony was one of the main attractions tennis and the ATP held for me. Dividing Europe from the United States would have been a negation of that and, no matter how difficult our problems were at the time, I did not feel that splitting the ATP in two so soon after it had established itself as a force in the game would be good for tennis or its players in the long run.

So I let the moment pass and decided to search for other solutions during the course of the summer although I knew that working with Briner would become increasingly difficult. Estep duly handed him the list of names asking that I be allowed to run for the Council but the reply was predictable. Briner simply said he was not interested in locker-room politics. As many players will attest, his trouble was that he wasn't interested in the locker-room and the people who occupied it.

The extent to which Briner was a bad administrator was revealed at the ATP board meeting at the Gloucester Hotel during Wimbledon. In an effort to clear the air or at least to get the Executive Director to show his hand in front of the entire Board, I asked him to spell out exactly what was bothering him about the Paris office.

Given the fact that he obviously wanted to get rid of me, one would have expected that a senior executive heading for a collision with his No. 2 would have armed himself with a few facts and figures for the kind of situation I had precipitated and which he must have been expecting. But the only thing he could say was that I was not spending enough time in the office. When I pointed out that the problems that arose at tournaments on a daily basis could not be handled through a telephone system that did not work nearly as well as the one in America, he didn't have a coherent reply.

McManus, revealing himself in his true colours for the first time, jumped in to try and support the man he obviously saw as his long-term boss by saying that the Paris office didn't function quite as efficiently as the one in Dallas.

Those board members who had visited our cupboard in Benny's shop looked as if they wished McManus had kept his mouth shut. 'No kidding, Jim,' I replied. 'With a staff of five, an American telephone system, a telex machine, a computer and all the space you need, it would be pretty amazing if Dallas didn't work better. You've got to come up with something better than that.'

But they couldn't and it was obvious that the relationship between us was becoming a farce. I sought Dell's help at Wimbledon but it was equally obvious that he was prepared to sacrifice a 10-year friendship for what he considered important political motives. Through Briner, he could control the ATP, but he couldn't control me. Even though I had stood up for him in numerous arguments with the players, he knew I did not take kindly to being ordered about and he also knew that I knew too much. I had been standing on the kerb of Avenue Franklin Roosevelt near our office in Paris one day not many months before, when Donald had turned to Briner and said, 'When we control the game...'. At that stage Donald still thought he could, but he needed his supporter Briner in place and so my presence represented a threat to that.

So a stony-faced five-minute talk in the Wimbledon locker-room was all I got out of my friend Donald and, three weeks later, after another row with Briner over closing down the Paris office for August (he couldn't grasp the concept of Paris closing down every summer as it does) I received a letter saying 'Thank you very much but...'.

Although he had had one conversation about my position with John Newcombe — who had succeeded Ashe as ATP President — at Wimbledon, Briner took the decision to fire me without the agreement of the ATP Board. Staff appointments, he insisted, were his domain. Happily for me, the players thought otherwise.

After a somewhat fraught few weeks spent in Hollywood with an actress friend of mine, which offered a nice little close-up of an industry that made Briner look positively benign, I turned up for the US Open at Forest Hills to find yet another petition being bandied around the locker-room on my behalf. This was getting absurd.

Ego-boosting as it was to get such a show of support — genuine in some cases and a bit of the 'Oh, where do I sign?' syndrome in others — it was having absolutely no effect on Briner, who was turning out to be about as responsive to the feelings of the players he was being paid by as Allan Heyman had been to Cliff Drysdale's efforts to find a solution to the Wimbledon boycott. That was a sad irony but one that became the biggest tragedy of the Briner administration. Instead of regarding the ATP as their own association, a parent body created to serve the players' needs, the players started to regard Briner's office in the same way as they had looked upon the ILTF — as an adversary.

Kramer, no matter how much he disagreed with some of the top players, had always gone out of his way to maintain a dialogue, and enjoyed the daily contact with the rank and file to such an extent that in the Los Angeles office he was often reaching for the phone before his assistant Cindy Parks could lay her hands on it. Some youngster ranked 210th in the world would suddenly find himself asking the boss if he still had time to enter the qualifying round in San Francisco. But Jack loved all that and was, incidentally, far more reluctant than I was to fine the players for breaches of discipline. The Code of Conduct was a pretty thin book in those days, but we still had a few rules that needed enforcing and when Drysdale broke one of them in Boston I went after him for the fine.

'Oh come on,' he began lamely, sensing the thinness of the ice, 'I'm a friend of yours and...'

'Precisely,' I cut in. 'That and the fact that you are a board member is precisely why you're going to pay.'

Trying to look noble about it, he paid the 100 bucks — but there was a great deal more at stake for the ATP, for me and for a lot of people at Forest Hills that year. Naturally it was to Cliff and Newk that I turned for advice about the next move and both said that if I put my name forward for the spot vacated on the Board by Kramer, which had not yet been filled, I might have a chance of getting it. That would, of course, create the most enormous embarrassment for Briner but I wasn't particularly concerned about his personal feelings and so, at Newcombe's invitation, I went along to say my piece at the board meeting which was being held at a rather nasty-looking hotel in Queens not far from Forest Hills. With Briner sitting there, I said that, despite the support the players had given me, I could never work under his leadership again, but that I was putting my name forward for the non-player position on the Board. With that I left.

There were obviously certain votes I was not going to get, including that of Ashe, who had told me that he was pushing for

Joe Cullman who would, without question, have added a great deal of prestige and business expertise to the Association.

However, by what I suspect was the narrowest of margins, I was elected and for that I owe a debt of gratitude to Cliff Drysdale and Ray Moore, to Patrick Proisy, Adriano Panatta and Ion Tiriac as well as, I presume, to Newcombe and Argentina's Lito Alvarez who had always offered great support on the tour in Europe. My election was, naturally, a defeat for the Dell faction and a major slap in the face for Briner who would now have to report to a Board that included the man he had just fired.

Strangely, Briner and I share one thing in common as a result of that vote. We are the only two non-players ever to have been elected to the Board of the Association of Tennis Professionals and, given the state of my backhand, I regard it as the greatest honour I have ever received.

The months that followed were interesting to say the least. Increasingly the ATP was being divided, not simply by the distance between continents, but by a rift between those players who were content to let Dell pull the strings in Briner's ample shadow and those who were not. Had Newcombe been as combative in the board-room as he was on court we might have managed to head off the looming crisis within the Association, but Newk was not a politician and was primarily interested in running orderly meetings. He admitted to me later that he used to freeze in embarrassment when I went after Briner on various matters that he had refused to act on after the Board had instructed him to do so. Newk proved to be a very skilled, neutral President but that was all to Briner's advantage.

No one could ever accuse Briner of not being a hard worker but there was a cynicism about his business methods that hardly matched the outward image of a solid, church-going Texas citizen. When Len Owen of Benson & Hedges first approached the ATP with a view to sponsoring a major new tournament at Wembley, Briner promised him that he would have no competition from any other tournaments in the world that week. Owen went ahead on that basis and I represented the ATP on the tournament committee. After six months' preparation, with everything just about in place for the first event in November, Briner told me before one of the Benson & Hedges meetings to inform Owen that it had been decided to run a small Grand Prix event in Santiago in the same week as Wembley. At first glance that would seem no particular threat, but Vilas was a big draw card at the time and other top players like Fillol and Tom Koch of Brazil would also opt for a South American tournament.

But, more than that, it was the fact that Briner had gone back on his promise that bothered me most.

Predictably, Owen was incensed. 'I've dealt with a great many people in a great many sports over the years,' he said, staring at me across the table. 'But the ATP is the limit. I don't like dealing with people who won't keep their word.'

I could not have agreed with him more and I remember sitting there in front of a roomful of people, many of whom were friends, feeling not so much embarrassed as furious at having to work for a man with Briner's ethics.

A year later we were at Mission Hills Country Club in Rancho Mirage, one of the beautiful Californian desert towns near Palm Springs, which had become the new home of the American Airlines Tennis Games. I was functioning as a journalist again by that time but, after six months as a board member, I had seen the rift that was emerging between Briner, along with the small coterie of Dell-managed players he felt comfortable with, and the membership at large.

The magnificent tennis facility which that die-hard enthusiast Tommy Tucker has now transformed into one of the best of its kind in the world was not entirely finished in 1977. The desert sand began a few yards behind the seating that had been erected for the tournament, whereas today greenery, interspersed with tennis courts, stretches as far as the eye can see. Dennis Ralston, who was later to hand over to Tucker, was tennis director at the time and he arranged for the ATP to hold a players' meeting in the squash court. From the attitude of some of the players as they filed in, it was obvious some of them had come to play hard ball with their Executive Director.

As with the players' meetings I used to hold in Europe — often just to let the guys have their say and let off steam — the questions came thick and fast. No matter what the popular perception is of athletes in general, many tennis pros have minds as sharp as razors and you had to be quick on your feet to avoid being left groping in the wake of some of their better verbal volleys.

Before this particular meeting was very old, Briner got himself in a tangle trying to explain how he had negotiated some complicated sponsorship deal and virtually admitted to having lied. You could feel the hostility bouncing off the walls of the court.

Suddenly, releasing the tension, Nick Saviano, a swarthy young man from New Jersey who had graduated from Stanford University, went for him in front of the whole meeting. 'Who gave you authorization to lie on behalf of the ATP?' Saviano snapped. 'You're supposed to represent our best interests, not get us a reputation for shady practices. We don't want someone lying for us.'

Saviano should have been a lawyer. He had a mind that saw round corners and would have torn anyone to bits on the witness stand. Briner groped his way out of the situation as best he could but one was left wondering how the spirit of 1973 had descended to this.

My job in Paris had been taken over by Paul Svehlik, a former England hockey international of Czech origin who had worked briefly for WCT in London. His sporting background and linguistic ability made him a sound choice but Paul was more of a bureaucrat than I was and lacked the experience to lead any revolt against Texan domination of Europe. And, anyway, Briner never gave him the scope. One of my first utterances as a new board member had been on behalf of the players I had left behind; pleading for a greater awareness of how things were handled on a continent that prided itself on its cultural boundaries of tradition and language.

'Don't worry,' Briner assured the Board. 'The Paris office is being upgraded.'

I had heard that sort of talk before — officials standing up and saying the opposite of what they actually mean — and when Briner stood up in front of the full player's meeting at the Roosevelt Hotel in New York and used the phrase again, I didn't know whether to laugh or cry. Upgrade the Paris office? It was a good bluff but it did not bear scrutiny. The truth always frightens frightened people and it seemed to me that Briner was scared to tell the European players in the audience that his true intentions were entirely different. Having replaced an experienced man with an inexperienced one, he had scrapped the title of European Director and replaced it with that of Paris Office Manager and, just to make sure Svehlik understood his position, had refused to allow my successor to attend Board meetings. The world would be run from Garland, Texas and if the Europeans didn't like chilli-beans, too bad.

To be fair the Paris office was *up*graded in one way but its elevation was somewhat literal. The office was moved from the Rue du Colisée to a floor high up in the Montparnasse Tower. The view was as great as were some of Svehlik's assistants like Anna Blackney, Andrea Richards, Carol Harvey and Heather MacLachlan, most of whom had stayed involved with the game in various capacities. But just a few doors down the hall, Darmon took a room from which to run his own business, so Dell's man wasn't very far away.

It is an old cliché to point out that it is at moments like this that you discover who your friends are. Kramer and Dell offered perfect opposing examples. When I went out to Los Angeles to cover the Pacific Southwest in September 1976, I dropped by Jack's office in the now-demolished annexe to May Co. store on Pico Boulevard and he said how sorry he was that it had all worked out that way.

'Bob and I have always got on well so I was sad to hear you two were having problems,' he said. Then he went on to tell me about an old friend who was trying to get a commentary written for a documentary film he was wanting to make. He suggested we both meet back at his office next day. Jack went through the motions of saying how interested he was in the project and ended the meeting by pulling out his cheque book and writing me an advance for $2,000 to help his friend with the project. It wasn't the greatest idea in the world and although we both made a genuine effort to help it get off the ground, it never did. I don't think Jack ever believed it would. But he knew I had worked fairly hard for three years for the ATP on a $14,000 a year salary — in 1976 Pato Cornejo, the 99th highest money-earner, won over $16,000 — and wanted to show that he cared. You don't forget that sort of gesture.

After our abortive meeting at Wimbledon I never heard a word from Donald. He avoided me completely at Forest Hills and eventually sidled up to me at Wembley, four months after his man had fired me, and muttered something about it being sad that business got in the way of friendships. I was tempted just at that moment to remind him of an incident that had happened a few years before.

We had been leaving the Westbury Hotel together and had crossed the street to where my hired car was parked. It was facing towards Regent Street so that the passenger's side was next to the kerb. I had just turned on the ignition when Donald said, 'Damn! I've left those Ted Tinling papers in my room. I'll have to go fetch them because Ted will be wanting to go over them later tonight.'

So he got out of the car, passed in front of me to cross the road back to the Westbury and got caught broadside-on by a car accelerating away from the Bond Street lights. That was what saved him. If the lights had been green and that car had not been in second gear Donald would be dead. As it was he had a broken leg and was lying in the road in pretty bad shape when I got to his side. He had, of course, fallen foul of the British traffic system and looked the wrong way. He was dazed, concussed, in pain and, quite naturally, frightened.

He looked up at me and said, 'Richard, I don't know what hap-pened. I just ... but Richard, don't leave me. Please, don't leave me.'

Somebody rushed over with a blanket from the concierge desk in the hotel and I stayed with him as he lay in the road for five minutes until the ambulance arrived. Then I got his room key, went upstairs and phoned Carol in Washington. Luckily the number was in my own phone book because I had stayed at their house not long before. I tried to collect my thoughts before talking to Carol. Waffling is the last thing you need to do because as soon as you mention the word accident on a long-distance phone call, the seconds become hours.

'Carol, this is Richard. Donald's had an accident but he's OK so don't worry,' I said in one breath. After letting that sink in, I went on, 'Actually he's broken a leg so it's hospital for a few days I'm afraid.'

I have always adored Carol and she remained as calm and sensible as I would have expected. She was planning to fly over to London in any case and merely caught an earlier plane. By the time she arrived at Donald's bedside at the old Charing Cross Hospital, which was actually at Charing Cross in those days, a whole gang of players led by Charlie Pasarell and Zeljko Franulovic had been along to assure Donald that he was in the best place and that not being able to rush about making phone calls for a few days would do him good.

It probably did, but standing there at Wembley all those years later, I couldn't help hearing that voice, 'Don't leave me, Richard ... please don't leave me...'

15

BORG—McENROE

Two years after Arthur Ashe had felt it was his destiny to win Wimbledon, Virginia Wade arrived at the All England Club for the Championships' centenary in 1977 with the same instinctive belief that her moment had come. Despite her magnificent athletic prowess and the best serve a British woman had ever displayed on the Centre Court, Wimbledon had been a catalogue of disasters for this proud but brittle star. Since her victory at Forest Hills nine years before, the cry of 'Oh, Virginia, not again!' had become an annual wail of lament at Wimbledon as the British No. 1 managed to present some less talented rival with a victory that should have been hers for the taking.

Yet, after beating a 16-year-old Bristol schoolgirl called Jo Durie in the first round, Miss Wade strode into the subterranean room in which the press conferences are conducted and started telling us how she was finally going to do it.

'As the Queen will be coming to present the Cup I think I had better win it,' she joked. But that was just to soften us up. Underneath the banter, there lay an obvious conviction that there was something special about her chances of success. 'I know I've had a lot of disappointments in the past but this year I am absolutely confident in my ability to handle the pressures and win.'

We smiled a little at that. Virginia had proved often enough that she was capable of losing to anyone and the entry that year was stacked with talent. Chris Evert and Martina Navratilova were the top two seeds but even as good a player as Kerry Melville Reid was ranked no higher than eighth. Everyone said 'Good luck, Virginia!' and waited for the fall. But there was no sign of it that first week. Miss Wade disposed of Betsy Nagelsen (later to become Mrs Mark McCormack) 6–2, 6–1; Yvonne Vermaak of South Africa 6–1, 6–2; Marianna Simionescu (later Mrs Bjorn Borg) 9–7, 6–3 in the first match that gave her pause, and then Rosie Casals 7–5, 6–2. All that was great, but now that she was in the semifinal it was the future Mrs John Lloyd who was going to present the biggest problem.

The reigning champion had dismissed Billie-Jean King, one of her most illustrious predecessors, 6–1, 6–2 in the quarter-final, and it was only when Miss Wade began serving with real consistency and penetration that any real hope of a British victory began to seep into the consciousness of the packed Centre Court crowd. But even after she had allowed Chris back into the match in the second set, Miss Wade's nerves were, as she had assured us, steeled to withstand the strain and, with an almost imperious air, she swept into her first Wimbledon final by the wholly deserving score of 6–2, 4–6, 6–1. Whether those nerves could have taken another battering two days later had a player of Miss Navratilova's quality been on the other side of the net is questionable, but destiny, once it is riding with you, can remove all manner of troublesome problems from your path. Betty Stove, the big Dutch woman who would go on to make a career of coaching Hana Mandlikova, had stepped in to do destiny's bidding by beating Martina 6–1 in the third set in the quarters, and followed that up with a victory over the other British star of this centenary Wimbledon, Sue Barker. Unlike Ashe and, indeed, unlike the Miss Wade we had known before, Virginia went on court for the final as the odds-on favourite. Keeping her promise that Her Majesty would be handing the huge gold platter to a British player, Virginia duly won, but not before Miss Stove, who was on a loser to nothing with the crowd and was not very happy about it, had won the first set. In the end it was sure enough — 4–6, 6–3, 6–1 — but really the score didn't matter. Virginia Wade had saved her only good Wimbledon for the perfect occasion and, in doing so, had made the whole country feel proud of itself.

But it was not solely because of Virginia that Rex Bellamy was moved to write, 'The hundredth anniversary of Wimbledon's first championships came as close to perfection as anyone could reasonably have wished.'

The men also played their part and while Connors was ending the whirlwind introduction of a peculiar-looking youngster from New York with a southpaw style all of his own who was to win the title four years later, Borg and his good friend Vitas Gerulaitis were offering a semifinal that remained one of the most talked-about matches seen at Wimbledon for years.

Borg was not having an easy time defending the title he had won so surprisingly the year before. In those days, before we realized just what he was made of, Borg's grass-court game was not considered good enough to win Wimbledon and, even though he had beaten Nastase in the final the year before, that had been looked upon as something of a fluke. Out of a panel of experts — ex-players as well as writers — invited to predict the winner in *World Tennis* magazine in 1977, not one picked Borg to retain his crown. In the first round the burly Australian Open champion Mark Edmondson showed just what havoc a natural server and volleyer could cause with a base-line game by leading by two sets to love and then having Borg teetering on the brink of extinction at 4–4, 30–30 in the fourth. Bjorn survived but his duel with Gerulaitis took us on to a different plane altogether. For a start they were the two fastest men playing tennis at the time and few, before or since, have matched the speed with which these two supreme athletes could cover the court. In addition they both knew each other's game inside out because Vitas was Bjorn's regular practice partner. Therefore anticipation joined hands across the net, forming an invisible tracer for each shot as the ball sped to corners of the court that would normally have been empty. But not between these two. Time and again they were moving to head off a drive or even a volley before the ball had left their opponent's racket and, as a result, the tennis was breathtaking. And it never flagged, either, as Gerulaitis checked Borg's surge for victory in the fourth set to fight back and win it 6–3 and then get his nose in front for the first time in the match by breaking serve in the fifth. Borg needed to summon everything he had ever learned about championship tennis from deep inside himself to turn that fifth set around and win it 8–6.

That loss set a pattern that was to become a continuing thread of frustration through Gerulaitis' career. He could never beat Borg. A different result that day could have changed both men's lives but as it was, Vitas, bitterly disappointed inside, headed for the West End after a meal and a shower and it was near to 2.00 am that I found him dancing alongside me at Tramp's in Jermyn Street. Somehow the legs were still moving and, apparently, continued to do so long after I headed off to bed. The match he had just played that afternoon would have finished most players but Vitas always had a reservoir of adrenalin left over for a little boogie.

The effort Borg had put into beating Vitas nearly cost him the final against Connors. This, too, was a fine match and when Jimmy, pumping away as manically as ever, grabbed the fourth set 7–5, Borg admitted to feeling as exhausted as he had ever done on a tennis court. But basically he had Connors' number and retained his crown 6–4 in the fifth.

But that was only Championship No. 2 for Sweden's greatest ambassador. Connors, in straight sets this time, was his victim in the 1978 final and the next year, as Fred Perry's record of three successive wins went up in smoke, Borg survived another severe test from Roscoe Tanner, whose wicked left-hand serve spat fire at the champion over five sets in the final.

By now the experts up in the press box and, more importantly, the players in the locker-room, had given up trying to explain exactly what it was that kept happening out there on Wimbledon finals day.

No one was disputing that Borg was a great player but what was he doing winning Wimbledon year after year with a volley that was never in the same league as Hoad's or Laver's or Newcombe's? Well, in a sense, Borg got lucky. Just as Ivan Lendl would prove to be over the years 1984–87, Borg was the most durable winner of his era. But, unlike Ivan, Borg came along at a moment when Laver and Newcombe had just faded from the scene and McEnroe had not quite arrived. A window opened up as far as serve and volley grass-court experts of the highest calibre were concerned and Borg jumped right through it. Lendl, on the other hand, keeps getting beaten at Wimbledon — and used to in the Australian Open, while it was played on grass at Kooyong — because either Becker or Cash or Edberg can expose his limitations on the volley. They are natural volleyers, Lendl is not. Yet, along with McEnroe who was to give Borg so much trouble once he reached his peak, all three are a class above Tanner or anyone else Borg had to face in his Wimbledon winning years.

Having said that, I must add that Borg's achievement was monumental, and in the late 1970s when he was the undisputed king of Wimbledon and Roland Garros — the two extreme tests as far as disparity of surface is concerned — an aura fell about his shoulders that even retirement from the game has failed to dispel. Bjorn Borg. The name took on an extra dimension and that aura of excellence it represented reached out to the world at large, far beyond the confines of a tennis court. He became, quite simply, a phenomenon.

But there was a phenomenon of another kind on the horizon and, having made a hash of his two Wimbledons since reaching the semifinal in 1977, John McEnroe was ready to make his move. In 1978, Erik Van Dillen, the doubles expert with the droll wit, made life very unfunny for McEnroe by beating him in the first round, and, the following year, the All England Club committee missed a great opportunity to douse the ill-disciplined fires that burned so fiercely inside the New York teenager by failing to default him during his fourth-round defeat at the hands of Tim Gullikson on Court One. On a couple of occasions during a generally appalling performance, McEnroe was out of control and should have been thrown off court.

'If it had happened, it might have done me good,' McEnroe was to admit to me later. 'I might have grown up a bit.'

So his reputation as a loud-mouthed brat was already established as he walked on court to a cacophony of boos for his first appearance in a Wimbledon final in 1980. It had been a wet and miserable Wimbledon and Borg began as if the damp had got into his bones. McEnroe, undeterred by his reception, handled the Swede's serve with skill, breaking twice to take the first set 6–1. At 4–4 in the second, three break points on Borg's serve gave McEnroe the chance to make his lead even more decisive, but Bjorn came up with three service winners to the backhand and was suddenly a new man, or at least the champion of old. A run of five consecutive games to Borg put McEnroe back on his heels for the two losses of serve effectively cost him the second and third sets. McEnroe might have lost the initiative but the streak of genius was still running freely through his game as he countered the champion's blistering groundstrokes with those angled, feathery drop volleys that became his trade mark. The fleetness of foot and quickness of eye of both men were something to marvel at and the crowd, in between outbursts of spontaneous applause, were frequently hushed into fleeting moments of silence as one player or the other brought off a seemingly impossible piece of athleticism or racket control.

At 4–4 in the fourth set, one of those vicious top-spin passes off the two-handed backhand beat McEnroe as he raced in behind his serve, and Borg had broken. Serving in the next game, he reached two match points at 5–4, 40–15. McEnroe went for a backhand pass on the first and scored. Then, revealing the outrageousness of his talent as well as his nature, he saved the second with the most dangerous shot in the game, a forehand drive volley from mid court. Six successive points won by the American ripped the prospect of imminent victory from Borg's grasp as McEnroe took the fourth set into the tie-break. *The* tie-break — the 20-minute sequence of 34 points that will be talked about for as long as the game is played. The 12-point tie-break had been introduced at Wimbledon in 1971 after a couple of years' disastrous experimentation at Forest Hills with the nine-point sudden-death version favoured by its originator, Jimmy Van Alen. The 12-point tie-break could, theoretically, go on for ever but, in singles, the record stands with the 20–18 breaker Borg himself won against India's Prem Lall at Wimbledon in 1973. Now he and McEnroe were going to come perilously close to matching it statistically. Artistically, of course, it was in another realm.

At 7–6 Borg began a sequence that brought him five more Championship points but, each time, McEnroe thwarted him, mixing precision passes with a couple of desperate dives to retrieve seemingly hopeless situations. It wasn't just his brilliance but his courage that was winning him the appreciation and even the support of a crowd that had booed him a couple of hours before. Nine all; 10 all — on and on it went with the tension reaching such a pitch that I actually saw a man tear at his hair. Now, having seized a Borg service point with another daring return, McEnroe was into a sequence of set points and it was Borg's turn to fight with his back to the wall, twice throwing up well-disguised lobs that were just low and fast enough to beat McEnroe's despairing attempts to race back and retrieve them. Six times it was set point to McEnroe and then, with the electronic scoreboard showing a barely credible score of 17 points to 16, Borg missed a forehand volley and McEnroe punched the air in jubilation. The match was even, as were the honours.

But there are no draws in tennis, nor is there a bell or a clock that allows a player to put up his defences and win by virtue of what he has already accomplished. In tennis you have to go over the horns for the kill. No amount of brilliance will win you the match if you do not have the courage to win the final point. Many don't, and that is why tennis is one of the most brutal mental games in the world. Now the champion's mental strength was tested to breaking point, and Bjorn admitted later that he'd had a tough time getting his head together in time to deal with the fifth set. He lost the two opening points on his service but then everything snapped back into place. In a fantastic display of serving which, incredibly, allowed McEnroe only one more point against it in the entire set, Borg retained his crown with a score of 1–6, 7–5, 6–3, 6–7, 8–6 after three hours 53 minutes.

As he sank to his knees to create a picture that would flash around the world, Borg was also painting himself into the record books. His fifth consecutive Wimbledon was a record that had been bettered only by William Renshaw a hundred years before and equalled by Laurie Doherty between 1902 and 1906. But, with respect, they had played a different game. Borg's 35th consecutive victorious match at Wimbledon was also a record, one that would be extended by six more the following year until the moment McEnroe exacted his revenge by winning the first of his three Wimbledon titles.

Borg won the French Open for the sixth time 11 months later but he had, in fact, reached the pinnacle and would never be as dominant again.

16

SEX AND THE SINGLE PLAYER

Apart from being bored and lonely, Bjorn Borg was drunk. Nothing catastrophic, just a couple of beers too many in a hotel bar in Madrid. The loneliness factor was relative as well. He had me and a middle-aged Swedish journalist for company. What was missing, of course, was something young, attractive and of the opposite sex.

Bjorn, to a more serious degree than most of his public realized, was very keen on the opposite sex. Prior to his marriage to the Romanian player Marianna Simionescu — and even during its rockier moments — the way for an attractive young girl to get to know Bjorn Borg in the biblical sense was to follow the advice in Matthew 7:7: Knock, and it shall be opened unto you. All you needed to seek out was the right room number.

That worked fine for our restless Swedish star in London, Los Angeles or Hamburg, but Madrid in the Franco-ruled days of 1975 was not exactly overflowing with young ladies who were willing to throw off the strictures of a rigid Catholic upbringing and offer their bodies to the next virile teenage tennis player to hit town.

Being beaten by Adriano Panatta in the Madrid Open was bad enough but being ignored during the long night that followed was proving even more irksome. Finally, as the midnight hour approached and the little bar started to look more and more deserted, Bjorn gave my journalist colleague a dig in the ribs and nodded towards the barman. So the question was asked, the phone call made and not long afterwards a young woman appeared out of the night.

Youth was, perhaps, her greatest attribute. She was not so much unattractive as dull, both in appearance and in personality. She spoke no English. Bjorn ordered drinks and, with the help of the Swedish journalist's basic Spanish, an attempt was made at conversation.

It did not take long for Bjorn's patience to run out. 'Ask her what the deal is,' he muttered.

If one remembers that this was 1975, and when one considers what percentage of their life's savings half the teenage female population of northern Europe would have given just to have Bjorn kiss them on the lips, the 'deal' was a little unrealistic. The girl wanted $100 to sleep with Bjorn Borg.

The nasty chauvinistic attitude is that girls are supposed to look better after midnight but, as far as Bjorn was concerned, this one didn't.

'You've got to be joking,' he said, signing the bill, picking up his room key and heading for the door, the broad shoulders rolling just a touch more than usual under the weight of alcohol. We sent the poor girl home.

Admittedly this was Madrid and not Manila but if Borg could experience a night like that, it does not require too much imagination to realize what life on the tour can be like for ordinary mortals searching for company after a bad loss in a strange town. It is fondly imagined by some people that a man can go off into the night and pick up anyone who takes his fancy. While it is true that certain members of the tour in the 1970s did possess a quite amazing ability to frog-march females of some 15 minutes' acquaintance straight upstairs to bed, the 'sure thing' simply does not exist for the average man. Possibly because of this, marriage at an early age became quite popular amongst the new breed of touring professional.

Tito Vasquez, a bright and inquisitive Argentine who explored most of the world's pleasures during his time on the circuit before falling happily for the matrimonial institution himself, took a somewhat cynical view of some players' motives. 'The guy thought it would suit his tennis if he didn't have to go screwing around every night,' said Vasquez, referring to one young star who had married a beautiful but hopelessly young teenager. 'Somehow the urgency to do it all the time is not there if it's the same girl in your bed all the time.'

Although there was some truth in Vasquez's observation, time has proved that most of the players' marriages were based on values a great deal more solid than a need for the guys to solve their sex problems. The list of couples who have survived the incredibly disruptive life-style of the touring pro is endless. Stan and Margie Smith have to take top seeding position as the archetypal all-American couple, but Brian and Windy Gottfried, Harold and Jan Solomon, the Gullikson twins — Tim with Rosemary and Tom with Julie — Bob and Sharon Lutz and Charlie and Shireen Pasarell all proved that divorce may be as American as apple pie but it need not be inevitable. There were equally impressive examples of family solidarity elsewhere, too, with the inseparable Balazs and Bori Taroczy from Hungary, Australia's Mark and Vicki Edmondson — who must be in the top 10 for miles travelled together — and the Amritraj brothers from Madras, Anand, who broke with tradition by choosing a blonde New Yorker, and Vijay, who stuck with tradition by allowing his parents to present him with a list from which to choose. Both methods are proving to be eminently workable.

But, perhaps, the greatest understated love affair of all has been that between Ken and Wilma Rosewall. In 1956 Wilma was told, 'Don't worry, dear, I'll just tour for a couple of years and then we can settle down.' But the bag never quite got unpacked and when Wilma tends to it now, it's to kit Kenny out for the Grand Masters tour. But she understands. The little maestro just loves to play tennis.

Rosewall, in fact, always used to enjoy playing tennis more than having a party which was not strictly true of many of his great Australian contemporaries. He was always wary, however, of the need to avoid staleness towards the end of a long tour and when the WCT troupe reached Barcelona in late October 1972, Ken was worried about being fresh for the first WCT finals which were due to be played in Houston and Dallas a month later. So one night, at a dinner given at the Real Club, Ken decided to have a couple of glasses of wine too many. It was for him a sort of cathartic exercise. But whereas a couple of bottles only increased the power of Emmo's back-slap or lowered the tone of Newk's latest story, two glasses too many for Kenny inspired more eye-catching behaviour. He danced on the table. Not just on it but all the way down it. Later, determined to fall in with the Spanish spirit of things, Rosewall took off his jacket outside the club entrance and, using it as a cape, made elegant, matador-like passes at the passing cars. His timing was, of course, perfect otherwise he might no longer be with us. The bonnet of a Seat at 30 mph has much the same effect as the horns of a bull.

'It was bloody unbelievable,' said Fred Stolle whose intake of Rioja had not dulled his senses to the point of his being unable to appreciate the transformation that had overcome his doubles partner. 'No one had ever seen Kenny behave like that before.' Or since.

It was, of course, with Lew Hoad that Rosewall had first burst on to the scene, and there names will be for ever linked as a result of their teenage triumph in 1953 when they won the Davis Cup for Australia against a pair from the United States. But not since the dashing Tony Wilding and the conservative Norman Brookes had teamed up for Australasia just before the First World War had two players, blessed with a talent for the same game, been quite as different in looks, personality and style of play. Black-haired as opposed to blond; cautious as opposed to adventurous; cunning and precise with his stroke-play as opposed to powerful and full of flair, Rosewall and Hoad made a very odd pair of twins. But even if they live on opposite sides of the world, Rosewall in Sydney and Hoad on Spain's Costa del Sol, their respect for each other remains intact.

Hoad would have been just as surprised as Stolle had he been in Barcelona that night because he had seen even more of Rosewall's abstemious habits than Fred. It was typical, however, that Kenny's binge was a premeditated tactic to freshen him up for Dallas, where the ultimate victim of this unusual method of preparation was, of course, Rod Laver who lost both WCT finals he played against Rosewall. Once in Texas, one could be sure that the man his mates called 'Muscles' — probably because he didn't have any — was back on his customary one-beer-before-an-early-night routine. Hoad was never like that.

Like Emerson, who rivalled his great predecessor in his ability to handle large quantities of golden liquid and come up next morning, if not quite like a million dollars, then at least with money in the bank, Lew was just as likely to be led from the straight and narrow on the eve of a big match as he was at any other time. The most remarkable example of this, perhaps, occurred on the final Saturday of the French Championships in 1956. Lew and his partner Ashley Cooper had been involved in a very late doubles semifinal and it was almost midnight by the time Lew and Jenny sat down to dinner at a restaurant near their hotel on the Left Bank. There they fell into the company of some Russian diplomats who plied them with vodka and champagne and then invited them back for a very prolonged night-cap at their apartment. It was 6.00 am when the Hoads got back to their hotel, and when Lew lay down on the bed the ceiling revolved. 'This is no bloody good,' muttered Lew. 'I'm pissed.'

Hoad's remedy for this particular ailment was to put on his track suit and run to Stade Roland Garros which was not exactly around the corner. Arriving well before nine o'clock he found the gates closed and so took himself off into the Bois de Boulogne for another little jog. On finally gaining entry to the stadium he tried to have a hit with a freckle-faced young man on his first European tour called Rod Laver. 'But I was still seeing two balls and didn't know which one to hit,' said Lew who promptly repaired to the locker-room for a kip. The first attempt at breakfast failed — he threw up — but another attempt to hit balls back to Laver proved more successful and after a bite to eat that stayed down and another brief rest, Hoad marched out on to the Centre Court to perform in front of an admiring and unsuspecting crowd and to become the only man to anyone's knowledge who has won a Grand Slam title after omitting to go to bed the night before. It was not even very close. Hoad beat the clever clay-court specialist from Sweden, Sven Davidson, 6–4,

8–6, 6–3. Try telling that story to a member of today's pro tour and he will stare at you in utter disbelief.

On the occasional night (only occasional because, even at a young age, I needed my sleep) I was witness to the way Emerson and Stolle dominated the US Eastern grass-court circuit on absurdly little sleep and absurdly huge quantities of beer. In South Orange, New Jersey in 1965 we all ended up staying at the same house near the tennis club and I took a bottle count of Emmo's beer intake for the evening. Eighteen. It was a few minutes before 5.00 am when the party broke up and I distinctly remember Emmo's last words to Fred before they headed for bed. 'On the golf course at eight, Fiery!'

Fat chance, I thought. But sure enough I was woken by the less than melodious sound of Roy Emerson singing at 7.45 am and Stolle, who may well have earned his nickname as a result of coming up less than full of fire after a night out with Emmo, dutifully emerged, haggard but awake, to follow his mate off to the first tee. They went for a run at lunchtime and played each other over a five-set final in sticky summer heat that afternoon. Then they got in a car and drove to Southampton on Long Island and started all over again. By the time they reached Boston, Fred was having trouble getting his arm above his head to serve and a week later Emmo put himself in hospital in New York suffering from various debilitating effects that go along with exhaustion. But he was fit for Forest Hills.

The legacy of this kind of behaviour was carried over into the first years of Open Tennis because the tour leaders still spoke with an Australian accent. Ever since I have been associated with the game, the tour has been under the influence of the example set by the best players of the moment. Throughout the sixties and very early seventies, Hopman's strict training routine allowed the best of the Aussies to play hard off court, train even harder to sweat the alcohol out of their systems and then play just as hard on court. Without Hopman alongside to make sure that happened, it took enormous reserves of self-discipline as well as stamina to make sure all three things happened. But somehow, spurred on by the pride that makes a champion, Emmo, Newk, Roche and even Laver, who was not averse to a couple of beers, all managed to keep up their winning ways.

Once the Hopman line started to peter out, the Americans, who were a very different breed, took over. Most were great guys and good sports who enjoyed a fun time but they had no sense of the instinctive camaraderie shared by the Australians, and as soon as the money increased and players started travelling with coaches and arranging dinners with their managers, the mood changed completely.

But one American at least tried to ensure that night-life on the tour was not forgotten. By the mid 1970s Bjorn Borg had not only a friend, a look-alike and a rival but someone who could outlast him on any disco floor in the western world. Vitas Gerulaitis, one generation out of Lithuania, was a New Yorker to his fingertips and the last lock of his curly, shoulder-length blond hair. He was a perpetual-motion man who would hit half a dozen night-clubs in the space of three hours — the search always being more fascinating than the catch. Girls and money slipped through his fingers as he skimmed over the surface of a supersonic life-style made much easier by the invention of Concorde. Bored in the middle of a European tour, Vitas would hop on the droopy-nosed bird and spend a couple of days hitting his haunts in Manhattan before winging it back mach 2 to his suite at the Plaza Athénée in Paris or the Sheraton Towers in London.

Vitas' vitality was incredible. And so was his appetite. Before checking out the action in Tramps, Castels or Club 54, depending on whether it was London, Paris or New York that particular week, Vitas would replenish his energy at the best restaurants in town. He certainly knew where to find them. A Gerulaitis Good Food Guide would certainly be worth buying.

It was typical of Vitas that when Bjorn said OK to the idea of a bachelor party before his marriage to the Romanian player Marianna Simionescu, Vitas, with the assistance of his pal Rick Fagel, one of the pros on the tour, went to considerable lengths to ensure that this would be the kind of bachelor party that most bachelors merely fantasize over. A penthouse suite was arranged at Turnberry Isle in North Miami; every beautiful, available and free-spirited girl in Florida — as well as a few who flew down from New York — was invited, and male guests were very strictly vetted. I have it on good authority that it was a wild success. Bjorn spent much of the night in a large jacuzzi — never alone.

Today there are plenty of players around who have the money for such extravagance but few who would feel inclined to spend it on each other. The Swedes are the only really close friends amongst the world's top 20 and although Mats Wilander, contrary to his public image, enjoyed a drink and a good party as much as anyone on the circuit in the years prior to his marriage, the Nystroms, Jarryds and Edbergs of this world, although better company than one might imagine, are never going to challenge Borg's capacity for excess during the midnight hours.

Yannick Noah, who has a huge appetite for life, could challenge anyone to anything and would have enjoyed the days when the players moved as a group and created their own entertainment on tour — an impossibility now with practically all the top-ranked players travelling with at least a coach, probably a girlfriend or wife and possibly even a bodyguard or guru. More and more, the players are forming friendships away from the tour, partially to ease the pressure and partially in a deliberate effort to keep their distance from someone they will be attempting to deprive of $100,000 the next afternoon.

Some of the evenings we spent in various exotic places around the world in the 1970s would now be unthinkable. Copenhagen was one of them. After a week that saw half the players on that segment of the WCT tour finish each evening on the roof-top discothèque of the Sheraton Hotel, I can safely say, at the risk of incurring the wrath of any Danish feminist group that may exist, that Danish girls do everything that Swedish girls are supposed to do but don't. Or at least they did. Presumably the current climate of conservatism and fear has had an effect.

Apart from Roscoe Tanner, who discovered his chamber-maid was an American student who was just homesick for some down-home lovin' — and therefore rarely emerged from his room — and Tom Gorman, who made the mistake of falling hopelessly in love (just for that week, you understand) with the only girl in the place who insisted on behaving like a nun, a fair-sized percentage of the 32-man draw spent an invigorating if slightly exhausting week asking girls to dance, popping the question, whisking them downstairs to bed (slightly confusing that) and depositing them back at the top-floor bar in the hope of finding another local lass who knew exactly what she was there for. I think the record for any one player was five in a night.

It may all sound like a terrible tale of male chauvinism run amok but it was the girls who were calling the tune — don't they always? — and they saw absolutely no point in messing about with social protocol. Most even refused the basic opening offer of a drink. The most confusing aspect of it all was the presence, on most evening, of certain ladies who were obviously professionals. I presume they found some clients amongst the elderly businessmen who occasionally appeared, but any form of prize money was far from the minds of the tennis players' girls. They were there strictly for the game.

Over the years I have noticed that a tennis player's appeal cuts right across the social, educational and nationalistic spectrum. There have been English actresses who have fallen for wild Bolivians; French disco queens who have seduced poetic Argentines (no, not Guillermo Vilas in this instance); devastaing Hong Kong models who have chased blue-eyed Californians, and, on a considerably more serious basis, the daughter of the Mayor of Palm Springs who eventually married a former ball-boy from Barcelona called José Higueras. It is, after all, an international game.

Certainly a superior social background has rarely been an obstacle to desire. One year during Wimbledon I was seeing a young lady who was sharing a sumptuous Mayfair flat with a couple of other girls who were constantly being featured in the society columns at the time. I had arranged to take her out to dinner and duly arrived at the flat at about eight o'clock. On being ushered into the drawing-room I found Syd Ball slumped in an armchair, reading the *Evening Standard* and occasionally checking his watch.

'My mate's in there with your friend's friend,' said Syd by way of explanation. 'I'm giving him half an hour. That will help calm his nerves before tomorrow's doubles final. Any longer might be too much of a good thing. So I'll have him out of there in a minute and make sure he gets an early night.'

They knew how to look after each other, those Aussies. Ball wasn't playing with the guy in the bedroom at the time but he always had a fatherly instinct and later became a good coach. No wonder.

That was not the only time I shared a drawing-room with an Australian while others enjoyed themselves, but the other occasion was very different. It was in Manila in the days of President Marcos who may or may not have been aware of one of the side-effects his midnight-to-4.00 am curfew had on certain sections of the population while it was in force in the 1970s. Basically it meant that anyone who found themselves still at a party at someone else's house at midnight was stuck there for another four hours. Basically the curfew got a lot of people laid.

That was certainly the case in 1973 when a couple of sisters managed to arrange for their parents to be away on holiday when the tennis tour hit town. Their large house, surrounded by a garden overflowing with tropical plants, was perfect for a party and a party we had. It would have been pretty successful even without the curfew but the sudden inability to leave meant that every bedroom in the house, of which there were several, was soon occupied. Someone always loses out on these occasions and by one o'clock I found myself in the drawing-room, with soft breezes billowing the curtains by the Frenchd winows, staring at Allan Stone, Jurgen Fassbender and a

Filipino girl the German No. 1 was obviously determined to get to know better. Not a man to be thwarted by such mundane matters as lack of bedroom space, Jurgen promptly seized one of the sofas and dragged it out into the garden, across a flower bed and into a hedge. The girl followed.

'Well,' said the man who was inevitably known as Rolling Stone by his Aussie mates, 'I think you and I had better have another beer.'

Allan, who has since become one of Australia's premier tennis commentators for Channel Seven, would have had a hard time describing the rest of the night. If the Marx Brothers had ever wanted to make a blue movie, that night in Manila would have provided an excellent screenplay. Before we had got half-way through our beer, the cricket's nocturnal song was momentarily silenced by a piercing cry of pleasure emanating from Fassbender's hedge. Not long afterwards, the naked German burst forth, the girl in his arms, and strode with Teutonic grandeur across the garden his white skin gleaming in the moonlight, and, without further ceremony, threw the focus of his ardour into the swimming-pool. Within seconds the night was rent once more by the cries of love.

'Jesus,' muttered Stone admiringly, 'Jurgen's gone berserk.'

Considering the amount of noise they were making about it, Fassbender's movements could hardly have gone unnoticed inside the house and one player, in particular, had been taking note of the proceedings. Bill Lloyd, yet another Aussie on the tour with a highly developed sense of humour, saw his chance and took it. Unseen even by Allan and myself, he had left his curfew partner, climbed out of the window of the bedroom he was occupying and stolen Fassbender's trousers.

And so it was that, at four in the morning, Stone and I were roused from our post-beer snooze by the sight of an enraged German in his underpants, with a dressed, bedraggled but obviously contented young lady at his side, threatening us with all manner of retribution. We were, after all, No. 1 suspects as far as trouser-snatchers were concerned. When we finally convinced him of our innocence, Jurgen stormed into the house shouting, 'Vere are my trousers? I vill kill the man who has stolen my trousers!'

Bill Lloyd survived and moved on from trouser-snatching to selling Nike shoes back home in Australia but he, like the rest of us, will not have forgotten the opportunities presented by the Marcos curfew.

On the Virginia Slims tour, the women had a curfew all of their own. It was in place at all times and in all cities and it was called social etiquette. No matter what the feminists want to say about it, there is still a social stigma attached to the idea of a young woman picking up men in bars, restaurants or even off the street for her own amusement. And even if there weren't most women simply don't want to behave like that. So it was inevitable that some members of the tour would turn to each other in an effort to combat the loneliness of a nomadic and highly competitive existence. For a period in the 1970s lesbianism was the tendency amongst some of the players and both Billie Jean King and Martina Navratilova have talked openly about it.

In this instance adverse publicity helped. Parents recognized the facts of the situation and made a greater effort to accompany their daughters to tournaments, especially those who were still at an impressionable age. The sensationalism, which intensified, of course, when the women broke away to form their own tour, has largely subsided and the whole subject is being treated with an air of greater sophistication. The fact that Martina makes no attempt to hide her relationship with Judy Nelson, who is now totally accepted on the tour, is nicely balanced by the fact that Martina's two greatest friends amongst the players are Pam Shriver and Chris Evert, two totally heterosexual women.

It was the irrepressible Miss Shriver, naturally, who took a bet that she would not dare walk into the men's locker-room at Kooyong during the Australian Open a few years ago. Just as inevitably, if you know how her mind works, it was the then Mrs Lloyd who put Pam up to it. Chrissie knew Pam would do it and she did.

'Hi, guys, don't be scared. I'm just doing this for a bet,' was Pam's opening line. Soon Chris and some of the other girls joined her and a wet afternoon was spent with a faintly amazed group of young men swapping dirty jokes with some very celebrated female tennis players.

'It was real college dorm stuff,' Pam said, laughing about it later. 'But my timing was right off. When I walked in there wasn't a single guy without his clothes on. It was a real bummer!'

As no one has offered me huge sums of money to try it, I have never, as yet, entered into the women's domain at a tournament and apart from Ted Tinling who was always in there fixing someone's hem-line or untangling their bra-strap, only a handful of trusted male trainers have been allowed into the inner sanctum.

One of them was Stan Nicholes, a champion Australian weight-lifter just after the war, who became trainer to several winning Australian Davis Cup teams and later helped both John and Chris Lloyd add some much-needed muscle to their game. Stan told me of the occasion when he was giving Margaret Court a message in the locker-room. 'Big Marge', a devoutly religious lady, was covered in towels, revealing one limb at a time, but most of the others girls had practically forgotten Stan was there.

'Then I felt this cold spray on the back of my neck,' said Nicholes. 'When I looked round there was this very lovely young Swedish girl, still wet and still very naked after her shower, flicking her long blond hair over her head so as to give me a good soaking. She was laughing like crazy but Margaret was most embarrassed and apologized for the way some of "those young girls behave". I said "No worries, Marge, I don't mind one bit!" '

Nicholes' experience aside, tennis could do with a bit more mixing of the sexes on tour. Gladys and Billie Jean did a great thing for women's tennis in starting their own circuit but it would be a happier, healthier and more natural sport if the men and the women played more tournaments together.

17

CHRIS AND MARTINA

Martina Navratilova and Ivan Lendl took time to mature but once they had acclimatized themselves to the great big world outside Czechoslovakia, it was the world that had to sit up and take notice. By the mid eighties Martina and Ivan had redefined the word 'professional' in tennis.

Making use of every scientific and technological device that had become available to the modern athlete, these two Czechoslovaks set themselves up in the United States, Martina as a defector, Ivan as a resident alien, and, like so many immigrants, promptly became more American than America. The nation, it must be said, was ready for them. The world's greatest democracy had undergone some searching self-examination since I had first spent time there in 1965. That was the era of the five-Martini business lunch, the calorie-laden steaks that literally fell over the side of the plate and the naïve belief that American goodwill and American wealth could move mountains. Then obese business executives started dropping dead from cardiac arrest on the commuter trains carrying them back to equally overweight wives in the suburbs, and the little yellow men in pyjamas began testing and thwarting the resolve of the US Cavalry in the jungles of South-East Asia. Suddenly America started to face reality.

Exercise, diets and health care became industries overnight and Perrier arrived in little green bottles. For those who still needed something stronger, wine from the Napa Valley and Europe replaced hard liquor as a socially acceptable cocktail as America, probing ever deeper for cause and effect, analysed every organ in the body. After a few years of self-indulgence, during which she understandably rummaged around in the good life like a kid in a candy store, Martina took one look at a somewhat pudgy outline in a mirror and started analysing her body and her career like a true believer. A diet devised by Dr Robert Haas in Florida, accompanied by weight training and a fearsome regimen of gym work, changed the way Martina looked and, very soon, the way she played. One tends to forget that Martina was 25 before she became a regular winner of Grand Slam titles.

Born in Prague in October 1956 she had won just two Wimbledon singles crowns prior to her first success in Australia at Kooyong in 1981. That was the first of 15 Grand Slam titles she would win in the following seven years.

Lendl's career has followed a remarkably similar pattern. By the beginning of 1984, Ivan, who turned 24 in March, was starting to be regarded as a nearly-great player who could not win the big ones. He had lost two finals at Flushing Meadow and one each at Roland Garros and Kooyong, and it was not until McEnroe let him come back from the dead in the French Open final that same year that he was able to gain the confidence he needed to make the final push to the top of the world ladder.

That match in Paris has haunted McEnroe ever since because he knows that, with a two-set lead in his pocket and nothing to worry him except the glare of the sun and his own combustible temperament, he was as close as he is ever likely to come to relieving Tony Trabert of the unwanted record of being the last American to win the French title. And that was in 1955.

McEnroe may well have suffered from a touch of sunstroke in that match but the fact that Lendl was able to survive the ordeal in better physical condition was highly significant. He, too, had started to follow the low-fat, high-protein Haas diet and the results were remarkable. On several occasions in previous years I had seen this apparently strong young man fade in the final stages of a long match through sheer fatigue. But Lendl has little sympathy for the frailties of the human condition, especially his own. He seems to take a masochistic delight in punishing his body which he regards as an instrument designed to suit his needs. It requires fine tuning but, just as he can judge the sound coming from the engine of his Porsche, Ivan knows instinctively which gear to choose. He was telling us once how he looks at himself in the mirror every morning during his training session at home in Connecticut and asks his body how it feels.

'Sometimes after a real hard session the day before, my body tells me it is really tired and I realize I need to take it a little easy for a day,' Ivan said. 'But some mornings I know that it is just being lazy and trying to fool me and then I let myself have it and go twice as hard just to teach myself a lesson.'

A 20-mile bicycle-ride around the roads of Greenwich, Connecticut is Lendl's idea of a good finish to a day of non-stop physical exertion either in his specially designed gym or on court under the demanding eye of Tony Roche, who spends time at the Lendl compound attempting to make friends with the German Shepherds who guard the precincts during the weeks preceding major tournaments.

'I don't have to push Ivan,' says Roche, who was tutored in the art of on-court torture by Harry Hopman. 'He is a naturally hard worker and has made use of every aspect of modern sports medicine and technology to help maximize his abilities. He is the complete professional.'

One senses that Lendl enjoys the rigours of discipline while Martina has always had to steel herself against distractions and the wayward flights of a wild imagination in her determination to make the most of her natural talents. She can be an impulsive, inquisitive and exasperating person who, despite moments of unpardonable thoughtlessness, has a good heart. She spends a lot of time and money on the charities she has adopted near her home in Fort Worth, yet can refuse to spend 10 minutes hitting with a junior during an exhibition tour 'because I never do that'.

She can nit-pick over a word like 'entourage' which we inevitably use to describe the caravan of people and animals that accompany her around the world, and yet the sweep of that amazing mind can carry her, in one sentence, from talking about the sliding roof at Flinder's Park to anti-apartheid demonstrators, President Reagan and Iranian terrorists. Like one of her opponents on court, you have to be on your toes when Martina gives a press conference. The objection to 'entourage', incidentally, came when she looked it up in the dictionary and discovered that it suggested subservience amongst a group of followers. Martina prefers 'coterie'.

Considering how many differences in style, taste and personality set them apart, it is strange that the names of Martina Navratilova and Chris Evert will be linked for ever in the annals of sporting history. No matter what happens from now on these two remarkable women have established a sporting rivalry without parallel for longevity, intensity and skill.

It began on an indoor court in Akron, Ohio in 1973 and Miss Evert won that first-round match 7–6, 6–3. It was not until her sixth encounter, in the quarter-finals of the Virginia Slims of Washington, that Martina eventually beat Chris, and right up to the semifinal of the US Open in 1981, which she won after a thrilling duel 6–4 in the third set, the girl from Prague trailed decisively in the head-to-head duels. Then the new slimmed-down and determined Martina emerged and Chris found herself being swamped by the sheer power generated by Martina's big left-handed serve and superb athleticism. In a sequence that very nearly sent Chris into retirement, Martina won 13 consecutive matches between the Toyota Championships of 1982 and the US Open final of 1984 which, once again, went to Martina 6–4 in the third. Chris stopped the rot in the Virginia Slims of Florida early in the following year and then revitalized her career by beating the new American citizen in that memorable French Open final that captivated a packed Centre Court at Roland Garros and woke up an entire nation to the skill and entertainment value of women's tennis.

Armed with a new graphite racket, Chris has kept after Martina ever since, beating her on the Virginia Slims tour in Houston and Los Angeles and running her close in a three-set Wimbledon semifinal in 1987. By the time they had completed their semifinal in the 1988 Ford Australian Open at Flinder's Park, they had played 76 times in official tournaments and Martina had established a 40–36 lead. The set score after 15 years' competition played on four continents was 96–84 in Martina's favour, with Martina also leading in tie-breaks won — by the wholly appropriate tally of 7–6. And through it all, they have remained genuinely good friends.

Fifty-seven of those meetings have come in the final round of a tournament and, of those, 14 have been the final of one of the four Grand Slam events. I have been lucky enough to see all but two of those and none of them lingers in the mind quite as dramatically as that Saturday in Paris in June 1985 which did so much to persuade Chris she still had plenty to offer as a world-class player.

To reach the final Mrs Lloyd, as she was at the time, had to overcome a little piece of history in the making. A stunning newcomer from Argentina with a name that sounded like a hot breath from the pampas, Gabriella Sabatini, had beaten the young Bulgarian clay-court specialist Manuela Maleeva to become, at the age of 15 years and a few days, the youngest player ever to reach the semifinal of a Grand Slam championship. Parisians can never resist feminine beauty, and, seeing it flower suddenly on a tennis court, they cast aside past prejudices to pack the Centre Court for Gabriella's match against Chris.

The teenager looked beautiful and the spectators cheered her every move but Chris had played that role herself once and remembered how a Forest Hill crowd had reduced poor Françoise Durr to tears when she had played that delightful French girl at the very start of her own career. So Chris refused to be rattled and concentrated furiously as she knew she must, allowing Gabriella only five points in the last five games to win 6–4, 6–1.

It was noticed in passing that Chris had beaten another teenager of talent on her way to the final, a 15-year-old from West Germany called Steffi Graf. In their press conferences, both Martina and Chris were being asked how long they would keep going and Miss Navratilova replied that she didn't see anyone who posed a threat. 'I don't see anyone taking over until we retire, which isn't so far away,' she said.

Three years later, both are still at it and both have been beaten, if not entirely supplanted, by those two youngsters Chris brushed aside so imperiously in the spring of 1985. Alan Trengove, who had been reporting on tennis since the days of Quist and Sedgman just after the war, read the situation correctly at the time by noting in his magazine, *Tennis Australia*, that their rivalry was such that each would keep the other going. That has proved to be true and the upward surge of Steffi and Gabriella has only fuelled their incentive.

Considering she had managed only one victory in their last 14 meetings and had been soundly beaten 6–3, 6–1 by Martina in the corresponding final the previous year, Chris did not walk out on the huge Centre Court on that warm Parisian afternoon with the spring of confidence in her stride.

'She had killed me the year before,' Chris told me recently. 'All I remembered was how well she could play on red clay even though it was the surface that gave me the best chance against her.'

In her semifinal against the powerful West German Glaudia Kohde-Kilsch, Martina had looked a little tentative on occasion and the lack of rhythm which had developed in that match carried over into the final. Her service, in particular, was affected and Chris was able to capitalize on that in the early stages, moving with authoritative ease to a 6–3, 4–2 lead, and then led 0–40 on Martina's serve. Cornered, the left-hander struck back, claws flashing, and some devastating serves, backed by equally punishing volleys, allowed her to hold serve, break back and, in a sudden turn around, grab the tie-breaker by seven points to four to level the match.

But the damage had already been done. Those opening games had lifted the air of inferiority that had hung over Chris in her matches with Martina in the previous couple of years and suddenly she was her old assertive self again.

'Right from the start I realized I was playing even with her and then I was winning,' Chris recalled. 'It was an unfamiliar position to be in but it felt good, especially when I realized the tactics John had thought out for me were working.'

After their separation of the previous year, John Lloyd was back at Chris' side in Paris that June and, having watched the pair play so many times through the expert eyes of a top player, he had devised some unorthodox tactics in an attempt to break up Martina's game.

'John suggested I stay back and hit more looped balls to the forehand,' Chris explained. 'Before I had been hitting flat and that had enabled her to chip and come in. She'd do that off the backhand very effectively, too, so switching the point of attack helped.'

These tactics had been tried out during practice sessions against Jerome Vanier, a French left-hander who had been at SMU under Chris' long-time coach Dennis Ralston. Now, in the heat of battle, they were paying off and even if the tennis, disrupted by the gusty wind and nerves that jangled in both women's elbows, was too patchy to be rated at the very highest level, the excitement never abated and the crowd was totally captivated by the spectacle of these two great champions duelling with an intensity and pride that only seemed to increase with the passing years.

Refusing to be disheartened by Martina's sudden revival, Chris quickly regained the initiative at the start of the third set and led 3–1 before the left-hander broke back again to level at 3–3. Again Chris edged in front, threading backhand passes down the line after punishing returns of serve to lead 5–3. But by now the tempo was quickening with every step, like a cancan of the courts, hearts aflutter, the sensation of a swirling skirt or a flashing racket upping the beat until it seemed as if the whole match had been transported on to the great windmill of the Moulin Rouge. But there was no choreographer to bring us to the end of this cabaret. The magic of sport is that no one can design the ending; no one knows who will end up at the top of the windmill.

One minute the money was on Mrs Lloyd and then, once again, Miss Navratilova pounced, allowing a shocked opponent only one point out of the next 12 to pull back to 5–5 and 0–40 on Chris' serve.

'I thought I'd blown it,' Chris admitted. 'On the next point I went for a winner, like you do when you're so far behind.'

'And Martina missed the forehand volley,' said Ted Tinling with instant recall. 'That was the shot that lost her the match. It was one of the most outstanding cases I have ever seen of a match being lost on one point.'

Sure enough, as Tinling noted, Chris' chin came up, the eyes narrowed and the dainty little strut appeared once again in her walk. She was back in business. With the crowd in a state of Gallic frenzy, Chris held serve, and when Martina chipped an approach to her backhand on match point in the next game, the lady from Fort Lauderdale hit the backhand she may remember most when the racket finally gets thrown in the closet; the ripping two-hander that sped up the line to earn her the French title for the sixth time.

'I was ecstatic,' said Chris. 'Beating Martina is always rewarding but doing it in a Grand Slam final is enough to keep you going for another six months.'

It kept Chris going for rather longer than that. She returned the following year to win at Roland Garros for a record-breaking seventh time — on this occasion with a somewhat less hair-raising three-set defeat of Martina — and so complete the 13th consecutive year in which she had won at least one Grand Slam title. If Steffi Graf wants a goal in life, I suggest she chase that one and may I wish her good luck.

The rapid advance of Steffi and Gabriella has, of course, provided the perfect period of transition in women's tennis, in which two proven champions of immeasurable stature are battling with obvious relish to remain on equal terms with two wonderful newcomers. All four have played their part in making the women's game rather more interesting than the men's at the moment and, back at their new home in Santa Fe, New Mexico, Gladys and Julius Heldman must be gratified to know that the tour they pioneered in the face of such odds in the United States can now hold its own in Europe, too. They have all come a long way, but will two champions ever tread a longer or more golden path than Martina and Chris? We will be exceptionally fortunate if they can.

18

DAVIS CUP

The silly British, mad dogs and Englishmen and all that, thought deserts were hot. There were obviously no veterans of Montgomery's Eighth Army in the Coachella Valley in December 1978 because we were back at the Mission Hills Country Club for a Davis Cup final between the United States and Britain and when the sun went down and the lights came on, everyone froze. No one had thought to bring their winter woollies from frost-bound blighty and when Gerald Williams tried to do his BBC Radio reports from the top of the clubhouse his lips nearly stuck to the microphone.

No matter. Britain had worked a miracle just getting to the final of the Davis Cup with a team that comprised Buster Mottram, John Lloyd and his elder brother David. Maybe it needs a family effort to get unfancied teams to the Davis Cup final because the next rank outsiders to make it that far, the Indian team in 1987, also had a pair of brothers, Anand and Vijay Amritraj, playing doubles. But, like the Indians in Gothenberg, the British were outclassed at Rancho Mirage, despite Mottram's gallant first-day victory over Brian Gottfried. Britain were outclassed because, apart from a top-flight doubles team in Stan Smith and Bob Lutz, the United States had a mop-haired left-hander from New York called John McEnroe.

McEnroe had already made a name for himself in tennis, having reached the Wimbledon semifinal as an unknown 17-year-old qualifier the year before and then revealing the true extent of his extraordinary talent by winning Colgate Grand Prix Super Series titles in San Francisco, the Stockholm Open, and the Benson & Hedges at Wembley in quick succession in the autumn of 1978. After a week's relaxation in Montego Bay, McEnroe was due to beat Ashe and so claim his first Masters crown at Madison Square Garden before the year was out.

But here at Mission Hills, he was making his début as a singles player for the United States in the Davis Cup. One could say it was a historic moment because McEnroe turned out to be the most successful player in US Davis Cup history. But it was historic for a rather broader and more important reason than that. It was the beginning of the career of a man who would single-handedly save the Davis Cup from extinction.

I make that statement without hesitation despite the fact that McEnroe, in many people's eyes, went on to behave in a manner that brought disgrace to America and that nation's sporting image, and was eventually suspended from the competition by a USTA President, Randy Gregson, in 1986. Let us examine the facts. By the mid 1970s it was becoming unfashionable for the big stars to play the Davis Cup. Bjorn Borg played for Sweden — and had led them to their first Davis Cup triumph over Czechoslovakia in 1975 — as long as he was not having a row with the Swedish Federation, a not infrequent occurrence, and it was much the same story with Argentina's two great players, Guillermo Vilas and José-Luis Clerc. Sometimes they found better things to do. But it was in America that the real erosion of interest was taking place, primarily because the format of the Davis Cup in those days took anything from six to eight weeks out of a player's schedule, and although all that nonsense about only authorized players being allowed to play had been done away with, the money was minimal and the effort required considerable.

Before the traditionalists start spluttering on about it being one's duty to play for one's country, let me try and put it in perspective once again. How many weeks in the year would business executives give to represent their country, say at an international symposium in Bogota, Mexico City or Toronto if they knew it would cost them in the region of £20,000 per week? Not, I will wager, anything near six.

Yet that is the sum, even in those days, that a Jimmy Connors or a John McEnroe could expect to earn from exhibition matches in Davis Cup weeks if he chose to do so. On most occasions Stan Smith and Arthur Ashe chose not to do so and were almost, if not quite, one hundred per cent loyal to the Davis Cup. Jimmy Connors and Vitas Gerulaitis, however, felt less obligation to come running when the USTA called because neither felt that he owed very much to his national association when he was trying to make the grade. Eddie Dibbs, who finished as the top money-earner in the world in 1978 with $575,000 ($300,000 in bonuses for coming first on the Colgate Grand Prix points table), felt the same way. Davis Cup discipline was not quite Fast Eddie's style and, after a couple of none too successful forays into Latin America, he decided his time would be more profitably spent at the Miami dog track.

That was the trend and by the time McEnroe appeared on the scene it was threatening to turn into a stampede. Had McEnroe joined in and galloped away on the exhibition circuit, the efforts of Chatrier and David Gray, who had joined him from The *Guardian* as Secretary of the ITF, to streamline the Davis Cup and pump some much-needed sponsorship money into the world-wide competitions would have come to naught. Without their top stars bothering to turn out, American audiences would have turned off the Davis Cup so fast that no promoter worth his dollars and cents would have touched a Davis Cup tie with the end of an outsize racket. And if America had not continued to be a leading Davis Cup nation, no major international sponsor would have been interested either. Dwight Davis' marvellous idea, which had produced so many glorious sporting moments since its inception in 1900, would have been reduced to a second-rate competition between second-class tennis nations. Only one person prevented that happening. John McEnroe.

John and Kay McEnroe will admit to various errors of judgement in bringing up their eldest boy, but if you can blame the parents for some of the sins of the son, they should also receive the praise that is due for instilling into him a sense of patriotic pride. Personally I think that patriotism can be taken too far and, after the way John Jnr whipped up the crowd in a flag-waving assault on the senses in the 1987 relegation battle with West Germany at Hartford, Connecticut, I know that many Americans will agree with me. But those critics who damn McEnroe at every turn almost certainly have not had to endure the cockpit of hysteria and fury that awaits visitors to Davis Cup ties in Latin America. McEnroe has, having twice put himself on the line with no top-class clay-court support against Argentina in Buenos Aires. If you have been through that, maybe you have earned the right to wave a flag when you get home.

But until he brought officialdom down on his head after the disastrous loss to Sweden in the 1984 final in Gothenberg, McEnroe's motto was simple: 'I'll go anywhere, anytime to play Davis Cup for the United States.' That was a commitment no other top American star was prepared to make. It was that commitment that rekindled interest in the competition in America and was instrumental in allowing the ITF to find a sponsor of the calibre of the Nippon Electric Company (NEC) to take over world-wide sponsorship to the tune of one million dollars.

The equation is very straightforward — no McEnroe, no America; no America, no NEC; no NEC, no future for the Davis Cup. That is how it was in 1981 when David Gray unveiled his new format for the Davis Cup, comprising a World Group of 16 nations with various zonal groups fighting each year for promotion to the top echelon. First-round losers in the World Group would have to play off against each other and the losers would be relegated. Hence the disappearance of the United States into the forbidding South American zone, after Boris Becker had led West Germany to victory over McEnroe, and the flags in Hartford. Just to keep up to date with the heroes of our story, the captain of the German team on that occasion was a newly-naturalized West German citizen called Nikki Pilic. One way or the other Nikki can't get the Davis Cup out of his hair.

Although there is a move afoot, supported by Chatrier, to have the Davis Cup played as a two-week bonanza, Olympic Games style, with all the leading nations competing in one spot, I think Gray got it absolutely right. The new format gives the opportunity for the smaller nations, most of whom do not have major professional stars, to play almost as much Davis Cup as they used to in the past, while in the World Group a player has to commit himself to only four weeks' play to take his nation all the way to the final. But the essence of the competition remains in the advantages and disadvantages of playing every round at home or away. To take it to neutral territory for all but one team each year would destroy that essential element.

By virtue of some lucky draws, no nation has made better use of home court, and therefore of home surface advantage, than Australia. Against all the odds Neale Fraser has led his team to victory four times since assuming the captaincy in 1970, and only once in all the years since has Australia failed to get at least as far as the semifinals. That is a quite extraordinary feat of consistency. Considering the world ranking of many of the players he has had to choose from, the former Wimbledon champion must take a fair slice of the credit for a record that bears comparison to the halcyon years of Harry Hopman, who had a whole line of champions to help him to no less than 15 Davis Cup victories in the post-war years.

Only once, against the United States in Cleveland in 1973, could Fraser call upon the calibre of players Hopman routinely had at his disposal. Then his team was so strong that Fraser had to make the most difficult decision of his life. Taking a deep breath he told Ken Rosewall that he would not be wanted for the doubles and left one of the world's great players on the bench while Rod Laver and John Newcombe proceeded to play the whole tie themselves, justifying Fraser's decision by routing the Americans 5–0.

After that Fraser often took the court without a single top-20 player in his squad, but the arrival of Pat Cash enabled the tradition of Christmas-time Davis Cup finals at Kooyong to be revived, and twice, in 1983 and 1986, Cash proved too powerful on grass for Sweden's all-round talents and inflicted the only defeats the Swedes have suffered in five consecutive appearances in the final up to 1987.

Bjorn Borg's legacy of a veritable army of top-class Swedish players has been the most astonishing feature of men's tennis in the 1980s. For the past five years Sweden has regularly provided five or six of the top 20 players in the world, and sometimes more. Not only that, but Mats Wilander, Stefan Edberg, Anders Jarryd, Joakim Nystrom and their colleagues have played everywhere and excelled on all surfaces, indoors and out. Strangely, only the US Open has not fallen to the Viking hordes — for although the new generation have not yet conquered Wimbledon, Borg, of course, reigned there for years. However, like his successors, the greatest Swede of all found both Forest Hills and Flushing Meadows impenetrable fortresses.

With so much talent at their disposal, it was only a matter of time before Sweden would start to dominate the Davis Cup, a competition that had been won only by the Big Four — the United States, Australia, France and Great Britain — until, sadly, South Africa took it by default in 1974 when India refused to play them in the final for political reasons.

Far more appropriately, Borg's Swedish team in 1975 became the first genuinely to break the mould and then, almost a decade later, on a specially-laid clay court in the vast Scandinavium Stadium in Gothenberg in 1984, the real take-over began. Ironically, the team Arthur Ashe took to Gothenberg was, on paper, one of the strongest American teams in history. Connors had agreed to make one of his rare Davis Cup appearances that year, and, with McEnroe and his long-time partner Peter Fleming still at that stage unbeaten in Davis Cup doubles, Sweden should have been given the severest of tests.

But Connors is no team man; McEnroe could never fathom Ashe's laid-back attitude to captaincy, and team spirit never surfaced from beneath an unhappy atmosphere of superstar individualism hampered still further by poor preparation. Connors lost the opening singles to Wilander, bitched over line calls and ended up, after an appalling display of petulance, by shaking the umpire's chair in fury. McEnroe, ill at ease as usual on clay, then lost comprehensively to Sweden's fleeting star Henrik Sundstrom but made a huge point of shaking the hand of just everyone he could find at the end, including linesmen, the opposing captain and the umpire. When Edberg and Jarryd won the doubles in four sets, this juggernaut of an American team had been humiliated to such an extent that it had managed to win only one set in three live rubbers. McEnroe recovered some semblance of pride by beating Wilander in the dead reverse singles but Connors did not even bother to play, leaving the task of wrapping up the disaster to Jimmy Arias, who lost to Sundstrom.

Despite the strength of the Swedes it had been an appalling performance by the Americans and the general behaviour of the team came over extremely badly on television back home. As a result the USTA, urged on by their embarrassed Davis Cup sponsors, tried to get every player in line for Davis Cup duty to sign a good-conduct pledge before selection. The 'shocking' behaviour of McEnroe and Connors in Gothenberg was cited. When pressed as to exactly what McEnroe had done wrong in Sweden apart from lose, the USTA told us that he had laughed while the national anthems were being played and criticized the court surface.

There have been moments during his brilliant Davis Cup career when McEnroe has indeed left himself open to censure and has been lucky to get away with such light penalties. But Gothenberg was not one of them. If the USTA were trying to make out that McEnroe had been disrespectful to the United States flag, they must have been joking. Since birth he has been draped in the Stars and Stripes and for years made a point of wearing his Davis Cup jacket with 'USA' on the back at Grand Prix tournaments. As for being critical of the court, McEnroe was right, as he so often is, because it is very difficult to get a perfect clay court when it has been laid for only a week. But if criticism of another country's preparations for Davis Cup matches was supposed to be just another example of deteriorating standards amongst the disrespectful new generation, then the USTA should read a little history and see what H. Roper Barrett, captain of the British team, had to say about the conditions he found at the Longwood Cricket Club in Boston where the first Davis Cup tie in history was played in August 1900. Said Barrett: 'The ground was abominable. The grass was long. The net was a disgrace to civilized lawn tennis, held up by guy ropes that were continually sagging. As for the balls, I hardly like to mention them. They were awful — soft and mothery-looking – and when served with the American twist came at you like an animated egg.'

Poor old McEnroe. He will have to brush up on his vitriolic vocabulary. He has got nothing on H. Roper Barrett, a true Victorian gentleman. At any rate McEnroe refused to sign and it eventually became apparent that Gregson, the incoming President whose sunny smile concealed a ruthless political ambition, was not going to allow McEnroe to play Davis Cup for as long as it was in his power to prevent it.

This was never spelled out to Tom Gorman when he was interviewed for Ashe's captaincy job. But suddenly, in the summer of 1986, when McEnroe had indicated that he was ready to rejoin the team in Mexico City, Gorman was told flatly by Gregson that he could not pick him.

It was a shabby way to have treated a new captain, especially one of Gorman's integrity. The President should have been up front about it to start with but then someone as devious as Gregson could never have been expected to match up to Gorman's standards of honesty. Between 1971 and 1973 Gorman had reached the semifinals of Wimbledon, the French Open and the US Open but it had been in Barcelona, where the third Masters was held, that Gorman had produced one of those acts of sportsmanship that stick in the memory. In the semifinal he had been completely outplaying Stan Smith, who was the reigning Wimbledon champion, and duly reached match point. But Gorman had suffered for most of his career from a chronic back complaint and, a few points earlier, he had felt his back go. He knew that it would stiffen up over night and leave him totally immobilized the following day, so instead of winning one more point, he kissed goodbye to a place in the Masters final by walking up to Stan and shaking hands.

'I couldn't deprive the tournament and the crowd of a final the next day,' explained Gorman. 'It just would not have been fair.'

Gregson appeared to be less interested in fairness than in scoring political points with his USTA constituents. It is quite true that a vociferous group were putting pressure on him to banish McEnroe and, in this, he was even getting support from his good-natured predecessor, Hunter Delatour, to whom McEnroe had been rude the previous year. One of McEnroe's blind spots is his inability to realize that people with badges on their blazers are capable of being his friend if only he would give them a chance. But John is paranoid about officialdom and lashes out childishly and unthinkingly at anyone in authority. Delatour could have been a friend, but McEnroe had taken care of that possibility.

Even when Gregson's term ended and Gordon Jorgensen arrived with his conciliatory manner and hopes for restoring some of the family spirit that Gregson had done little to foster, Gorman was still left with a major problem. He could hardly expect McEnroe to come running as soon as the green light came on, especially when the first tie of 1987 would take the Americans in Asunción in Paraguay, where powerful Czech and French teams had perished since Victor Pecci had recruited the Puerto Rican-born Francisco Gonzales as his No. 2. On a technical level McEnroe knew he would struggle on the clay that would be used in a new tennis stadium built on the banks of the River Paraguayos, and on a temperamental level he felt that he was not ready to face the trauma of playing in front of a South American crowd.

'I've still got to get the bad taste out of my mouth,' he told me when I phoned him one day at his Malibu beach house near Los Angeles. 'Whatever I may have done wrong, I think I deserve to have been treated a little better after all I have given to the Davis Cup. If Tom still wants me, I'll be around later in the year.'

He lived up to that promise but by the time he did appear, in Hartford, Gorman's team was fighting for survival as a World Group nation and, with Becker playing his best tennis of the year, even McEnroe could not save them.

Looking back I think McEnroe was probably right to opt out of Paraguay. His presence would only have given the thermometer another boost and I am not sure we could have endured anything hotter than we got. The air was hot, the music was hot and the atmosphere boiled. The Davis Cup unleashes extraordinary passions and, over the years, it has produced some of the most memorable moments I have ever witnessed in a sporting arena. It is a beautifully designed sporting contest in the first place and when allied to unbridled emotions it can turn into the purest drama imaginable.

I think of Mike Sangster staring down a whole wall of hysterical Milanese and willing them to silence before powering an ace past Nikki Pietrangeli; I think of poor Alex Metreveli suffering the wrath and hatred of an entire nation as the Czechs booed and hissed his every move when the Soviet Union played in Prague soon after 1968; I think of the tears of humility and pride that trickled down Yannick Noah's cheeks when a packed stadium in Grenoble cheered his name. That day only the opposing captain, Arthur Ashe, really understood why Yannick was crying.

Tears have often mingled with triumph in Davis Cup play but in Asunción in 1987 there was an element of fear, too, as the Americans fought to survive in a concrete bowl surrounded by steel-helmeted militiamen with the aged dictator Stroessner staring down from his presidential box which, in itself, was guarded by a pistol-packing posse of plain-clothes henchmen. The cymbals clashed, the drums sent the rhythms of the pampas echoing out into the night and across the river into Argentina and the crowd danced and chanted and willed their players to beat the damn Yankees.

Orchestrated to perfection, the music stopped the instant a player was ready to serve, and, although there was a handful of real trouble-makers amongst them who tried to turn a scene of celebration into an ugly confrontation, the crowd were not as bad as some of the American players tried to make out. It was scary and Ken Flach was rightly concerned about his wife's safety when a small group of nasty-looking characters came surging forward at the end of one of the matches, yelling anti-American obscenities. But the real villain of the piece was Senor Velasquez Ugarte, the President of the Paraguayan Federation, who actually tried to intimidate the Danish referee Kurt Nielsen in the middle of the dramatic fourth rubber between Jimmy Arias and Hugo Chapacu. Nielsen, twice a Wimbledon singles finalist in the 1950s, had all the pressure he needed without that and did well to respond by clamping down on some of the outrageous foot-fault calls that were being made against the Americans on crucial points.

The Arias–Chapacu duel was one of the most exciting matches I have ever witnessed. Being a base-line top-spin specialist Arias could not complain about the clay court, but the general conditions were something else and I am not sure even he knows how he managed to let slip a 5–1 lead in the fifth set. Three match points went begging as little Chapacu, seemingly on the point of exhaustion at one time, fought back to claim a famous victory and so allow the national hero Pecci to clinch the tie 3–2 by defeating Aaron Krickstein in the final rubber.

Chapacu, another recent recruit to Paraguy's multinational team, could have been in danger of being kicked back across the river to his native Argentina had he lost, but such is the incongruity of sporting fate that, less than an hour after staring defeat in the face, he was being pressed to Stroessner's ample bosom on national television, his place amongst the pantheon of Paraguay's sporting heroes assured for ever.

Shocked by more horror stories from Asunción, Chatrier, who had seen the way his French team had been treated there two years before, encouraged the Davis Cup committee to slap a ban on Paraguay playing any more ties at home for the remainder of the year. What Chatrier did not realize at the time was that things had improved considerably in many aspects, not least the completion of the fabulous Golf and Racket Club Paraguayos right next to the stadium, which offered the players the most comfortable modern accommodation they had seen all year. So when one of the owners, Richard Kent, arrived in Paris to plead Paraguay's case and hint that a change of President might be on the cards, Chatrier relented and Paraguay would have been allowed to play at home again, had they beaten Spain in Caracas, Venezuela. But they didn't and Pecci, Gonzales and Chapacu had to wait another year before they had the chance to conjure up more miracles for their expectant compatriots.

A test run for what was to follow — left to right, Pierre Barthes, Jaime Fillol, Patricio Cornejo, Alex Olmedo, Ray Moore (later to become one of the game's leading politicians) and Terry Ryan discuss the possibilities of Player Power at the Los Angeles Tennis Club in 1971. *Photo: R. Evans*

Jack Kramer and Donald Dell prepare for another of their many roles, television commentators, while Bjorn Borg who was trying out for a role as colour man, looks rather less comfortable than he did on court. *Photo: Eugene L. Scott*

Grim faces at Stade Roland Garros in the early 1970s as French Federation official Benny Berthet wants to know why the WCT pros aren't playing the French Open. John McDonald (left, in the raincoat), Lamar Hunt and Mike Davies try to explain. *Photo: Albert Evans*

'This is the saddest statement I have ever had to make. . .' ATP President Cliff Drysdale announcing the Wimbledon boycott at the Westbury Hotel in 1973. Weary Board members Jim McManus, Stan Smith, Arthur Ashe and Ismail El Shafei back their President. *Photo: Ed Fernberger*

Winning the WCT Dallas Final at
Reunion Arena in 1974 — John
Newcombe's volleys stayed hit ...
a little doubles in the US Open
ten years later and Newk and Fred
Stolle stayed pals. *Photos:
R. Evans & Michael Cole*

Bjorn Borg and Jimmy Connors are generally credited with introducing the two handed backhand to modern pro tennis but Cliff Drysdale's two hander was a lethal weapon that kept Cliff in the top five of the powerful WCT tour for four years in the early 1970s. Here he uses it against Connors in a WCT event. *Photo: Russ Adams*

Rod Laver and Lew Hoad flank host Pierre Barthes on the terrace of his lovely house near Versailles during the 1986 French Open while the author looks suitably content to be in such exalted company.

A moment for celebration during the JAKS Awards Dinner at the New York Hilton in 1985 as the two Panchos, Gonzales and Segura, are honoured for their services to the game.
Photo: Russ Adams

Blonds from different eras — Vitas Gerulaitis caught in a rare moment of introspection in the locker room at Forest Hills when the dreams were still real and Stefan Edberg whose dreams may yet become reality.
Photos: R. Evans & M. Di Giacomo

Typical poses for the two Rumanians who have made such an impact on the Open Tennis era — Ilie Nastase looking as cute as custard as he leaves the Grand Hotel during the Stockholm Open while, in the days when Boris Becker was still a baby, Ion Tiriac has plenty to say about something at a tournament in England. Britain's Gerald Battrick listens.

Not too much imagination was needed to turn Stan Smith into a fair Gary Cooper understudy during the American Airlines Tennis Games in 1975.
Photo: R. Evans

Bjorn Borg, the supreme athlete. *Photo: Michael Cole*

That visit to Asunción only served to dramatize the effect the Davis Cup can have on some of the smaller nations and how it can lift the game of tennis from a country-club pastime to a sport that engages the passions of the entire populace. Paraguay became a force in the Davis Cup because they suddenly produced a giant of a man called Victor Pecci whose natural talent for the game enabled him to reach the final of the French Open in 1979 and take a set off the great Borg. He should have gone on to even greater things but Victor decided that life was to be lived and confined his serious bouts of training to coincide with the Davis Cup. With Francisco Gonzales to help him, not to mention the old fast boards they used to play on in Asunción where the linesmen's calls could be even more difficult to verify, Paraguay burst out of the backwoods to become a leading Davis Cup nation.

In all probability it will last as long as Pecci does for Paraguay, but even though the relegation of the United States is hardly what the NEC would have wanted, the Japanese company's involvement should ensure that this venerable competition, begun under less than auspicious circumstances so long ago, will continue to carve a prominent niche for itself in the professional game.

Because fewer ties are played each year now, it will be impossible for McEnroe to come close to challenging Nikki Pietrangeli's record tally of 120 matches won out of 163 in a total of 66 ties. Even Ilie Nastase, placed second in the all-time list of Davis Cup stalwarts, is safe with 110 wins from 146 matches in 51 ties. However, despite what his critics may have to say about it, the Davis Cup will benefit from more of McEnroe for as long as he can manage it. Thanks to his insistence on swimming against the tide, the competition doesn't need him quite as much as it did a decade ago but if he can help the USA escape from the treacherous clay courts of South America, he will have done the Davis Cup another favour.

19

OUT OF CONTROL

The All England Club were not the only culprits in failing to deal with bad behaviour when they had it in their power to do so. Despite the appointment of Grand Prix Supervisors, pro tennis by the end of the 1970s was on the verge of running amok. Big-time promotional hype had hit the sport like a whirlwind and there was a great deal of chaos to be reaped. It was never quite as bad as my profession made out, but then it is a journalistic fact of life that none of us is going to write about Stan Smith and Jaime Fillol playing a match brimming over with the milk of human kindness when Nastase and McEnroe are at each other's throats on the adjoining court. That is not just the way of journalism, that is the way of the world.

In fact Nastase and McEnroe were never mortal enemies, but they did manage to light the fuse that created a notorious dynamite of an evening at Flushing Meadow, a night that was to give tennis its first real inkling of what it was like to be a sport for the masses. Invitingly, the two most controversial characters in the game were drawn against each other in the second round of the 1979 US Open and a new sort of tennis crowd quickly accepted the invitation. Over 10,000 people turned up for the evening encounter, which had been given the kind of billing the New York press usually reserved for fights at Madison Square Garden. The fans came looking for a fight and, in reality, neither McEnroe nor Nastase had to do very much to ensure that they got one. McEnroe only had to look like McEnroe to set the wise-guys off with their smart remarks — but it was Nastase who started the fatal dialogue with some ringside spectators and followed it with a little stalling.

Ilie, even more than McEnroe, has always been a veritable maestro of the art of instituting bedlam and when the first beer cans hit the court he knew he was into his best orchestration. From then on the players didn't have to do much, except stand around and look innocent while the officials made fools of themselves. When Nastase said he was not ready to receive a McEnroe serve, umpire Frank Hammond docked him a penalty point. Nastase protested and was docked a game. All hell broke loose. For 17 minutes chaos reigned and during that time we had the absurd spectacle of Nastase being defaulted and then, eventually, reinstated when tournament director Bill Talbert, fearing a complete riot from a crowd that had turned into a howling mob, overruled the Hammond default, which had been supported by referee Mike Blanchard, and replaced Hammond in the chair with Blanchard! By this time Grand Prix Supervisor Frank Smith was in on the act, supporting Talbert's decision, and there were more officials out there on the court than one could count. When order was finally restored, McEnroe went on to win the match and, eventually, his first Grand Slam title, one of four he would win at Flushing Meadow.

Even though the vast majority of players were perfectly well behaved, McEnroe, Nastase and Connors were far from being the only ones to daub the game's lily-white image with a kind of graffiti that mirrored the age. McEnroe's doubles partner, Peter Fleming, a quiet, shy giant off the court, had a very short fuse when he was on it, but even he paled in comparison to the massive Fritz Buehning, another of the young Americans who used to stomp around the court like a one-man Panzer division on heat. Buehning was lucky to escape expulsion on several occasions while Nastase, of course, would never have hit a ball at all if he had been playing under the Code of Conduct as it is implemented today.

Even in those more lenient times, he met his match on a couple of occasions, once at a Grand Prix event in New Orleans, when a comparatively trifling incident during his first-round match against Bob Lutz ended up in a default, and once, more spectacularly, when WCT were running a television special in Salisbury, Maryland. When Nastase started acting up, the Executive Director, Mike Davies, was in the truck directing the show which was to be sold to stations as a tape-delayed event through WCT's own network. Finally the antics were more than Davies could bear, so he threw down his headphones, stormed out of the truck and straight on to the court, kicked down the singles stick and said to an amazed Nastase, 'Right, that's it, you're defaulted.' The crowd were equally amazed, because Davies, not expecting to be on public view that day, was dressed in a shirt and jeans and looked as if he had walked in off the street.

But Davies had not only the authority to take drastic action of that kind but also, in that particular event, the leeway, because he knew that they had one match more than they needed for the show, so one would never have been aired anyway. That, of course, was a unique situation and one that highlights the problem tennis faces when a player deserves to be defaulted. If it is a final or the second semifinal, that's it for the day. Sorry, folks, but Joey here has been a bad boy and so you don't get to see any more tennis. There are crowds who don't take kindly to that and it was the threat of a riot that persuaded me to bend the rules when I was helping to run the Italian Open one year at the Foro Italico. Mexico's Raul Ramirez was stuck in traffic; Nastase was ranting on quite rightly about a ten-minute time limit and the tournament officials, only too happy to let the ATP make the tough decisions, asked me what to do. I took one look at the huge, restive crowd, which had already been bored to tears by a very brief and one-sided women's match and said to Ilie, 'Sorry, you're going to get screwed. We are waiting for Raul.'

The net result was that Ilie went to pieces and Ramirez went on to win the Italian title. The rule book said Raul should never have walked on court. But the rule book wasn't written with Roman crowds in mind.

The problem with the state of the game at the beginning of the 1980s was that the officials were not being much more sensible than the players. Leaving aside for a moment the internal problems that Briner's stewardship of the ATP had created, the game was taking a battering from the press on a whole range of issues. The totally needless lawsuit that erupted between the MIPTC and Lamar Hunt created yet another split which achieved little other than to make players and lawyers rich. Owen Williams, the former South African player and promoter, who used to fill Johannesburg's Ellis Park when it was politically acceptable to play in South Africa, had stunned his former colleagues on the Pro Council by accepting Hunt's offer that he should take over as WCT Executive Director when Davies decided to call it quits after 13 years. With cries of 'Traitor!' ringing in his ears, Williams went off to organize a 22-tournament tour, totally separate from the Grand Prix, which would offer the winner of each event the nice little sum of $100,000. With Lendl virtually turning himself into a millionaire with the prize money alone, Hunt soon decided that the whole thing was costing more than his bank balance would allow and the schedule was cut back drastically the following year. Peace was made when the lawyers decided they had earned enough for themselves, and WCT was allowed to crawl back into the arms of the Grand Prix which has since all but smothered WCT's once proud identity.

Davies had seen it all coming. 'Lamar was a decent guy, a good man to work for,' Davies told me. 'But even his pockets weren't bottomless and in 1981 we needed another huge injection of cash like the million-dollar tour we had launched in 1971. Then I had insisted he guarantee the million and let me go out and sell off as much as I could through sponsorship deals. I promised him an 80 per cent return and ended up giving him 96 per cent. But it had been a battle and 10 years later I was tired. In some ways WCT had lost its usefulness as a trail-blazing organization for the professional game and it needed somebody else to define its role.'

Neither Hunt nor Williams is the type of man to walk away from something close to his heart, however, and, as long as WCT does not go on costing Lamar money, World Championship Tennis will continue to play a part in the game.

But the split in 1982 did nothing to enhance the game's image, and the previous year the Masters, sponsored at the time by Volvo, had gone into reverse gear in its attempt to show off the sport at its best. The mass-circulation *New York Daily News* ran two tennis stories on its back page the day after the tournament ended at Madison Square Garden. One headline screamed, 'Masters Flop Forces Scheduling Changes' and the other, lower down, against columnist Mike Lupica's byline, was a real beauty which read, 'Players, Masters Cheat, Lie to Fans'.

The copy didn't get any better. This was Lupica's first paragraph: 'Tennis is the worst-run sport in the world. It is filled with shifty politicians and greedy players, and hardly anyone gives a damn about the people who pay to watch. The Grand Prix Masters was a flop, saved only by Bjorn Borg who absolutely annihilated Ivan Lendl to win his second Masters title and another $100,000. Thank God. Even if he had played better, Lendl did not deserve to win the tournament after going into the tank against Jimmy Connors in a meaningless match Friday night.'

Apart from that overworked word 'greedy', Lupica had got it about right. Under fire from the press, Donald Dell's partner Ray Benton, who was running the tournament for Volvo, was forced to admit that the round-robin format might not be conducive to the best tennis. How so? Well, it was possible for a situation to arise whereby it would benefit a player to lose his last round-robin match, once he was assured of reaching the semifinals, because by doing so he might avoid having to play the strongest member of the last four. This had happened with Lendl. By losing to Connors, he had avoided playing Borg. As a move by a professional who maintains that his priority is to win the tournament, it was smart. As a move by a professional who is also an entertainer and therefore has a duty to the public, it was a disgrace. So what is a player in such a situation supposed to do?

Basically no system should force a player to answer that question. It is totally unfair.

Benton admitted as much, but by then the tournament and tennis in general had received an enormous black eye. That was nothing new. The game was asking for it.

To a lesser extent it still is, because Marshall Happer, the lawyer from North Carolina who was appointed very soon afterwards as the first Chief Administrator of the MIPTC, resolutely refuses to tackle the public relations problem. Tennis is the easiest target in the world because, despite all its administrative foul-ups and on-court outbursts, it is incredibly successful and therefore makes people green with envy. Despite an influx of socialistic Swedes, communist-reared East Europeans and stars like Zina Garrison and Lori McNeil who have come straight off the public park courts of Houston, tennis cannot rid itself of its snotty, country-club image — not, at least, in the minds of many American sports writers, who still feel they have to explain everything in baseball terminology and apologize for the fact that the crowd are generally well-heeled. After all the time I have spent in America I still find this attitude bewildering. But it exists and it is just one of the problems that need to be tackled by a visible, high-profile personality to whom the average American sports writer will listen.

If, for example, Dave Anderson, the sports columnist on the *New York Times*, needs 'insider' information about some aspect of the game, how is he to find someone who is not aligned with a politically orientated group like WCT or the ATP? The Pro Council offices in New York should be his best bet, but Happer, by his own admission, is not comfortable dealing with press enquiries, while John Hewig, who held the title of Director of Communications for a few years soon after Happer assumed his position, had a history of PR work in ice hockey and basketball. What could he have told Anderson that would have been worth quoting or even using as background information? And if Hewig had tried to present the game's case after the kind of gratuitous attack launched on it by Pete Axthelm in *Newsweek* in 1987, would Axthelm have bothered to listen? However, if someone of Tony Trabert's stature had been on the phone to him next morning, he would have listened and the game might actually have had a chance of being defended instead of becoming the most convenient punching-bag for the next writer who felt it was time he wrote a good, tough piece — the kind that editors always love.

I use Trabert's name because, as a former Wimbledon champion and still the last American to win the French title on that most un-American of surfaces, red clay, Tony has kept his name in the public eye with his CBS television commentaries which, along with those by Cliff Drysdale and Fred Stolle on the ESPN cable network, are now considered to be the best in the business. Trabert is the type of tennis personality writers would listen to and respect. There is, of course, one snag. Trabert would hardly be interested in taking a full-time PR job in New York, so when Happer, who remains the most genial of men, even under fire, hits back at my criticism of his handling of the PR question with a demand for specific names, I admit it is not easy. But someone of the Trabert type has to be found. There is no other multimillion-dollar organization in the United States — and very few in the world — that does not have a high-powered public relations officer looking after its interests. Until the pro tennis administration does, it is very difficult to argue that the game does not get what it deserves, largely by default.

Association of Tennis Professionals (ATP)

Briner was another top administrator who in my view had virtually no idea of how to conduct a reasonable relationship with the press, but by the time Happer appeared, Briner's inglorious years with the ATP had come to an end. I don't know how hard the Board had to push to get rid of him because I had been eased out by then (a convenient reduction in size from 13 to 11 making Darmon and myself redundant), but he must have known the game was up because the fears voiced by Drysdale and others at that meeting in Tucson five years before had materialized to an even greater degree than we had anticipated. To the tune of a $600,000 overdraft the ATP was broke. Or as near as made no difference. When the Board had asked for detailed accounting of the Texas office expenditure, only the most rudimentary figures were produced.

Briner seemed to have no luck with the board members he had to deal with. Having seen me off, he got landed with another British Richard who was just as inquisitive and persistent in his demands as I had been. Richard Lewis — who, in 1987, took over as head of Britain's junior training programme — became ATP Treasurer soon after being elected to the Board in 1978, but it was a title without access.

'We could never get our hands on the proper accounts,' Lewis told me. 'We kept being handed two pieces of paper with "income" and "expenditure" written on them. I was no expert but they just didn't look right somehow so I got Colin Dowdeswell to see if he could decipher them.'

Dowdeswell, the former British No. 1, whose dreamy appearance conceals an intellect that allowed him to work for a high-powered financial outfit in the City in London for a while, could not make much headway without the information that was consistently being denied the board members.

'Briner kept telling us everything was OK but the whole thing was becoming a farce,' Lewis continued. 'We got ourselves involved in yet another lawsuit over the decision to set up an ATP championship near Cincinnati in opposition to our former site, Boston, and although the move had received Board approval, many of us were unhappy about the way it had been handled.'

Briner, defensive as ever in front of the players, shrugged off this latest legal battle by telling them that lawsuits and counter-suits were just common occurrences in his life.

'Then I think your life's sick!' thundered Lewis, banging the table.

Briner's colleagues on the Pro Council, of which he was Chairman, were also beginning to tire of his methods. The ATP's dispute with Boston's Longwood Cricket Club was as needlessly complicated and boring as most of the conflicts in which various factions of the game kept getting embroiled but, like most of the others, it raised the temperature and at one stage, in June 1979, five of Briner's colleagues on the Council felt obliged to write him a strongly worded letter which included, in its second paragraph, the following admonition: 'We further feel that by selectively revealing Council voting figures you are in violation of Council ethics and that you have misused your position as Chairman of the Council in dealing with the Boston issue . . .' The letter was signed by Derek Hardwick, Stan Malless, Brian Tobin — now President of Tennis Australia — Owen Williams and Lars Myhrman, the young Swede who served as a representative of the European Tournament Directors.

On reading it, I was reminded of Len Owen's lecture during the Benson & Hedges meeting and of Nick Saviano's outburst at Mission Hills. The players demanded leadership of a higher moral tone than Briner was giving them. And they demanded, too, a greater response to their wishes concerning the way in which their affairs should be run. In the most literal sense they were frequently ignored.

'At players' meetings you would sit there like a dummy with your hand raised,' Mike Estep recalled. 'And if you didn't belong to that small group who owed their allegiance to Dell, Briner would simply ignore you.'

The relationship between Briner and the rank and file became so bad that he actually threatened to sue the outspoken Australian Bill Lloyd after the player had dared to criticize the man who was receiving upwards of $80,000 a year to represent their cause.

'That just shows the state we had reached,' commented Estep. 'How can you have a players' leader suing the players he is working for?'

Briner was eventually dissuaded from following that course of action but, as Lewis had stated so bluntly, the whole thing was becoming sick and the sickness had to be rooted out. The problem was that Briner was only a symptom. In my view, the real problem was Dell.

Despite the manner in which he had sacrificed our friendship for his own political ends I took not the slightest satisfaction in arriving at that conclusion. I was, and I remain, a true admirer of Donald's enormous energy, foresight and determination. In all probability the ATP would not have grown so strong so quickly without his dynamic leadership and legal expertise. Nevertheless, tennis players are, by nature, suspicious and Dell's apparently insatiable hunger for power and influence aroused their suspicions at every turn. Compromise was a word Dell never seemed to understand and, as he launched himself into each meeting, no matter how low-key the client or how unimportant the subject, the list of the enemies he made grew longer and longer.

Like any inspiring leader, Dell enjoyed total loyalty from his original troops and this, of course, only exacerbated the situation within the ATP because jealousy was aroused every time Pro Serv, the management company Dell had formed, pulled off a deal for Ashe or Smith or Ralston. For a long time the fact that Donald's closest friends were of such unimpeachable character themselves tempered the hostility towards him, but in the end, his supporters on the Board could protect him no longer and, just before Briner finally resigned, the battle was joined to get a Board elected that would carry a majority of anti-Dell players so that, apart from cutting the strings of the puppet, the ATP could also get rid of the puppeteer.

Cliff Drysdale and Ray Moore lobbied with a great deal of political skill during Queen's in 1979 but, inevitably, personalities got involved, feelings got hurt and friendships were damaged. The anti-Dell faction needed Ashe's position on the Board to go to one of their own men and Arthur, understandably, was terribly hurt at being opposed by colleagues he had always considered to be his friends. I knew how he felt.

In the end it was a close call and when Richard Lewis, Lito Alvarez and Briner sat down to count the votes, the Executive Director pulled a wad of ballot papers from his pocket, saying that they had been received at ATP headquarters in the last few days.

'They were virtually all for Ashe and those extra votes saved him,' said Lewis.

Nevertheless, the new Board contained a sufficient number of players of the Drysdale / Moore persuasion to ensure that, within a year, Briner would have gone and the arrangement whereby Dell acted as the ATP's legal adviser would be terminated. He would, however, retain the right to act as a negotiator for television rights on behalf of the ATP.

After interviewing such disparate personalities as Dave Grant, who was President of Penn Balls at the time, and Allen Fox, tennis coach at California's Pepperdine University, the ATP Board appointed Butch Buchholz as Briner's replacement. He was the safe choice and the desire to play safe was understandable after all the ATP had been through. A fine player himself in his time, Buchholz had been a leader amongst the remnants of the old Kramer tour and, through involvement in well-run tournaments in St Louis and a player-coach job with the Hawaii WTT franchise, he had stayed in close touch with the game. Above all he was a throughly nice guy — presentable, personable and a dedicated players' man. The ATP needed that.

Buchholz made a good start on the salvage operation that was required after the financial catastrophe that Briner had left behind, but very soon the more ambitious members of the Board, led by its new President, Harold Solomon, realized that Buchholz's limitations as a top-level business executive would prevent the ATP from regaining its rightful place as a powerful entity in an increasingly business-orientated game.

'Butch had taken us up from the bottom to a certain level and we were grateful for that,' Solomon explained. 'But we felt he could only take us so far.'

Once again Drysdale was instrumental in the further change of leadership that came years after Buchholz's appointment, in 1980. Although it might have been handled in a more sensitive manner — Butch was left hanging around outside a board meeting for nearly an hour while the players decided his fate — it at least freed him to pursue one of his life's ambitions, that of building a fifth two-week, 128-player draw championship for men and women to go alongside the four Grand Slams. It wasn't easy, but after a couple of false starts at Delray Beach — where Vitas Gerulaitis now has his camp — and Boca West, the Lipton Players' International has finally settled on the lovely island of Key Biscayne and tennis is all the richer for it.

Despite renewed talk about going outside the game for a leader, the players instead appointed Mike Davies as their new Executive

Director. It was an obvious, if ironic, choice because it was Buchholz who had brought Davies into the ATP as Marketing Director when the Texas-based Welshman left WCT. For a while it worked, but with the benefit of hindsight one can see that the appointment was always going to run into problems because Davies was losing sympathy for the players' cause. There was a generation gap that was just too wide to bridge. Davies, an idealist who had fought long and hard in the trenches to make professional tennis a true profession, would have been a better choice earlier on, as Kramer's immediate successor, while there was still time to discipline the new generation. But contact had been lost and Davies' standards, deeply entrenched in the past, made it difficult for him to conceal his dislike of modern manners.

Sooner or later a crisis was going to erupt between Davies and the outspoken group of players who had been elected to the Board. After a period on the sidelines, Ray Moore was back in harness in a big way, moving towards election to the Pro Council; Solomon and Estep were as forceful as ever in their demands for players' rights, and, apart from Lewis and Dowdeswell, Brazil's Carlos Kirmayr, the future President Matt Doyle and his great friend Mats Wilander all exerted pressure on Davies to push for the new cause that erupted in the mid 1980s — a player pension fund. The Board instructed Davies to get the four Grand Slam championships to contribute large slices of their television revenues to the fund, but All England Club Chairman Buzzer Hadingham, who had done so much to improve Wimbledon's relationship with the players since taking over from the austere Sir Brian Burnet in 1983, was the first to express horror at such a suggestion and, after months of negotiations, the Board decided Davies did not have his heart in the task.

When the ATP's demands for a pension plan became public, the press had a field day with the word 'greedy' all over again, despite the fact that the ATP tried to point out that this was not an attempt to make rich players richer. A player can spend 15 years of his life making a good living ranked between No. 30 and No. 50 on the ATP computer — which means he is a terrific tennis player — and still not have enough money in the bank to secure his family's future. This is why the ATP wanted a pension plan and, given their history in fighting for players' rights, it was very difficult to suggest that Solomon and Brian Gottfried, who succeeded Doyle as President in September 1987, did not have the credentials to lead the battle to extract some kind of a percentage from the considerable sums of money that were now pouring into Wimbledon, Roland Garros, Flushing Meadow and, to a lesser extent, the Australian Open.

Back in the mid 1970s Solomon, Gottfried and several other ATP board members who were concerned about other people's bank balances as well as their own, had spent hours in hotel rooms around the world arguing with tournament directors for a more equitable prize-money spread. Too many tournament directors were all for giving the winner a nice round figure such as $50,000 — or even double that — and letting the early-round losers scratch around for the crumbs. Solomon and Gottfried were top players at the time and both would have become richer had they kept their mouths shut. Yet both felt that the middle-ranked pro as well as the youngster battling to get through the first couple of rounds needed a better break, and soon forced through legislation to that end. Shortly afterwards, Solomon and his wife, Jan, became active at tournaments on behalf of the World Hunger Project and in the course of several years many top players, including McEnroe and Gerulaitis, flew down to Florida to spend a day supporting Harold's adopted cause. One read about it occasionally — but mostly one read about greedy tennis players.

If not greedy, the ATP Board were certainly ruthless about terminating the contracts of their executive directors, and Davies found himself out of work before the end of 1986. By this time Moore, the one-time King's Road hippy who had put himself through a variety of cosmetic changes while never losing his capacity to work for change within the game, had emerged as the most potent force, not merely within the ATP but also on the Pro Council — of which, in a surprise move following Davies' departure, he had been elected Chairman. It was a nice title, and an influential one, but as all voting posts on the Council were purely honorary, Moore had to find something else to do now that his playing career was at an end.

After all those years battling over conference tables in every corner of the globe, Moore teamed up with Charlie Pasarell at the new Grand Champions' Resort which Pasarell had created out of the desert dust at Indian Wells. It was in his office in the pro shop, handling his day-to-day problems as Director of Tennis, that Moore gave me one of his deadly, impish grins and said, 'We are interviewing three guys for Davies' job and when I tell you the name of one of them, it will knock your socks off!'

As the man who had taken Jimmy Carter out of the Georgian backwoods and got him elected to the White House, Hamilton Jordan was indeed something of a surprise candidate for the role of tennis administrator, but Moore, backed up Solomon and other members of the Board, was determined to go outside the game for a change, providing the man concerned was of sufficient stature. As a former White House Chief of Staff, Jordan was, at first glance, somewhat over-qualified for the role but, as he admitted after a few months in the job, there was no shortage of politics for him to grapple with in the Byzantine world of pro tennis. Being a prudent politician, Jordan took his time finding his way through the labyrinth and one suspects his true influence on the game has yet to be felt.

Men's International Professional Tennis Council (MIPTC)

As soon as Happer arrived to take charge at the MIPTC, two of the biggest names in the game, Bjorn Borg and Guillermo Vilas, became the victims of its growing pains. Although Chatrier has only recently admitted as much, it was the Council's decision, under his chairmanship, to refuse Borg's plea for a lighter Grand Prix load in 1982 that hastened the Swede's departure from the game. Bjorn wanted to cut down on his schedule and, to make a long story short, the Council said no. Borg threatened to quit, and if they had stopped to think about precisely what characteristics are required to create a champion of Borg's pride and determination, they would have realized he was serious.

Borg's farewell appearance in the Monte Carlo Open of 1982 was a media event of extraordinary proportions, and when he lost to Henri Leconte in the second round it seemed as if everyone just packed up and left. The tournament continued, however, and was won, appropriately enough, by Mats Wilander who would assume Borg's mantle with dignity and skill, but for Borg the story was over.

In fact Monte Carlo was merely the epilogue. I had seen the final chapter being written some months before in the beautiful Parc des Eaux Vives in Geneva, where Borg had beaten the indefatiguable Tomas Smid to win his very last Grand Prix title. It was clear then that Borg was becoming bored, not so much with being Borg, but with having to play like him. In the semifinal against Manolo Orantes, Bjorn had offered a little vignette of just what kind of effort and concentration was required for him to remain at the level he had set himself.

Orantes, whose muscular frame was always suffering from some kind of pull or strain, was hobbling around trying to be competitive as Borg worked his way routinely through the first set, raking the clay court with deep penetrating drives. Then, seeing how immobilized Manolo was by his niggling injury, Bjorn decided to throw a lifetime's training to the winds and to serve and volley his way to victory.

Orantes could hardly believe his eyes. With his consummate racket skill, Manolo didn't need two good legs to pass a net rusher on slow clay. Picking his spots with barely concealed glee, the Spaniard sent little left-hand chips and drives whistling past Borg's outstretched racket and raced through the second set to win it 6–1. Borg's square shoulders rolled a little more wearily as he strode back to the baseline, a prisoner returning to his cell. He never spelled it out in so many words afterwards but I have always felt that we had just witnessed the moment that terminated Borg's career. To win, he knew he would have to go back to the old routine of grinding it out from the back court, an exhausting and often joyless method of winning tennis matches, and after 13 years of it Borg's patience was running out. He wanted to have some fun on the court and if that was not possible then he wanted to kiss the court goodbye and have fun somewhere else. Grass was a splendid summer's interlude which he had learned to master, but clay was the bread and butter of his career and the taste was beginning to sour. If the Pro Council insisted on force-feeding him, he would quit. But first, being a true champion, he would finish the task in hand, so he ground out the third set against Orantes from the baseline and, after all his appeals had failed, a few months later he simply walked away. People as close to tennis as those nine wise men on the Pro Council should not have been so surprised.

At the end of 1987, the MIPTC were being criticized for having learned its lesson. Refusing to be caught out again, it gave Ivan Lendl special dispensation to play 12 instead of the designated 14 Grand Prix events required for eligibility to participate in the bonus pool in 1988. 'Why should Lendl be a special case?' was the cry heard from those locker-room elements who still like to think all players should be treated as equals. They have a point, and the MIPTC could accommodate them so easily by simply making it a rule that *any* player who competes in a certain number of tournaments over a certain number of years, say 10, while maintaining an ATP ranking in the top 200, becomes eligible for a reduction in the number of tournaments he has to play. Then it would not matter whether his name was Ivan Lendl or Ray Moore. With a serve that had brought them triumph or disaster, they would be treated just the same.

Guillermo Vilas was not treated in the same way as other players who might or might not have been taking under-the-table guarantees from Grand Prix tournaments. For that reason, if for no other, Vilas had good cause to feel victimized in 1983 as Happer made a quite inadequate attempt to solve an insoluble problem. Someone in Rotterdam ratted on Ion Tiriac and supposedly offered Happer evidence that Tiriac had accepted additional payment for Vilas to play in the Netherlands' premier tournament. Happer seized the opportunity of making an example of Vilas and suspended him under the Grand Prix Code of Conduct, which states that players are allowed to accept only the published prize money awarded by each tournament. The case dragged on all through 1983 and, in the meantime, the proud Argentine found himself slipping out of the world's top 10 for the first time in 10 years. Happer had a right to go after Vilas but the amount of time it took to get the case heard was a disgrace.

The problem of guarantees is yet another weapon that tennis has handed to its critics on a silver platter with an invitation to perform a full frontal stabbing. 'Illegal' makes for a wonderfully emotive headline but the fact is that guaranteed-appearance money is illegal only because pro tennis, trying to be whiter than white, says it is. Golf doesn't say so. Sevvy Ballesteros or Sandy Lyle would not dream of setting foot on a golf course in Europe without having made a pre-arranged deal through their agents for appearance money. But tennis decided that, in the best of all possible worlds, a player should be rewarded only for how he performs in a particular event. Terrific. And the sun always shines at Wimbledon, too, I suppose.

If we return to the real world we discover that some players sell tickets and others don't. So a tournament director who is able to advertise John McEnroe's name ahead of time is going to have dollars in his bank account ahead of time. So no matter what the rules say, that tournament director is going to go to McEnroe's agent — or Lendl's or Edberg's because I am not picking on individuals here — and suggest a means of making it especially worthwhile for the player in question to play his tournament. Nowadays nothing so crass as cash in the hand is suggested. Other arrangements can be made whereby the tournament plays only the most distant part in the actual paying of the money. A store in the town concerned might offer the player $20,000 to make a five-minute appearance in the sports department. Nothing illegal in that. Or a local company might be persuaded to offer a deal for an endorsement during the week of the tournament. Happer discovered that was outside his jurisdiction, too.

'The guarantees have beaten the system,' Phillippe Chatrier admitted when we were discussing what he would do about the new Paris Open, which in 1987 had a weaker entry than the Stockholm Open, played in the same week, despite the fact that it was putting up 50 per cent more prize money. 'Tiriac told me immediately after Becker won last year that they would be going to Stockholm this time because of some contract he had lined up for Boris in Sweden. There was nothing illegal about it. But the only answer for us is to go on putting up the prize money. In 1988 we'll put a million dollars on the table and tell the players to come and play for it if they want to.'

Happer's fine sense of humour was strained to breaking point when I teased him about having joined the guarantee system a little while back when the Pro Council decided to introduce an involved system of rewarding top players with cash bonuses if they played more than the stipulated number of Grand Prix events.

'You can dress it up in whatever name takes your fancy, Marshall,' I said. 'But you can't escape the fact that it's a form of guarantee.'

The answer, of course, is not to make unenforceable rules. The no-coaching rule which does not allow any communication between player and coach during a match is another that often reduces the game to the level of farce and, yet again, it was Tiriac's man, Becker, who found himself being victimized at a whole string of tournaments in 1986. Boris was still with his original coach, Gunther Bosch, at the time and it got to the point where Gunther had only to shift position in his seat for the umpire to 'warn' Becker under the no-coaching rule. Once, at La Quinta, during the Pilot Pen Classic, the umpire saw Boris glance at Bosch and nod and immediately issued a warning. That was too much for Tiriac. 'Now Boris is being warned for coaching his coach,' shrugged the Romanian. 'How stupid can you get?'

In the wrong hands the rules can make everyone look a fool, but happily in the last couple of years there has been a marked improvement in the standard of officiating on the men's tour, thanks largely to the programmes instituted by Happer and his Grand Prix Supervisors, now headed by the sensible Ken Ferrar. On occasion Ferrar has been made to appear very lenient in his interpretation of alleged obscenities by one or two of the regular culprits, insisting that he never heard certain words uttered which had been picked up by some members of the press. However, as I have mentioned, we are talking about a very small cast of villains, now that the days of the early 1980s when things really were teetering on the brink of anarchy are long gone.

In 1987 three MIPTC umpires, Richard Kauffman of the United States, Gerry Armstrong from England and the young Australian Richard Ings established themselves as a trio of chair officials whom the players felt they could trust, even if they did not always agree with their interpretation of the contentious overrule law. There is always room for improvement, but these three are producing, at last, the levels of consistency needed to let the players know what is expected of them and how they will be dealt with if they transgress.

Thanks to the foresight of the ATP under Davies' leadership there was another emotive issue that pro tennis headed off at the pass before the cowboys could really go to work on it. Drugs. Given the problem that other sports are experiencing with all manner of drug abuse, it was a brilliant move on the part of the ATP to decide that it would become the first sport to police itself voluntarily by instituting drugs tests at randomly selected Grand Slam championships during the year.

During those difficult years in the early 1980s there was a handful of players on the men's tour who were having a problem with social drug-taking. Cocaine flowed freely at virtually every party they went to in New York and Los Angeles and it would have been a miracle if a bunch of young men in their twenties with ready cash to burn had not got hooked up in the glitzy habits of the super-rich. A couple have retired from the tour and I personally know of three who faced the problem, cleaned up their act and put their shattered games back together again.

Cocaine may give you a confidence high going on court but, as no one knows how long a tennis match is going to last, it is almost impossible to prescribe 'performance' drugs for a tennis player, and in any case, no one has yet devised a substance that makes you jump higher at the net or hit a smoother backhand.

Like any social activity of the times that encroaches on the way in which sport is played, the drug problem will need watching, but on that the Pro Council and the ATP are united. There is no drug problem in tennis at the moment and, under the current leadership, every effort is being made to ensure that there never will be.

20

THE EIGHTIES

By the start of the 1980s, the game was demanding, and receiving more attention than ever. The volume had been turned up and, as the money continued to pour in — the top prize for the Volvo Grand Prix bonus pool doubled to $600,000 in 1982 and then went up to $800,000 in 1985 — no amount of backstage wrangling amongst the politicians seemed to damage a sense of armour-plated affluence.

The critics went on hurling bricks at the sport, but although some sponsors expressed justifiable dissatisfaction with the new trend, Len Owen of Benson & Hedges was not hypocritical enough to complain when the uproar created by Connors and McEnroe in the Wembley final of 1981 ended up emblazoned across three columns on the front page of the *Daily Telegraph*. Sponsors were in the game for exposure and they were getting it.

Someone had to control the volume, but we were moving into an age oblivious to noise. The yells of a new breed of spectator, the sound of McEnroe's voice — 'You can*not* be serious!' — and even the very sound of the game itself, a new sound created by graphite rackets, were heralding an era of dramatic change.

There was another sound, too, but it was strangely insidious — severing communication rather than relaying it, deadening the atmosphere of the tour rather than embellishing it. It was the sound pumped into an individual's ear through the headphones of a walkman — an instrument that must have done more to destroy the art of conversation than anything since the advent of television. No sight became more prevalent on the tour than that of young men and women, laden down with gear, slumped in the seats of buses, hotel lobbies or airport lounges, isolated from the world and their fellow-travellers by the blast of music.

Again, this is not wholly the game's fault. The Western world, feeding off a steady diet of narcissistic advertising, is still enveloped in the I-me-myself generation, and tennis, as an individual sport, is the perfect carrier for just such an affliction. As the pressures to gain the competitive edge increase, so players are encouraged to turn away from comrades who are also rivals and seek ego-soothing support from a favoured few whose job it will be to offer the reassurance and praise that can no longer be found in the locker-room.

I am convinced this is not healthy. Inflated egos never had much chance of swelling past acceptable limits when faced with the withering wit of Australians like Owen Davidson or Fred Stolle. Even later, in the years of American domination, Erik Van Dillen and Eddie Dibbs used to ensure that no one got carried away by their own importance. Reverse psychology was Van Dillen's speciality.

'Don't worry, Tom,' he would say, picking on some puffed-up player who had just played quite a good match, 'no matter what people say about your forehand volley, I think it's terrific.'

With that Van Dillen would sweep out, leaving his victim practising his forehand volley in the mirror and muttering, 'What's the matter with it? I thought I was hitting it pretty good.'

All this is good schoolboy stuff and very character-building, and although I don't want to give the impression that the locker-room today is a morgue, full of stony-faced players hating each other, much of the fun and camaraderie has evaporated and at least some of it might have a chance to flower again if the players would rip off those damn headphones.

On a technical level, nothing changed the sport more than the rackets the players held in their hands. The arrival of the huge Prince frame on the market in the mid-Seventies forced the ITF to come up with specific rules about precisely what constituted a racket. Astonishingly, the old amateur officials had never thought it necessary. 'Tried the big frame back in 1938, old boy. Thing fell apart. The fame wasn't strong enough.'

That was the level of complacency I discovered when I started asking why it was perfectly legal to walk on court brandishing anything from a frying pan to one of those five-foot tall display models Donnay produced for their shops at the time. The thought that new materials, some literally brought back from space, would revolutionize tennis equipment simply had not crossed some officials' minds.

Prince changed all that and the ILTF, whether they liked it or not, were forced to legalize the new size simply because they had allowed the company to get such a foothold in the market that any attempt to make large-sized frames illegal would have resulted in another costly round of lawsuits, quite apart from wails of discontentment from elderly club players who had found the large, lightweight racket a godsend.

But for the professional it was not the size of the frame that mattered so much as its composition. Graphite, later to be mixed with fibreglass, kevlar, boron, ceramic or just plain old metal, produced one ingredient that became indispensable to anyone seeking to survive on the tour — power. Today the little clay-court masters like Beppe Merlo, Juan Couder, Istvan Gulyas or even a Hungarian of later vintage, Balazs Taroczy — a tremendously gifted player who won the Wimbledon doubles title with Heinz Gunthardt as recently as 1985 — would be blown away not so much by the power of the modern player's arm as by the equipment he uses.

'Becker would never have won Wimbledon at the age of 17 with a wood-framed racket,' McEnroe states flatly. 'The guy has wonderful talent and was unbelievably strong for a teenager but it was the racket that made the difference.'

Being a highly complex person, McEnroe conceals the heart of a traditionalist behind the brash, pop-art exterior, and he would dearly love to see a return to the days when the touch and spin and slice he could generate from his trusty Dunlop Maxply were sufficient to win him Grand Slam titles. But in 1983 he, too, was forced to make a switch to more modern equipment and, after Slazenger's John Barrett had done all the groundwork, the parent company Dunlop insisted on sticking *their* name on the new graphite model which McEnroe was to use for much of the remainder of his career. And John, of course, was only one of hundreds making the switch.

Kevin Curren clung on to his Wilson wood longer than most before his new Kneissel graphite helped propel his serve to a Wimbledon final in 1985, and Tomas Smid loved his classic Slazenger Challenge so much that he continued using it for a couple of years even though Slazenger were forced to terminate his contract. After stretching their technology to its limits by making a special wood-framed mid-size racket for Guillermo Vilas, Slazenger took Jimmy Connors in from the cold when Wilson refused to make any more of those steel T-3000s that Jimmy loved but practically no one else could play with. After several prototypes had hit the scrap heap, Connors accepted the mid-size ceramic-coated graphite model with which, by the end of 1987, he had fought his way back to No. 4 in the world.

Amongst the women, Chris Evert was the last to desert wood, finally letting go of her Lady Wilson to add much-needed power to her game with the graphite Pro Staff.

McEnroe, who is not the spent force many people believe him to be, is still thristing for more power, and he may yet find it in the latest stringing innovation to have hit the market. There have been some weird and wonderful theories about how best to string a tennis racket, with the 'Spaghetti' strings used briefly by Mike Fishbach, Christopher Roger-Vasselin and even Ilie Nastase in the 1970s being the most bizarre. However, the ITF moved quickly to have double-knotted stringing banned.

But two young Australians, Mark Woodforde and Carl Limberger, are currently using Snauwaert's High-Ten graphite and fibreglass racket, so called because its widely-spaced strings require much higher tension than normal.

Both Woodforde, a red-headed left-hander of great promise, and Limberger are protégés of Barry Phillips-Moore, a player underrated in his day who reached the semifinals of the Australian on grass and of the Italian on clay in the 1960s. Now, a bad hip has left Barry with a pronounced limp, but that does not prevent him getting out on court to teach his group of aspiring champions, feeding them pin-point returns from his static position in mid court with the touch and accuracy that are the hallmarks of the naturally gifted player.

I found Barry hard at work one sweltering afternoon at Flinder's Park soon after Australia's new National Tennis Centre had been opened to wide acclaim. With the 15,000-seat stadium and its sliding roof providing an impressive backdrop and the equally new Rebound Ace cushioned, cement-style surface beneath his feet, it seemed an ideal setting for Phillips-Moore to talk about the latest technology as tennis launched itself into the twenty-first century.

'The greater space between the strings gives you more power,' he said. 'It proved a very temperamental concept when Snauwaert first started developing it. If it was not strung at the proper tension, balls used to fly everywhere but we have got it under control now. Forty kilos is about right, compared with the 30 or below that most players use for normal rackets.'

The High-Ten uses only 12 vertical strings and 16 across as compared with the 16 vertical and 20 across used in mid-size frames. The strings themselves are made of a combination of natural gut, which is still favoured by the majority of pros, and polymer strings. Thin strands of kevlar can also be wound into the gut to add strength to a 1½-inch gauge, which is the thinnest desirable for the High-Ten racket.

By the time the post-Borgian generation of Swedes was changing the face of the men's tour in the mid 1980s, wood rackets, widespread bad behaviour, sloppy officiating and top players who travelled alone were becoming isolated relics of a bygone age. Mats Wilander, wielding his mid-size Rossignol graphite, and with his deadly two-fisted backhand, served notice of the European take-over that was about to envelop the game by winning the French Open at the age of 17 in 1982. The following year everything that Chatrier had been doing to upgrade French tennis was justified when Yannick Noah snatched away Wilander's crown to become the first Frenchman since Marcel Bernard in 1946 to win at Roland Garros. Yannick is too genuine a person to hide his tears, and when his father practically fell out of the stands in a headlong rush to embrace his son on court it became a pretty special moment for those of us who remembered the skinny kid playing under the yellow lights of that court in Yaoundé 12 years before.

The following year saw the genius of McEnroe in full flower. In between hysterical outbursts, which he was finding increasingly disruptive to his own game, the New York left-hander with a style all of his own produced some sublime tennis that was designed for another planet. Certainly few of the players who tried to breathe the same air knew which way to turn after a few minutes on court with this incredible athlete, who could slice an advantage-court serve into the first row of the stands, take a first serve as powerful as Lendl's on the rise and come in behind it and turn full-blooded forehand drives into little feathery drop shots with the split-second timing of an exquisitely turned wrist. McEnroe played 82 Grand Prix and Davis Cup matches in 1984 and lost only three. He obliterated Connors in the Wimbledon final and Lendl at Flushing Meadow, and won tournaments in such diverse locations as Philadelphia, Madrid, Toronto, Stockholm and even on clay in the WCT Tournament of Champions at Forest Hills. If he had kept his head together in that agonizing final against Lendl in Paris it would have been the greatest year of tennis anyone had played since Laver's second Grand Slam. Even so, it wasn't so shabby and in January 1985 he added the final brushwork to his canvas by painting Lendl all colours of the rainbow in the Masters final at Madison Square Garden with a score of 7–5, 6–0, 6–4.

It was difficult to believe that only 12 months had elapsed since the time when I followed him into a black Manhattan night after he had lost to Brad Gilbert 6–1 in the third set in the quarter-finals of the last Masters to be played in January 1986. 'Can I drop you at your hotel?' he asked when we found ourselves in the multi-storey car-park across the street. Unlike his millionaire peers, with their coaches and security guards and big black limousines, McEnroe had driven in from his home in the suburbs quite alone, just to play a tennis match at the Garden as he had done so often before, because it wasn't supposed to be that big a deal, just a quarter-final — and it had all gone wrong. The colours of his palette had run and his brushes made scratchy sounds as if the paint had congealed. He had embarrassed himself and he knew he could not put himself through that kind of ordeal any more.

'I've got to take time off,' he said as we drove up Eighth Avenue towards the Essex House. 'The hip's hurting and my mind's not there. This relationship with Tatum takes a lot of my energy and with the baby due in May I just want to spend time with her. I want to do normal things like other people do for a change.'

There were echoes of Borg in those sentiments, the sudden realization that childhood, adolescence and young adulthood had been passed on tennis courts, on aeroplanes and in hotel bedrooms. When I talked to him a few months later at the Malibu beach house he had purchased from Johnny Carson (the price was lowered in return for a few tennis lessons), John said, 'Hey, man, this is great. I haven't been anywhere for eight weeks and I get up wondering if I need to fix something in the house. Is this how the real world lives?'

But John's mood on Eighth Avenue back in January was as sinister as the neighbourhood, shot through with false flashes of humour about as convincing as the neon-lit signs over the movie houses offering *Pets in Paradise* or other unlikely fare, and weighed down with morose complaints about the state of his hurting body as the car lurched from one pot-hole to the next. I wondered how many ex-prize-fighters, broken and broke, had staggered down that avenue of evil when the old Garden used to stand at the corner of 48th Street. At least John would never face that fate. He had a brain and a bank account that was a lot healthier than his body. If he would take as much care of one as he did of the other, a loss to Brad Gilbert might not be the end of the road.

'It's no use fooling yourself any more,' I said. 'You're about to be 27 and you can't just walk on a court and expect to beat these young guys with no preparation. You haven't even played doubles for the last six months, so how do you think you can maintain any level of fitness, training as you do?'

'You're right, I know you're right,' he mumbled. 'I'll start a proper training routine during these weeks off the tour.'

That was one side of the complex McEnroe brain talking. By the time we hit Central Park, another pot-hole had kicked the other side into action. Banging the steering wheel with the intensity that has pushed so many opponents back from the brink of victory, he suddenly blurted out, 'Hey, but I did it for eight years, didn't I? I stayed in the top two in the world for eight years without training, that wasn't bad was it?'

There was a glint of triumph in his eyes and I had to laugh. What is the point in trying to rationalize genius? Who else could have slopped around a practice court, using doubles finals to fine-tune a game that struck chords no one had ever heard before and lasted through the longest match in Davis Cup history — the six-hour-32-minute marathon in which he beat Wilander in Cincinnati in 1982? Amazingly, it was McEnroe himself who came within two minutes of matching that record when playing against Becker during the USA-West Germany tie in Hartford, Connecticut in July 1987. Who else could have behaved with such grotesque insensitivity on court while proving himself to be such a doting father and caring supporter of children in need?

It had been the previous year at the Garden that I saw McEnroe, having just a few minutes to prepare for the doubles final which he and the often underrated Peter Fleming would win for the seventh consecutive time, beckon to a youngster of 10 or 11 who was getting brushed aside at the entrance to the players' lounge. McEnroe chatted quietly to the boy for a few seconds and then said, 'You be sure to come back after the match so we can have a real talk, OK? And if anyone tries to stop you just tell them I want to see you.' The child was suffering from Cystic Fibrosis, the fatal lung disease that the ATP had adopted many years before, at the suggestion of *Sports Illustrated* writer Frank Deford, as its official charity. Apart from Stan Smith and his wife Margie, few players had made themselves as readily available to support the fight against CF as John. And no player made the kids feel more comfortable in his presence than the man who would walk out of that locker-room and, within a few minutes of having brought a great luminous smile to the face of a sick child, start yelling like a demented banshee at some poor linesman who was trying to follow a serve travelling at 120 mph. McEnroe himself can't really explain it, so it is futile for others to try. By the time he dropped me off at the Essex House that night in January 1986 I knew that the devil in him was still as alive as his talent and that both would surface again in good time. They did and they will do so again, rearing up to bewitch and bewilder us and bother others to the point of outright hatred. Personally, whether or not he wins another match or incurs another fine, I shall be happy to keep him as my friend.

Nothing had shocked McEnroe nor, indeed, the tennirs wold at large more than the flame-haired youth who hit Wimbledon like a meteor in 1985. With Lendl, Wilander, McEnroe and Connors starting to make routine appearances in the final rounds of Grand Slam events, the men's game needed an exciting injection of new blood and Boris Becker provided a tankful. I had first seen him in Luxembourg in 1984 and by the time he had muscled his way through to the quarter-final of the Australian Open on grass at Kooyong at the end of the year, it was obvious he was special. On returning to England I had a little bet with Onny Parun, the former New Zealand No. 1 who teaches at David Lloyd's club near London's Heathrow Airport, that Becker would be in the top 10 by the US Open that autumn. I won my £10, but what none of us would have dared predict was the manner in which this phenomenally powerful 17–year-old would bludgeon his way through Wimbledon to become the youngest champion in the 108-year history of the Championships. Looking back now Boris readily admits he did not comprehend the immensity of his achievement that first year, and that, in a sense, made his repeat victory in 1986 all the more remarkable. The pressure was on him the second time around but he came through again, revealing a superb big-match temperament to go along with a genuinely world-class serve and volley game.

It was obviously in Becker's stars that he should win Wimbledon that first year, for he was within a split second of defaulting his way out of his fourth-round match against Tim Mayotte on Court 14 when he twisted the ankle he had hurt at Wimbledon the previous year. I was doing the match commentary for BBC Radio at the time, from a cramped little eyrie that allowed one a diagonal view over the heads of spectators, and I have no doubt that Boris was on his way to the net to shake hands with Mayotte when a final, desperate glance at his coach Gunther Bosch and manager Ion Tiriac persuaded him to take the three-minute time out that is allowed for injuries. ATP trainer Bill Norris, who had to be called from the locker-room at the other end of the Centre Court complex, took about five minutes to fight his way through the crowds but by then the panic in young Boris had subsided and, after having the ankle strapped, he was able to complete his victory.

Becker became the overnight sensation West German tennis had been thirsting for. The game's brightest new star had appeared in the middle of the world's most prosperous sporting market and Tiriac's clever, hard-nosed bargaining ensured that he would be financially secure for life even before he won Wimbledon the second time. Apart from various other endorsements, Tiriac got Puma to agree to a contract that was worth in excess of $26 million over six years to make a Becker line of rackets, clothes and shoes. Even for a cat like Puma it was a huge leap into the big time, but initial sales of the racket justified the outlay as the numbers soared from 15,000 a year to over 200,000 as soon as Becker's name was attached to the project.

Fame and riches of the type heaped on this young man are not easy to handle and I have nothing but the greatest admiration for the way Boris has managed to remain as polite, approachable and sane as he has over the past couple of years. When I went to watch him play Yannick Noah in an exhibition in Stuttgart in 1986, the adulation was far from being confined to squealing teenagers. Grey-haired men and women in the packed auditorium waved little flags with 'Bravo Boris!' written on them, and when the young gladiator walked into the very staid, middle-class restaurant of the hotel he was staying in, everyone burst into applause. I know several 18-year-olds who would get a very distorted view of the world's values if they were treated like that, but when Boris lost the Wimbledon title of which he was so proud to Peter Doohan in 1987 his ability to keep things in perspective was revealed for an admiring world to see.

'I haven't lost a war,' he said. 'No one got killed. I just lost a tennis match.'

It was inevitable that Becker would suffer some kind of set-back after such a supercharged start to his career and, sure enough, a combination of illness, injury and simple loss of form plagued him through much of 1987. Yet he still finished at No. 5 on the ATP computer, and was preparing to regroup under his new coach Bob Brett, a tough, no-nonsense taskmaster who was trained under Harry Hopman and who has rightly been credited with revitalizing the careers of Paul McNamee and John Lloyd.

There is no doubt that Boris had taken time to recover from the sudden departure of his original coach during the Australian Open in January 1987. It had been Gunter Bosch who first spotted the child's great potential, and, as a contemporary of Tiriac during their early years in Romania, it had been Bosch who phoned Ion and suggested he come and have a look at his young protégé. Gunter and Boris had formed a father-son relationship in the ensuing years and, in the end, Gunter became too protective. Becker is an extremely self-willed and independent young man, and when he began a steady relationship with Benedicte Courtin he found the constant presence of Gunter constantly looking over his shoulder a little irksome.

Boris needed space to breathe and to discover what it was like to be a man capable of running his own life, at least part of the time. Frankly, I think Bosch was silly not to accept this. All Boris asked for, at a subsequently much-publicized meeting at the Regent Hotel in Melbourne following his fourth-round loss to Wally Masur, was for Bosch to take some time off and allow him to travel to a few Grand Prix tournaments on his own. Gunter, however, would not agree. He felt that he could not do his job properly if he was not with Boris at every match and, within a matter of hours, told Tiriac that he was resigning.

If decisions had not been made in such haste, a compromise could have been worked out, and although something needed to give on both sides I blame Bosch more than Becker for the simple reason that the older man should have had the maturity to understand what a teenager like Boris was going through. Had he played along with the youngster's wishes there would have been every chance that Boris, who had a genuine affection for Gunter, would have been calling him from every corner of the globe asking for advice and, even for an almost permanent return to his side. But the damage has been done and, in the long run, Brett may be better equipped to offer Becker the kind of hard-driving expertise he needs at this crucial stage of his career.

The manner in which Becker rocketed to the pinnacles of the game would have been remarkable in any age, but the overall standard is now so much higher than it used to be that the elements of surprise and sheer power in his game were not sufficient to provide an answer. In fact Becker offered another example of how true champions are born and not made. West Germany had produced a whole string of talented players such as Rolf Gehring, Uli Pinner and Werner Zirngibl in the 1970s and had lavished them with clothing contracts and deals to play for wealthy clubs in the Bundesliga. Although none was quite Grand Slam title-winning material all could have achieved a lot more than they did had they possessed Boris' burning desire to succeed. Not for Becker the comforts of a Mercedes, a nice flat and a little local adulation, Boris wanted the world and it wasn't his muscles or his Puma graphite racket that ensured he got it. It was his mind.

The way standards have improved was brought home to me many times on the tour as it developed and spread in the 1980s. I remember watching Tim Wilkison and Mark Dickson play a quarter-final in an ATP tournament in Bahrain in March 1984. There were barely 100 people watching on the court at the Holiday Inn. The desert heat bounced back off the shiny cement surface and there was nothing but ATP computer points, pride and a little bit of money at stake. Yet the two muscular Americans went at it hammer and tongs and sometimes the ball travelled so fast that it was difficult to pick up in the glare of the Arabian sun. Wilkison, whose insatiable enthusiasm for the game was given well-deserved opportunities to flower against Tim Mayotte at Wimbledon and against Becker at Flushing Meadow in 1987, went on to win that tournament in Bahrain but neither he, nor Dickson, nor the American he beat in the final, Terry Moor, was ranked in the top 30 in the world at the time, and I wondered how many top-20 players of the previous decade could have lived with the kind of tennis Wilkison and his colleagues produced that week.

A sort of bush telegraph lets other players know when a special match is in progress, which is why the whole locker-room emptied at the Yo-yogi Stadium in Tokyo during the Seiko Super Tennis Classic in 1983, when Ramesh Krishnan beat Mats Wilander in a match that had their fellow players swooning at the courtside. Because that was the way his grandfather taught him, Krishnan hits the ball flat, with virtually no top-spin, just as his father, the great Ramanathan, did. Despite a squat and rather unathletic looking figure, Ramesh is therefore blessed with a style as smooth as silk, and when it flows like a sari in the wind not even a man of Wilander's skills can unravel it. Aesthetically it will remain one of the most pleasing matches I have ever witnessed and for sheer sustained quality, it was also the Seiko of 1987 that demonstrated just what levels of excellence the game has reached. Lendl was playing Edberg in the final, and the Czech won the first set on the tie-break. People keep talking about Edberg's lack of fighting qualities and after the way Ivan had beaten him in the Wimbledon semifinal the previous summer, it would have been reasonable to expect Edberg to succumb to an apparently inevitable fate. But Stefan's British coach, Tony Pickard, is not interested in working with people who do not fight and although Stefan's on-court posture often suggests a man in despair, he has proved often enough in the last couple of years that Pickard's lessons have been absorbed.

Far from succumbing, Edberg kept serving and volleying on the medium-paced Supreme carpet, time and again countering Lendl's thunderous service returns with brilliantly played half-volleys. Often these were turned, almost involuntarily, into drop shots, so Edberg got Lendl where he wanted him — at the net — by unorthodox means. And when it came to quick-fire volley exchanges, eyeball to eyeball, the Swede could always back himself to come out the winner. One of the innovations of the Seiko that year was the introduction of a tiny camera eye attached to the central net-strap, which gave an ankle-high, upward-looking view of the volleyer as he charged in. One point, in which Edberg reacted to three Lendl forehands, power-driven from mid court, somehow getting his racket on all three in the space of a couple of seconds, made breathtaking viewing on the replay, quite apart from offering spectacular evidence of why Edberg was able to come back and win that match 6–7, 6–4, 6–4. Seldom has either man played better.

For sheer drama, nothing I have ever seen recently has surpassed the superb Benson & Hedges final at Wembley in 1986, when yet another young Swede, Jonas B. Svennson, introduced himself to British audiences by fighting back from two sets to love down against Yannick Noah to stretch the giant Frenchman to 7–5 in the fifth. In a way, it was an introduction to Britain for Yannick, as well, because his appearances at Wimbledon had been both brief and infrequent as a result of the catalogue of injuries that has plagued this superb athlete throughout his career and, as he admitted to me, he had never felt at ease in London. 'I have to feel good in a city to play well in it,' said Noah. 'I have just never discovered what makes London tick.'

That had changed on this visit as soon as Noah checked into the newly-furbished Piccadilly Hotel, now managed by the French chain Meridien, and his play immediately reflected his happier mood. The tennis he produced in warding off Svennson's wonderfully mature challenge in the fifth set was as spectacular as anything Wembley has ever seen — and, in tennis terms, dating back to the pros of the old London Professional Championships when the Kramer pros played there, it has seen a lot. Once again, slow-motion replays on television revealed just what kind of athleticism is required to win tennis matches in this modern age as Noah, heading into the fourth hour of a physically exhausting battle, lunged for a backhand and then, with muscles bulging, pivoted and projected himself back across the net to reach a forehand volley at full stretch. Finally British audiences came to understand what the French had been getting so excited about.

Roy Emerson, who found an attic hotel room for nine francs a night just off the Champs Elysées one year when he won the French title in the early 1960s, may have a hard time coming to grips with the fact, but living accommodation has become of primary importance to the top players on today's tour. Call them spoiled if you like, but Noah's satisfaction with his surroundings had everything to do with his winning at Wembley, and the following February, that moody Slav Miloslav Mecir offered further proof of the theory that a calm and unfussed mind is required to win big titles in the 1980s.

I refuse to believe it was coincidence that, of all the players competing in the 1987 Lipton Players' International, Mecir was one of the very few staying at a quiet, pleasant little motel on the island of Key Biscayne, where the tournament was being played, instead of at the official hotel which was a concrete monstrosity situated in a virtual no-go area of crime-ridden, downtown Miami.

The porter at the Bell Captain's desk, which caught the full blast of fumes from the underground parking lot serving as an inviting entrance to a hotel that started eight storeys up, actually advised us not to walk across the street to an Italian restaurant. 'Bad neighbourhood, mister,' he said. 'People get mugged around here all the time.'

So while most of the players wandered around the indoor shopping mall and whiled away their time between matches sitting in the gloomy lounge, Mecir was strolling along the beach at his motel, free of fumes, traffic, muggers and elevators filled with characters you just knew were armed to the teeth with switchblades if not actually with guns.

'I have my family with me and at night we walk under the stars,' Mecir told me one night as we dropped him off at the Silver Sands Motel, which looked as if it had been built when Alan Ladd was kissing Veronica Lake in some wonderful B movie that had Ronald Reagan in a supporting role. But Mecir looks a little out of date himself, not merely because of his quaintly old-fashioned preferences — he actually prefers Prague to New York — but also as a result of the deceptively leisured manner in which he plays the game. Like McEnroe, he is an individual talent with a very individualistic view of a world he was not quite ready for, and I'll warrant he would never have stayed around long enough to beat Lendl in the final had he been staying with the rest of us in downtown Miami.

Stefan Edberg was, and he lost to Mecir early on, producing one of his few inconsistent performances of the year. In 1988 Edberg was not planning to play the Lipton. 'There is no point in going somewhere if you don't feel comfortable,' says Pickard with irrefutable logic. This attitude is very tough on a tournament chairman who has worked as hard as Butch Buchholz and his brother Cliff have. They battled through untold problems with local authorities and resort-owners in Florida before finally finding what, one fervently hopes, will be a permanent resting-place for that Buchholz dream of a fifth Grand Slam Championship. But although the tournament site is fine — and will be spectacular when some permanent stadiums and locker-rooms are built — there are very few hotels of any standard in Florida that are interested in making deals on room rates in February and March, even if some of their discounted guests do bring prestige and publicity with their name-tags. If hoteliers can fill the rooms in their beachside palaces at $250 each a night and upwards, why bother with tennis players?

Only the tour millionaires can afford those sorts of prices, so Buchholz was forced to billet the tournament off the island, a solution that has definitely resulted in the event's having a weaker field in 1988 than its stature and level of prize money entitles it to. Knowing Butch, he will find a solution, but the problem illustrates perfectly the state of affluence that the game has reached. Although the Pro Council has won the right to 'hard-designate' players to a certain number of Nabisco Grand Prix tournaments each year, to ensure that no Super Series event is left without a reasonable quota of the top 10, the superstars can pick and choose as long as they complete the regulation number of 14 Grand Prix events in a calendar year. So the location of the tournament, the standard of hospitality and accommodation and the general ambience are — along with such technical considerations as the surface — the factors that determine where a player will compete. The choice is enormous and the temptations limitless and there is nothing more valuable to a player in heavy demand than a well-planned schedule that does not have him careering around the globe attempting to fulfil a never-ending series of commitments. IMG seldom got their priorities right with Bjorn Borg during the early part of his career, but sometimes it is the player's fault. McEnroe, who changes his mind every minute, has never got it right, and both his tennis and his temper have suffered as a result.

The success of the sport is such that the pressure is on everybody now, because a limitless number of cities want tournaments but they all want the top five players in the world to play in them. As this is a total impossibility, the market demand is far in excess of what the market can provide but, such is the appeal of the game and the excitement its life-style offers that, no matter how often they get burned, promoters keep coming back for more. People like Jochen Grosse in Cologne, Ken Catton in Hong Kong and Rolf Klug in Munich have all suffered the kind of set-backs that would have sent them off in search of some more profitable business had not tennis been so appealing. That is the game's strength and will continue to be so as it faces the challenges of the future.

It is ironic that so many tournaments are now thriving as a direct result of the involvement of the management companies such as the IMG and Pro Serv at a time when yet another lawsuit is questioning the very legality of that involvement. Ever since Philippe Chatrier found the man he was looking for in Marshall Happer, a full-time administrator with a proper staff who could run the day-to-day affairs of the Pro Council, battle has been enjoined with the agents to stop Donald Dell and Mark McCormack from seizing total control of the game. As we have seen, there was a time when Dell wanted total control, but I doubt if McCormack ever harboured such ideas and although Chatrier has been wise to be on his guard, the dangers have sometimes been exaggerated.

The one thing that, quite understandably, stuck in Philippe's throat was the fact that the Grand Prix's biggest showcase, the Masters at Madison Square Garden, was run and virtually owned by Dell and sponsored by Volvo, a company Dell had brought into tennis and with whom he had extremely close relations. This, of course, was a hangover from the days when Dell was intimately involved in setting up the whole Grand Prix tour with Kramer. Relationships had changed rather dramatically in the intervening years and as soon as the Volvo contract ran out, the Pro Council moved swiftly to sever the Dell connection, bring in Nabisco as the new Grand Prix sponsor and install *Tennis Week* publisher Gene Scott as tournament director.

The moves that followed were typical of the smash and grab, sue and counter-sue way big business operates in America. At Dell's urging, Volvo stayed in tennis — which was great for the game — and continued to sponsor individual tournaments that were now part of what was properly called the Nabisco Grand Prix tour. By virtue of some clever advertising, Volvo made it look as if they were still running a circuit themselves and Happer, reacting angrily, set the legal battle in motion by suing on behalf of the Pro Council. At the base of the Council's complaint was the fact that both Pro Serv and the IMG were beginning to manoeuvre themselves into a position whereby they owned, managed and ran an event in which players *they* acted for were playing and for which *they* handled the television rights. Although he does less of it these days, Dell even did the television commentary himself. It was great business but quite obviously unfair to those players who did not happen to be managed by the right firm.

Advantage International, formed by Dell's breakaway partners, Frank Craighill and Lee Fentress in April 1983, saw the problems and vowed to stick with managing players and to stay out of the tournament business. They also stayed out of the counter-suit that was filed by Pro Serv, the IMG and Volvo and which, but for a New York judge who obviously thought the whole thing was a waste of time, would have put the game back in the wrong sort of court. In his first ruling after wading through two years of paper work, US District Judge Kevin Thomas Duffy dismissed anti-trust claims filed against the Pro Council by Volvo and the two management companies, but said that Volvo could replead on cases of alleged breach of contract, fraud and defamation, all of which the Council vigorously deny. The Council itself is continuing the action because

Jimmy Connors, as vocal as ever with his new Slazenger Ceramic racket.
Photo: Christophe Guibbaud

Ouch! Treatment in Little Rock, Arkansas during one of his 'Tennis Over America' exhibition tours with Guillermo Vilas, reminds John McEnroe of all the times he had not paid sufficient attention to his body.
Photo: R. Evans

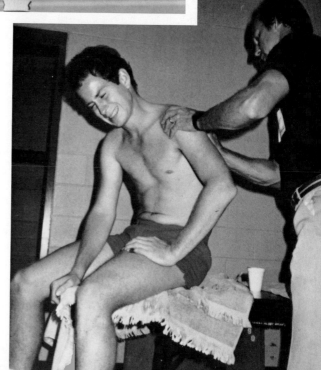

The Chris Evert smile we all so rarely see on court captured in all its
radiance by ace photographer Mel Di Giacomo.

But to call her Miss Stone Face would be misleading, too!
Photos: Melinda Phillips

The Victory Smile! Honed to a state of near physical perfection Pat Cash celebrates winning the Davis Cup for Australia over Sweden at Kooyong. Justifiably Neale Fraser, the most successful Davis Cup captain of the Open Tennis era, looks just as happy. *Photo: All-Sport*

Yannick Noah in action against
Eddie Edwards during the first
week's play at Flinder's Park
where the Centre Court Stadium
won unanimous plaudits from
all the players. The top tier of
the roof is the part that moves.
Photo: R. Evans

Steffi Graf won the second
Grand Slam title of her career
at Flinder's Park to cement
her position as the new World
No 1.
Photo: Christophe Guibbaud

Chatrier is determined to get a clear ruling, particularly in America, as to who, precisely, has a right to govern the world-wide game. It is reasonable to want the backing of the law to that end, but whether tennis needs the time and expense it will take to acquire it — let alone the poor publicity — is another matter.

As a result of this latest family squabble, all tournament directors involved in the Nabisco Grand Prix or the Challenger Series — which carries ATP computer points and is specifically designed for the up-and-coming player — are required to reveal the exact nature of the deals they make with the management companies, so as to prevent Pro Serv or the IMG being part-owners of tournaments in which their players compete. This has now become a Grand Prix rule and although it is basically a good one, it merely means that a certain amount of reorganization is taking place at a few tournaments so as to continue old relationships under a different guise.

Eric Drossart, a former Belgian Davis Cup player, is no longer officially associated with the Belgian Indoors — a tournament he was instrumental in creating — because he just happens to be head of the IMG's Tennis Division in London. Yet it was Drossart's marketing expertise that made the tournament what it is. This is something of an exceptional case because Drossart and the tournament grew together whereas, in most cases, it has been a question of tournaments calling in a management company to upgrade and modernize their entire marketing operation. At the very top Mark McCormack did the job personally on behalf of Wimbledon, and members of his staff have been equally successful in attracting huge amounts of sponsorship money to long-established but previously ailing events such as the West German Open in Hamburg and the Italian Open at the Foro Italico.

The sponsored tented-village concept started appearing at Wimbledon in the early 1980s and, as soon as the rebuilding programme at Stade Roland Garros allowed, the French Open soon had the champagne corks popping in tents bearing names such as Hertz, Lacoste and Daniel Hechter. Nowhere has the idea transformed the look and fortunes of a tournament so dramatically as in Rome, where the unmistakable figure of Cino Marchese, with his long silver hair, dark glasses and welcoming smile, has presided, on behalf of the IMG, over a new era for the Italian Open.

Since the matinée idol Adriano Panatta and his popular little sidekick Paolo Bertolucci had faded from the scene, attendance figures at the Italian Open had slumped alarmingly and it needed someone like Marchese, who understood the Roman temperament, to bring people back. By creating a sponsors' village behind the marble-tiered Centre Court and persuading Italian television to set up a live, late-night talk-show at one of the café tables, Marchese turned the Foro Italico back into a place where one just had to be. The days of La Dolce Vita on the Via Veneto may never return, but there is a little slice of that life simmering again every spring when the tennis comes to town, and Romans who like to think they know where the action is cannot afford to miss it.

In 1987 Marchese even persuaded Romans to come and watch women play tennis which, to those of us who had attended the event in the pre-Open days, was the biggest miracle of all. Back in the 1960s, great champions like Ann Jones and even local stars such as the delightful Lea Pericoli, who is now a huge television star in Italy, were scheduled for 9.00 am so that their matches could be got out of the way before the crowds arrived at noon. Either chauvinism is on the decline in Europe or the macho male is simply coming to terms with the fact that women can perform in an athletic arena. In any case, in 1987 over 60,000 people turned out to watch the women's Italian Open which, after a couple of years in limbo, had been moved from Perugia and was played the week immediately preceding the men's event. By mixing a little flair and imagination with some sensible support from the Italian Federation, Marchese had revitalized the game in Rome and given the city a new fashionable focus spread over two weeks in May.

In Canada, John Beddington, an Englishman who went to work for McCormack at the IMG headquarters in Cleveland in the 1970s, has created much the same kind of success story over a longer period. In 1978 Beddington moved to Toronto and took over the Canadian Open, which the previous year had attracted just 29,000 spectators for a championship for both men and women. Realizing the rivalry that exists between French and English-speaking Canada and sensing the need to satisfy both the nations' major cities, Beddington struck on the idea of alternating the men's and women's events between Toronto and Montreal. The format has proved such a diplomatic and commercial success that in 1987 the Canadian LTA, on whose behalf Beddington runs both events, cleared one million Canadian dollars in profit with a total of attendance of 196,000 — 118,000 for the men in Montreal and 78,000 for the women in Toronto.

'Like so many tournament directors I have to rely on a large volunteer staff,' Beddington told me. 'If I had to pay commercial rates for drivers, social hostesses and people who look after all the little incidentals of an enterprise this big, the profit margin would be cut to nothing.'

That, of course, is where tennis benefits in comparison to so many other businesses. Finding volunteers to staff an exhibition of cement-mixing equipment is not quite as easy. So even now, when so much has been streamlined and professionalized in this multimillion-dollar age for the sport, amateur volunteers still play a valuable role — providing they are serious about the task they have undertaken. Beddington's helpers obviously are and he is one of a small handful of tournament directors who make the players feel so well cared for that many write to say thank you afterwards. To return to my original point, it is no surprise, therefore, that the Canadian Open has enjoyed consistently top-quality fields over the past few years.

'For the superstars, money is not the incentive,' says Beddington. 'They can earn pots of the stuff anywhere they choose. You just have to work very hard to make sure they enjoy your tournament for all the usual reasons people enjoy visiting a place — the level of comfort, the hospitality, the warmth of the welcome. This is what makes them come back and, over the years, I really haven't had too many problems with any of the game's so-called bad boys.'

In San Francisco, Barry MacKay is another successful tournament director who would tell you a similar story. MacKay remembers what it was like to play in dreadful places and get treated like a hired hand in the darker days of the Kramer tour. The fact that someone as picky as McEnroe keeps going back year after year says all that needs to be said about the way MacKay looks after his players at the TransAmerica Open.

So, yes, the top players of today are pampered and not all of them are as gracious about it as they could be, but the cynicism and jealousy they have to contend with is largely unwarranted. They are simply extremely fortunate and they know it. Top-class pro tennis is very hard work, but basically they love it and get rich doing it. Is there something wrong with that? There have been one or two who played just for the financial rewards the sport brought them without really liking tennis at all. Gene Mayer was one. The son of a Hungarian coach who brought his family to America, where both sons were born, Gene was even more talented than his elder brother Sandy and, by 1980, had swept effortlessly into the world's top 10 with his wonderfully gifted two-handed game. But six years later, just as he was approaching 30, he took the fortune he had amassed and retired to Long Island to enjoy a family life with his wife. Rather than his having any lack of passion for the game itself, it was, I suspect, the itinerant life-style that Mayer could not take any longer and there have been many similar instances of less talented players leaving the tour because they simply could not stand such an unsettled nomadic existence.

But the suggestion that the majority of players are interested only in the money is refuted time and again when someone like Ken Rosewall, Ilie Nastase, Jimmy Connors or Guillermo Vilas reaches an age when most reasonable athletes would retire. Retire? How could they? They're hooked. They continue to play because they want to, not because they have to. Connors, Rosewall and Vilas are rich enough never to have to lift a finger, let alone a racket, ever again, but these people simply love to compete and love to be on a tennis court. Nastase loves it so much, he will play with anyone. In his insatiable, childlike enthusiasm for his chosen stage, he reminds me of Sammy Davis Jnr, one of the truly great entertainers, who admitted, 'I'm a ham. I know it. I open up the freezer; the light comes on and I do 10 minutes, immediately!' The love these great talents have for tennis transcends the embarrassment they feel at not playing as well as they used to. Their egos are accustomed to punishment and, like Rosewall's colleagues on the Grand Masters tour, they just take it on the chin and keep on going.

When he was guest of honour at the WCT finals in Dallas in 1987, Jean Borotra was complaining that his doctor had told him to lay off for a bit because of the fall he had taken at his home in Paris the previous winter. But Borotra refused to believe that was the end. Why, he wanted to know, should it be too late for a come-back just because you are 89?

Although Borotra plays purely for fun on private courts around Paris, the advance in sports medicine and the increased interest in the game at all levels has meant that more and more stars of yesteryear are still active in organized tournament play and this is one of the most pleasing aspects of the way tennis has developed through the last turbulent 20 years.

The number of players who are actively interested in putting something back into the sport is also increasing. Vitas Gerulaitis, whose foundation in New York was instrumental in helping to start up a little series of matches between Harlem and Brixton, is now in charge of a large camp at Delray Beach, Florida where the accent is on helping tomorrow's generation of players. Vitas, Arthur Ashe and Harry Hopman were all sufficiently committed to the cause to make their way out to Brockwell Park in south London for the first Brixton–Harlem match five years ago which had come about once I discovered what great work a Jamaican-born Lambeth

Council worker called Orville Brown was doing with his Saturday morning coaching sessions. Orville had come to watch a Britain v Jamaica match I had staged on Clapham Common with the help of Richard Russell, the most talented player ever to emerge from the West Indies, who brought two of his Jamaican players to compete against John Feaver, Richard Lewis and John Paish. The idea, then as now, was to show youngsters from the inner cities that tennis is not just a rich man's game played behind the walls of plush country clubs. I did not know Orville at the time but, by dangling the bait, I had hoped that someone like him would come to the Clapham Common match and make himself known to us. Happily that was precisely what Orville did and with the help of Vitas and his friend Peter Fishbach, who organized the first match in Harlem, we have been able to spread the word; taking it out onto the streets and parks of neighbourhoods where tennis is not normally considered a viable alternative to football, boxing or athletics.

It is a worldwide endeavour and in Melbourne Paul McNamee is involved in a scheme with similar goals. Prior to the Australian Open each year, McNamee hosts a fund-raising day to finance his VicTennis Foundation which is also committed to drawing some of the less privileged children into the tennis fold.

In Madras, a combined effort by the Nabisco subsidiary Britannia, which is funding the project, and the Amritraj family, has set up a training school under David O'Meara, a Peter Burwash coach, for eight of the best young players in India. Under the motherly eye of Maggie Amritraj, who dotes on them as caringly as she did over her own sons, they all benefit from the frequent week-long visits made to Madras by Anand, Vijay and Ashok as well as by Nabisco's roving ambassador Rod Laver. It remains to be seen whether they become champions but, whatever level they reach, they are sure to be a welcome addition to the tour because neither Mrs Amritraj nor any Burwash coach will stand for anything less than exemplary behaviour.

These are just some of the examples of how tennis is reaching out beyond its traditional constituency to draw in talent that otherwise might never have the chance to develop, and so offer children from all strata of society the chance to enjoy a life-style that has become one of the most envied in the world.

FLINDER'S PARK

'The future is now.' For once the giant frame of Ted Tinling was dwarfed by the tiered seating rising on all sides of him as he stood on the Centre Court at Flinder's Park to introduce the first day's play at the 1988 Australian Open. As usual Tinling had got it right. Cosy Kooyong, with its crumbling concrete bowl and picturesque old clubhouse, was now the past, and sat deserted and forlorn on this day of celebration for Australian tennis.

In fact it was more than that. It was a celebration for the game world-wide. The great, circular edifice, sprayed eggshell green to blend with the grassy banks of the River Yarra that flows nearby, was a tribute to the status tennis was enjoying 20 years after its radical transformation into a truly modern sport. The fact that the Premier of Victoria, John Cain, had dipped into government coffers to finance a vast multipurpose arena and adjoining complex that was built primarily for tennis and would, indeed, be run by Tennis Australia was a reflection of public interest in a game that had earned Australia so much international prestige over the years.

The new complex was to serve as a National Tennis Centre, to be used all year round by the public, and that had, of course, eliminated any possibility of retaining grass courts. Lovely to play on and lovely to look at, grass is a luxury that, perhaps, only a club like Wimbledon can afford. Apart from one mixed doubles to draw the sap just before the Championships start, no one sets foot on the Centre Court at Wimbledon from one year to the next. Flinder's Park would need something far more durable to weather the pounding of the public's feet and when the Australian players, led by Paul McNamee, convinced Tennis Australia President Brian Tobin that synthetic grass was still not ready for professional use, a new surface called Rebound Ace was introduced to the game and added to the feeling of newness that permeated every aspect of a championship that, possibly for the first time, put the Australian Open on an equal footing with its Grand Slam brethren.

Not surprisingly, a political feud lay behind the creation of what is now by far the most modern tennis facility in the world.

Factions amongst the committee at Kooyong, which is a private members' club, dragged their feet when Tobin told them that a major rebuilding job was needed on their grounds if the Open was to retain its status in the international game. Original proposals were blocked and, after several warnings, Tobin called their bluff and went off in search of funds to build an entirely new complex. By the time Kooyong realized they were about to be left with a cupboardful of cups and a lot of memories, it was too late. In the face of considerable opposition from conservationists who were loath to see concrete rise on another little slice of Melbourne's parkland, Premier Cain had given the go-ahead for the National Tennis Centre to be built just across the railway tracks from the Melbourne Cricket Ground. It is no more than 15 minutes' walk from the top of Collins Street — which means that its geographical equivalent in London would be a new Wimbledon built in Regent's Park.

Every politician likes to be associated with success, but Cain's frequent appearances at Tobin's side during the championships were well-justified and, when I found the pair of them peering over the head of some spectators out on Court 12, watching an Australian pair play doubles, it was obvious the Premier's interest was real.

'I've just done an interview for the BBC with Ivan Lendl and it seems he's your biggest supporter,' I told Tobin. 'He loves the place.'

'No, I'm Brian's biggest supporter,' Cain interjected and it was tough to argue with that. But for Tobin himself, the fortnight was to prove a triumph few could have foreseen just a couple of years before. Strongly tipped to take over as President of the International Tennis Federation whenever Chatrier decides to move on to greater things, Tobin has come a long way since his days as a bank clerk and a nationally ranked player.

Jenny Hoad, who was a top player herself before she married Lew in 1956, remembers going to collect the £20 pocket money on which amateur players of the era were supposed to exist for weeks on end, from a bank in Collins Street.

'I peered through the little grille and there was Brian counting out the notes,' Jenny recalled when the Hoads received their invitation to attend the opening with a host of other Australian Champions. 'It's a short hop from that bank to Flinder's Park but Brian seems to have travelled a bit further, doesn't he?'

That the Flinder's Park tournament was such a stunning success was not simply on account of a brilliantly designed stadium, or even of the fact that the whole event finished with a flurry of memorable and thrilling matches. It is the people who matter most, the people who run a tournament and add the personal touch. From tournament director Colin Stubs, top officials such as John McInnes, Colin MacDonald and Dr John Fraser to the guys who run the friendliest transport service at any tournament in the world and, most importantly for those of us who arrive to send back the written or electronic word, Tony Peek and Sharon Hanly in the press room, everyone radiates that warm, sunny disposition that is a hallmark of the Australian character. Just as much as cushioned acrylic courts and sliding roofs, it is this that has sent Flinder's Park soaring past Flushing Meadow in most people's estimation as the Grand Slam event they most enjoy visiting second only to Wimbledon and the French Open. The new team at the top of the USTA, Gordon Jorgensen and his vice-president, David Markin, are trying hard to add a softer touch to the US Open, but there are still too many people in positions of power whose brusque impatient attitude — outside New York it would be called rudeness — only makes the roar of the jet engines and the noise of the restless crowds all the more intolerable.

It is a pleasure to sit amongst an Australian crowd where you can listen to informed, intelligent comments about the players and their games from everyone from grandma to grandson. So as the tournament moved towards its climax, the spectators, as play on the outside courts tapered off, finally flowed in to fill the main stadium to its 15,000 capacity, where they revelled in a series of matches that will be remembered as much for their own merits as for the spectacular setting in which they were played.

Only Chris Evert's embarrassing slump in the middle of her final against Steffi Graf perplexed the spectators seated around me on the edge of the press area. 'Why's she missing so much?' someone asked. 'That's so unlike Chris.'

There were two answers to that. Firstly Chris had been completely thrown by the difference she found on returning to the court at 1–2 down after the roof had been closed because of a forecast predicting more prolonged rain. Steffi had practised indoors before the tournament while Chris had been playing an exhibition up at Sanctuary Cove in Queensland and for Steffi it was paying off. But, just as importantly, it was the weapon that the West German teenager was able to bring to bear on a disorientated opponent that was forcing Chris into error. The Graf forehand is the hardest shot women's tennis has ever known. Martina hits hers hard, and Chris is used to that, but the sheer velocity Steffi generates from that windmill wind-up and vicious top-spin is something previously experienced only on the men's tour. For a while Chris either got caught hopelessly out of position or was simply late on her shot as she tried to fend it off rather than hit it back. In the game's most futuristic arena, we were witnessing the first glimpse of the future of the women's game. Long-legged athletes who can hit the ball as Miss Graf does will soon become the norm.

Pride stood between Miss Evert and a humiliating defeat and pride won the day, as it always will with a champion of her calibre. Suddenly, from the very brink of defeat at 1–6, 1–5, Chris plucked enough first serves out of a previously troubled delivery to win her first game since the sky and, in psychological terms, her sky, had been shut out, and then proceeded to reel off a string of five consecutive games to lead 6–5 and come within two points of the set at 30 all. Concentrating on getting the ball deep to Steffi's backhand and then swinging it away wide to the forehand with far greater confidence and power than before, the woman who had never failed to reach the final of the Australian Open in the course of six visits to Melbourne was suddenly dictating the course of play. For the first time, Steffi looked her age as her backhand, carrying too much under-slice, plopped into the net and her first serve wavered. Even if she had not started dripping with sweat, the attack of nerves would have been obvious. But it is OK for champions to get nervous. It's how they deal with the nerves that counts.

'We all choke,' Rod Laver told me once. 'That's all right. We're not machines. What you have to learn to do is to accept the fact and not panic. It's the panic that loses you matches, not the nerves.'

One senses Steffi must have known that as she climbed out of the cot. Faced with the greatest winner in modern women's tennis, this 18-year-old, who had lost her last two Grand Slam finals — both to Martina — did not panic. Rather, she forced her way into the tie-break and then, shaking the tension out of her arm, got the forehand back in gear and simply out-hit Chris to take the breaker by seven points to three, thus claiming the second Grand Slam title of her young but already brilliant career.

Chris, of course, was furious with the way she had played in the middle of the match but relieved, too, that she had salvaged some honour from the occasion. And, in any case, the tournament had been a personal triumph for her from the moment she had made it to the final by beating Martina in the semis. At their 76th meeting, Chris' trombone had simply blown the more sonorous tune. You could tell by the sound of the ball coming off her racket that, having swept aside the promising young West German Claudia Porwik in the quarters, Chris had discovered the rhythm required to get the best out of the heavy and frequently fluffy South Korean balls which were Tennis Australia's least happy innovation. 'You have to really hit through them,' said Chris, 'otherwise they just don't go anywhere.'

The balls seemed to reduce the pace of the Rebound Ace court, thereby giving a baseliner time to pass and, as Martina struggled for timing on her volleys, Chris surprised her by going for many more passes down the line off her backhand than usual. Despite a brave fight back in the second set that took her to a 5–3 lead, it was not Martina's day and, after a net cord had finally offered her a tiny speck of luck, all she could do was turn to her new coach, Tim Gullikson, and let out a sarcastic laugh. Creating wonderful angles and pounding her two-handed backhand with ever increasing confidence, Chris broke serve twice in quick succession to narrow the gap in that incredible 15-year rivalry, claiming her 36th victory to Martina's 40. It was, incidentally, the first time Miss Navratilova had failed to reach the final of a Grand Slam championship since Helena Sukova had beaten her in the semifinal at Kooyong in 1984.

After her loss to Lori McNeil at the previous year's US Open and, even worse, a first-round defeat at the hands of yet another German, Sylvia Hanika, in the Virginia Slims Championships at Madison Square Garden in November 1987, there had been talk of retirement for Miss Evert. But Chris insists she never countenanced the thought, despite suggestions that she should from people who really had her best interests at heart. Now, of course, her determination to continue had been completely vindicated. Happy with her new boy-friend, ace skier Andy Mill, Chris was playing on for the same reason Nastase, Vilas and all the rest of them play on — because she loves it. Chris won't go on as long as some of her male contemporaries if her ranking starts to drop below No. 4 in the world but, after the way she played at Flinder's Park, there is no immediate danger of that, and anyway, as she told me one evening after practising with all the intensity of that little teenager I had first glimpsed at Forest Hills all those years before, 'One win over Martina in a Grand Slam is worth another six months' incentive to keep going.'

In the men's singles the fairy-tale ending that would have transported the nation off the end of the bicentennial rainbow was kept alive until the very last gasp. But reality tends to intrude sooner or later and, in the end, Mats Wilander won his third Australian title for the simple reason that he played the more consistent and effective tennis during the course of a final, against Pat Cash, that was as good as anyone could have hoped for.

Pat Cash's victory at Wimbledon the previous summer had been a greater triumph over pain and adversity than many people realized. Often criticized as a teenager for his abrasive personality, Cash, who has been coaxed as well as coached with great under-standing throughout his career by Ian Barclay, eventually learned to channel that Irish fire into his tennis. He used it, too, to fuel his determination to overcome a major back problem that took him off the circuit for nine months in 1985 and sent his top-10 ATP ranking plummeting into the 400s. After numerous consultations with specialists, Cash decided to opt for a chymopapain injection into a disc in his lower back. The injection would reduce the fluid in the sac bulging from the disc and so alleviate the pressure on the nerves.

As Bruce Matthews of the *Melbourne Sun* recounts so graphically in his book on Cash, the player was given only a local anaesthetic and it didn't do much to dull the pain. 'I thought I was going to die when they put the needle into the disc,' Cash told Matthews. 'I was moaning and I could feel my back go into spasms straight away. I was almost asleep and it was just like a nightmare. I was in so much pain I almost passed out.'

Worse than that, when Cash awoke next morning and tried to get out of bed, he found his legs wouldn't move. The inevitable thought flashed through his mind. 'They've done something wrong. I'll never be able to walk, I'm a cripple.'

But under the supervision of an unorthodox sports fitness specialist called Nigel Websdale and, later, of another expert on the subject, Ann Quinn, Cash put himself through various forms of torture back home in Ringwood, obsessed by the self-imposed goal of becoming the fittest player ever to walk on a tennis court. By the time he faced Lendl on the Centre Court at Wimbledon 18 months later, he had come as close as made no difference. It was his physical condition — the sheer power of those thigh muscles that enabled him to bend and bend, hour after hour, for the low volley — that enabled him to beat the No. 1 player in the world, fulfil a dream and break with tradition by clambering over the heads of the spectators to embrace his family and friends.

'We did it, Barkers!' he called out to his coach as he hugged his father. Now, at Flinder's Park, the question was, 'Could he do it again?' The fact that he came so close was confirmation of the all-round improvement in his game since that moment of triumph at Wimbledon the previous July. Throughout the fortnight in Melbourne he had looked like a Wimbledon Champion and played like one. By the time he had fought off three break points to seize the first set from Lendl 6–4, the galaxy of Australian champions — most of whom had won Wimbledon themselves — who were watching from the President's box must have felt that Cash was a worthy member of the club.

Neale Fraser, Ashley Cooper, Lew Hoad, Rod Laver, Ken Rosewall, Roy Emerson, Frank Sedgman and John Newcombe were all there, and if that cast was not dazzling enough the two elderly gentlemen sitting behind them knew a bit about winning titles, too. Fred Perry in 1934 and Don Budge four years later had won the Australian title in the days when you travelled Down Under by boat. Mind you, no one could accuse that very modern professional Ivan Lendl of just jumping off a plane in a smash-and-grab attempt to win something that had taken two months out of Budge's life 50 years before. Lendl had arrived three weeks before the Open to practise assiduously on a Rebound Ace court at Tony Roche's new club north of Sydney. The only problem was that he was now facing an equally determined competitor who had also been hard at work on the new surface. Cash had laid a Rebound Ace court at his Ringwood home, so advantages were even on that score as the match muscled its way into the second set, with Lendl suddenly forcing errors from the Australian's volley and winning it 6–2.

Obviously Cash was doing most of the attacking but, on occasion, he showed that he could stay back and rally with an opponent who was still loath to desert his post on the baseline. The tennis was athletic, powerful and rugged but, above all, it was a mental battle. Which iron will would buckle first? Whose concentration would waver longest? Cash's showed signs of wobbling in the fourth set, which Lendl grabbed 6–4 to level the match and send it into a fifth set that had the whole of Australia on the edge of its seat.

Both men held serve to take the score to two all, and then the Wimbledon champion seized the match by the throat and started blasting Lendl with a series of volleys that echoed like rifle shots around the huge arena. I have not seen volleys hit that way since Newcombe and Laver faded from the scene. McEnroe is as great a volleyer, but different. The power in Cash's legs enables him to get down so low for the really good returns and punish the high ones with such ferocity that all Lendl could do was turn away and stare ruefully at his racket strings. In a matter of minutes a match that lasted just four minutes under four hours had been torn from his grasp. The final score in the fifth set was 6–2 and it was as decisive as it sounds.

Cash, looking as exhausted as he usually does after a big match, refused to offer the press any gleeful quotes afterwards. 'I still have another match to play,' he said. 'The job isn't finished yet.'

The final was going to be won by strength of mind as well as body, both of which could impose themselves over the basic tennis skills of either player. Writing in the Melbourne *Age*, veteran sports columnist Peter McFarline got the point that so many others miss.

'Forget statistics... In modern tennis there is scarcely a shot between the top 10 players; their skill levels are so close the gap is minimal. It cannot be translated into games or sets or even points,' McFarline wrote. 'Surely more than other sports, the major championships of men's tennis are now decided on mind strength, mental fitness, the ability to absorb pressure and to keep the brain operating at high speed in concert with hands and feet.'

That was what this final between Cash and Wilander would be about and so it proved. Had it not rained, everything might have been different because Wilander was on a roll when the first shower caused a 33-minute delay, and if Cash had not been given the chance to regroup in the locker-room he could have been swept aside by the devastating accuracy of the Swede's service returns, which kept pinging at his ankles like the arrows of a Trojan archer searching for Achilles' heel. But when play resumed, with the decision having been taken not to close the roof, Cash tackled the small mountain of 6–1, 4–1 that faced him and scaled it with renewed vigour and determination. Wilander, who had been darting into the net himself to good effect at various moments in the early stages, put in a good deep volley at 4–2, 15–40, but found his service seized by a glorious forehand pass into the corner that he could not have bettered himself. Now we had a match. Cash, conjuring up two superb winning lobs off Wilander's service points, took the tie-break by 7–3 and, after serves had been swapped, broke again for 4–2 in the third set, which he quickly translated into a two set to one lead. There had been another brief stoppage due to rain during that set, but now the match would run its course and build to the kind of climax that is sometimes inspired by great occasions in great arenas. How quickly Flinder's Park had come of age!

Although Wilander opened the fourth set with his second double fault of the match, it was Cash who suddenly faltered just when he most needed to press home his advantage. Fatigue seemed to seep into his footwork for a while and a bundle of volleys ended up in the net. To the screaming delight of the handful of painted Swedes whose support Mats recognized generously afterwards, Sweden's favourite son swept through the set 6–1 and then broke in the first game of the fifth. But there was still gas in Cash's tank. Gas for the mind as well as the body, but it was sheer physical conditioning that allowed him to recover from a weak first volley on break point in the fourth game and, hurling himself to his right, punch away a superb forehand volley to level at two all. Strong first serves got him out of a

15–40 predicament in the next game and the match settled into a final test of wills, an emotion-charged fight to the death. At six all in any other sport it would have been called a draw, honours even, thank you and good-night. But in tennis, that supposedly gentle pastime in which no one is allowed to shout or scream or say 'boo' to a goose, let alone to a linesman, someone always gets carried out feet first. Blood is spilled in tennis. You don't see it because the haemorrhage is internal but believe me, it is still spilled.

And so it was now. You knew it from the howl of agony that Cash found unable to suppress when Wilander finally drove the dagger home and broke his serve in the 13th game. Quite rightly Rod Laver said that Wilander won because he didn't panic, but kept on concentrating on playing his game, forcing Cash to bend for as many low balls as possible off the return of serve. That was true, but in the end Mats knew that the deadlock would be broken by a single moment of inspiration or pure luck. Happily it was inspiration. The point that set up break point at 6–6 was the best of the championship — the best, you could say, ever played at Flinder's Park. Twice Cash seemed to have Mats and the entire court at his mercy as he lined up that lethal forehand volley, but twice Wilander read it and flung himself wide to his own forehand side, in front of the linesman's nose, to retrieve seemingly impossible balls, and Cash, hurried by such an unexpected riposte, suddenly found himself on the defensive, forced back by a lob and then having to lunge himself to get a racket on a Wilander smash. After almost four and a half hours of actual playing time at the end of a fortnight of heat, wind and torrid competition, a point as heart-pounding as that would have left anyone else gasping for control as Cash's return floated back above their head. But Wilander never loses control and the second smash settled it. He should have lost the point three times but that moment of inspiration had arrived and when he served for the match there was no doubt as to who was the champion.

Almost all the match statistics reinforced the feeling that Wilander won because he had rolled with the heaviest of Cash's punches and maintained the more consistent level of tennis throughout. For a start, Mats won six more games. His first-service tally was 76 per cent compared with Pat's 60 per cent and he made 21 unforced errors to Cash's 48 and served two double faults to his opponent's nine. But it was not just a question of making fewer errors.

Wilander mixed his game like the thoughtful player he is, drawing something from the all-out serve and volley tactics he had used to win the title twice on Kooyong's grass, and, despite losing his way a bit in the third set, he was stronger in the end and gave further evidence, in claiming his fifth Grand Slam singles title, that he is a thoroughly worthy leader of the post-Borg dynasty.

But if Wilander, with his inquisitive mind and timeless style, provides a link amongst the generations of this story, Cash tries very hard to be a thoroughly modern champion — a determined individualist with his diamond ear-ring, his rock-and-roll guitar and the love he feels for the girlfriend who gave him a son on his 21st birthday. As if to emphasize how far we have travelled, for better or worse, in terms of social behaviour, two other tennis stars (who like Cash also happened to come from good Irish stock) were presented with children in that very same week of May in 1986. And, at the time, neither Cash, nor John McEnroe nor Peter McNamara was married to his child's mother.

So, 20 years on, it is more than ceramic rackets, sliding roofs and Steffi's forehand that makes this a brave new world. But, as Pat will learn and, indeed, as he keeps on being reminded in strange ways, the future may be now but it is the past that has shaped it and great achievements can become truly satisfying only when put into proper historical perspective. Quirks of fate and one unbelievable coincidence will have offered Cash examples of what I mean. On two occasions, once while heading towards ultimate victory at Wimbledon and once on the way to a narrow defeat in the final at Flinder's Park, Cash was called upon to beat Paul McNamee, the man who has been his greatest mate, in the truest sense of the Aussie term, and on the second occasion the defeat effectively ended Paul's career. The fiercely patriotic Victorian, who with Mark Edmondson produced one of the greatest doubles performances I have ever seen in the 1983 Davis Cup final against Sweden, had announced that he would retire after the Australian Open, and when he had won his first two rounds, the luck of the draw pitted him against Cash.

Naturally it had to be scheduled for the Centre Court and although Cash, playing all out ('As I knew Macca would have wanted me to'), blitzed him in straight sets, McNamee was delighted to have ended it all in that fashion. 'I would have hated never to have played out there,' he told me after an emotional courtside handshake and farewell speech. As Cash watched his friend address the crowd, he was looking back down a long road that McNamee, often in partnership with the other Melbourne Mac, McNamara, had travelled while Pat was still a boy. The past flickered like a shadow over Cash's face at that moment as he recognized Paul's emotions — and it was not for the first time.

The previous September, Cash had been sitting on the beach early one morning up in Cairns on the north Queensland coast, when a solitary figure with a familiar gait loomed over his shoulder.

'Hello, Pat,' said Lew Hoad. For people who believe in fate it would be easy to think that there was a message in that meeting. After all, what are the odds on two Wimbledon champions, separated in their moment of glory by a full 30 years, being the only two people on a beach in Queensland at a time when one would normally be at home in southern Spain and the other, had he not lost very early in the US Open, would be competing at Flushing Meadow? As it was, Lew was stuck in Australia — after visiting his daughter Jane — for far longer than expected because Jenny had contracted hepatitis, while Pat had flown north simply to get away from all the hassles of being the 1987 Wimbledon champion.

Two of Australia's most famous sons chatted for a few minutes and then Hoad wandered off, leaving Cash to deal with so many problems and challenges that the older man had never had to face ... and so many that Lew had been handling in his own individual style long before Pat was born.

It has been a long journey — longer, more exciting and more rewarding than any of us dared imagine when we gathered for the first Open Wimbledon 20 years ago. The focus of attention centred on the sport today is so much more intense, with every shot played and every word uttered analysed and fussed over by those qualified to do so and by many who are not, that everything is magnified and stretched out of proportion. Some dear old thing was quoted in the paper two days after the Australian Open as saying that she didn't like tennis any more because of the tantrums. But there weren't any tantrums at Flinder's Park. Some columnist in London, searching for a new angle during Wimbledon, realized tantrums were old hat so he wrote a story about boring Swedes. But at Flinder's Park Mats Wilander was cracking jokes at the end of on-court interviews and, the week before, at the Rio Challenge exhibition matches, had done hilarious imitations of other players' service actions. Nothing is quite as it seems; nobody is quite what we want them to be. How many thousands of times have I heard, 'If only Nastase hadn't.... If only McEnroe didn't...' If they hadn't and didn't they would not be Nastase and McEnroe. The public want their heroes to be both special and normal at the same time. That is not reasonable but the press, hoping to catch the public mood, chastise them when they fail. There is still much to be done in improving the public perception of what it takes to succeed as a sporting superstar on the tightrope that leads to riches or oblivion, and maybe that is one of the challenges of the next 20 years. The only certainty, as we leave Melbourne with the Pro Council huddled in another session at the Regent and the players, like parts of a scattering caravan, heading off across the oceans, is that the shifting sands will offer up the mirage of new unbeatables and invincibles to enrage or delight us, all seeming larger than life because that is the way we want them to be. And yet the ones who rise to the very top are special in a way few can comprehend and, in future years, will become even more so — bigger, faster, fitter, but not necessarily better because no one knows how Cash would have played Hoad and no one ever will. All we know is that the game they play offers practically everything one could ask of a sport and that its popularity as a spectator sport, even in the United States, is still on the rise. In 1987 a whole variety of tournaments ranging from Philadelphia, San Francisco and Dallas to Brussels, the Sydney Indoors and the Seiko in Tokyo posted record crowds and, of course, as 1988 dawned, the Australian Open's new home ensured that more people than ever watched the championship that gave us a close-up look at the future. This was not entirely due to Flinder's Park for, if I may risk a prediction, Australian tennis itself may be on the brink of a revival. Jason Stoltenberg, the world junior champion for 1987, is a country boy like Laver and Emerson and appears to be made of the right stuff. And he is not alone. Ray Ruffels and Bob Carmichael, old comrades-in-arms who are now doing such a good job as coaches to Australia's next generation, have a whole crop of youngsters under their wing who may soon be ready to fall in step with Pat Cash and begin a new dynasty from Down Under.

But even as the cast and the styles and the setting changes and evolves, the constant is tennis itself and, being such a beautiful game, it will continue to prosper.

ATP COMPUTER YEAR-END TOP TENS

1973
1. Ilie Nastase
2. John Newcombe
3. Jimmy Connors
4. Tom Okker
5. Stan Smith
6. Ken Rosewall
7. Manuel Orantes
8. Rod Laver
9. Jan Kodes
10. Arthur Ashe

1977
1. Jimmy Connors
2. Guillermo Vilas
3. Bjorn Borg
4. Vitas Gerulaitis
5. Brian Gottfried
6. Eddie Dibbs
7. Manuel Orantes
8. Raul Ramirez
9. Ilie Nastase
10. Dick Stockton

1981
1. John McEnroe
2. Ivan Lendl
3. Jimmy Connors
4. Bjorn Borg
5. Jose-Luis Clerc
6. Guillermo Vilas
7. Gene Mayer
8. Eliot Teltscher
9. Vitas Gerulaitis
10. Peter McNamara

1984
1. John McEnroe
2. Jimmy Connors
3. Ivan Lendl
4. Mats Wilander
5. Andres Gomez
6. Anders Jarryd
7. Henrik Sundstrom
8. Pat Cash
9. Eliot Teltscher
10. Yannick Noah

1987
1. Ivan Lendl
2. Stefan Edberg
3. Mats Wilander
4. Jimmy Connors
5. Boris Becker
6. Miloslav Mecir
7. Pat Cash
8. Yannick Noah
9. Tim Mayotte
10. John McEnroe

A random poll taken amongst some of my colleagues who have watched as much tennis as I have over the past twenty years shows that the Borg–McEnroe 'Tie Break' Wimbledon Final of 1980 is the match that stands out above all others in most people's memory with the Rosewall–Laver 1972 WCT Final coming in second. Answers to the second question – what event or innovation has had the most significant impact on Open Tennis since 1968 – range across a far broader spectrum.

	MEMORABLE MATCH	MOST SIGNIFICANT EVENT
John Barrett (BBC Television)	Borg–McEnroe 1980 Wimbledon F	Failure of ILTF to foresee Open Tennis & prepare properly
Bud Collins (*Boston Globe*)	Rosewall–Laver 1972 WCT Final	ATP Wimbledon Boycott
Judith Elian (*L'Equipe*)	Rosewall–Laver 1972 WCT Final	Introduction of TV for good & evil
Fred Stolle (ESPN TV)	Borg–McEnroe 1980 Wimbledon F Navratilova–Graf 1986 US Open S–F	Rosewall–Laver WCT Final changed perception of tennis in USA
Ted Tinling	Borg–McEnroe 1980 Wimbledon F Evert–Navratilova 1985 French Open F	Introduction of tie-break. It kept TV in tennis
John Parsons (*Daily Telegraph*)	Borg–Gerulaitis 1977 Wimbledon S–F	Revolution in racket technology
Alan Trengove (*Tennis Australia Magazine*)	Borg–McEnroe 1980 Wimbledon F	ATP Wimbledon Boycott
Bjorn Hallberg (Swedish Freelance)	Borg–McEnroe 1980 Wimbledon F Newcombe–Emerson 1970 Wimbledon Q–F	The Borg legacy resulting in Swedish dominance on men's tour
Virginia Wade (BBC TV)	Smith–Nastase 1972 Wimbledon F	New rackets, emphasizing power, making game one dimensional
Don Lawrence (*Melbourne Herald*)	Newcombe–Connors 1975 Australian Open F	Introduction of tie-break

	MEMORABLE MATCH	MOST SIGNIFICANT EVENT
Ray Moore (Chairman, MIPTC)	Laver–Roche 1969 Australian Open S-F (7-5, 22-20, 9-11, 1-6, 6-3)	Borg perfecting top-spin & virtually removing net as obstacle because shots so high
Frank Deford (*Sports Illustrated*)	Borg–McEnroe 1980 Wimbledon F	End of US–Australia dominance & total internationalization of game
Gianni Clerici (*Repubblica*, Rome)	Rosewall–Laver 1971 & 72 WCT Finals	Disappearance of the sporting gentleman
Ron Atkin (*The Observer*)	Borg–McEnroe 1980 Wimbledon F Evert–Navratilova 1985 French Open F	Banning of spaghetti stringing & regularization of racket limitations
Lance Tingay (*Daily Telegraph*)	Gonzales–Pasarell 1969 Wimbledon	Chairs & mandatory stoppage between games has changed rhythm of game
David Lloyd (BBC Radio)	Borg–McEnroe 1980 Wimbledon F Evert–Navratilova 1985 French Open F	Borg's top spin changed way game is taught
Christine Truman Janes (BBC Radio)	Borg–McEnroe 1980 Wimbledon F Navratilova–Graf 1986 US Open S–F	Top players opting out of doubles & mixed has reduced fun & enjoyment for everyone

SINGLES WINNERS

Over twenty years of Open Tennis, Jimmy Connors is the runaway leader amongst winners of Grand Prix, WCT and ATP sanctioned tournaments in singles play. Only Ivan Lendl has a realistic chance of catching him in the foreseeable future.

	TITLES WON	LOSING FINALS
Jimmy Connors (USA)	105	52
Ivan Lendl (Czechoslovakia)	70	38
John McEnroe (USA)	70	28
Bjorn Borg (Sweden)	65	26
Guillermo Vilas (Argentina)	61	42
Ilie Nastase (Rumania)	57	38
Rod Laver (Australia)	47	21
Stan Smith (USA)	39	18
Arthur Ashe (USA)	33	32
Manolo Orantes (Spain)	32	34
John Newcombe (Australia)	32	20
Ken Rosewall (Australia)	32	20
Tom Okker (Netherlands)	29	25
Vitas Gerulaitis (USA)	27	28
Mats Wilander (Sweden)	27	23
Brian Gottfried (USA)	25	26
Jose-Luis Clerc (Argentina)	25	10
Eddie Dibbs (USA)	22	20
Harold Solomon (USA)	22	16
Yannick Noah (France)	21	12

NB These figures include the Australian Open 1988
NB It should be remembered that Laver, Rosewall & Newcombe were all winning titles prior to 1968.

DOUBLES WINNERS

Frew McMillan, of the white hat, South African accent and quick wit (much appreciated by me in the BBC commentary box) has been the pre-eminent doubles player of the Open era. Mostly in partnership with Bob Hewitt, McMillan used his unique two-handed style – so well suited to doubles – to devastating effect.

	TITLES WON	LOSING FINALS
Frew McMillan (South Africa)	74	45
Bob Hewitt (South Africa)	65	33
Stan Smith (USA)	64	30
John McEnroe (USA)	63	19
Peter Fleming (USA)	59	21
Sherwood Stewart (USA)	54	43
Brian Gottfried (USA)	54	42
Ilie Nastase (Rumania)	51	41
Wojtek Fibak (Poland)	48	36
Tomas Smid (Czechoslovakia)	47	38
Bob Lutz (USA)	44	29
John Newcombe (Australia)	41	27
Rod Laver (Australia)	37	18
Mark Edmondson (Australia)	35	34
Anders Jarryd (Sweden)	34	13
Heinz Gunthardt (Switzerland)	33	26
Pavel Slozil (Czechoslovakia)	32	28
Roy Emerson (Australia)	30	18

NB It is no coincidence that the first two names to appear on both lists – McEnroe and Nastase – are the two greatest natural talents seen in twenty years of Open Tennis. Considering how much fewer God-given skills they had to work with, the all-round achievements of Smith and Gottfried are also particularly noteworthy.

PRIZE MONEY

1968

Player	Official Earnings	Player	Official Earnings
1. Tony Roche	$63,504	6. Butch Buchholz	$31,786
2. John Newcombe	57,011	7. Roger Taylor	29,523
3. Cliff Drysdale	37,880	8. Pierre Barthes	26,516
4. Dennis Ralston	34,626	9. Marty Riessen	14,985
5. Nikki Pilic	32,846	10. Ray Moore	6,600

1975

Player	Official Earnings	Player	Official Earnings
1. Arthur Ashe	$326,750	6. Ilie Nastase	$180,536
2. Manuel Orantes	269,785	7. Brian Gottfried	167,960
3. Guillermo Vilas	249,287	8. Jimmy Connors	163,135
4. Bjorn Borg	221,088	9. Roscoe Tanner	150,459
5. Raul Ramirez	211,385	10. Jolon Alexander	138,050

1980

Player	Official Earnings	Player	Official Earnings
1. John McEnroe	$972,369	6. Guillermo Vilas	$378,217
2. Bjorn Borg	731,762	7. Wojtek Fibak	368,073
3. Ivan Lendl	583,406	8. Vitas Gerulaitis	340,823
4. Jimmy Connors	570,060	9. Brian Gottfried	296,800
5. Gene Mayer	397,156	10. Jose-Luis Clerc	280,697

1987

Player	Official Earnings	Player	Official Earnings
1. Ivan Lendl	$2,003,656	6. Anders Jarryd	$561,977
2. Stefan Edberg	1,587,467	7. Boris Becker	558,979
3. Miloslav Mecir	1,205,326	8. Emilio Sanchez	538,158
4. Mats Wilander	1,164,674	9. Brad Gilbert	507,187
5. Pat Cash	565,934	10. Tim Mayotte	458,821

WITA TOP 10 RANKINGS

1977	1980	1984	1987
1. Chris Evert	Chris Evert	Martina Navratilova	Steffi Graf
2. Billie Jean King	Tracy Austin	Chris Evert	Martina Navratilova
3. Martina Navratilova	Martina Navratilova	Hana Mandlikova	Chris Evert
4. Virginia Wade	Hana Mandlikova	Pam Shriver	Pam Shriver
5. Sue Barker	Evonne Goolagong Cawley	Wendy Turnbull	Hana Mandlikova
6. Rosie Casals	Billie Jean King	Manuela Maleeva	Gabriela Sabatini
7. Betty Stove	Andrea Jaeger	Helena Sukova	Helena Sukova
8. Dianne Balestrat	Wendy Turnbull	Claudia Kohde-Kilsch	Manuela Maleeva
9. Wendy Turnbull	Pam Shriver	Zina Garrison	Zina Garrison
10. Kerry Reid	Greer Stevens	Kathy Jordan	Claudia Kohde-Kilsch

CAREER MATCH WINNERS IN WOMEN'S PRO TENNIS (SINGLES) SINCE THE OPEN ERA, 1968 – 25 JAN, 1988.

		WON	LOST	TOTAL	DEBUT
1.	Chris Evert	1,221	126	1,347	1969
2.	Martina Navratilova	1,075	153	1,331	1973
3.	Virginia Wade	839	329	1,168	1968
4.	Billie Jean King*	695	155	850	1968
5.	Evonne Goolagong Cawley	695	158	853	1968
6.	Wendy Turnbull	572	301	873	1972
7.	Rosie Casals	528	303	831	1968
8.	Hana Mandlikova	515	161	676	1978
9.	Virginia Ruzici	490	279	769	1973
10.	Margaret Court*	464	78	512	1968
11.	Pam Shriver	458	152	610	1978
12.	Dianne Balestrat	449	247	696	1973
13.	Sue Barker	365	208	573	1974
14.	Sylvia Hanika	359	198	557	1977
15.	Mima Jausovec	349	243	592	1974
16.	Tracy Austin	337	71	408	1977
17.	Claudia Kohde-Kilsch	313	161	474	1980
18.	Helena Sukova	311	136	445	1981
19.	Betsy Nagelsen	297	295	542	1974
20.	Sharon Walsh-Pete	290	324	614	1973

*King and Court started their careers before Open tennis. These statistics reflect their careers since 1968.

INDEX